—Eighth Edition—

A Wesley Bibliography

by

Kenneth J. Collins

First Fruits Press
Wilmore, Kentucky
2019

A Wesley Bibliography, 8th Edition, by Kenneth J. Collins

Published by First Fruits Press, © 2019

ISBN: 9781621719434 (Print), 9781621719441 (Digital), 9781621719458 (Kindle), DOI: 10.7252/Paper.0000324

Digital version at https://place.asburyseminary.edu/firstfruitspapers/161/

For all other uses, contact:
First Fruits Press
B.L. Fisher Library
Asbury Theological Seminary
204 N. Lexington Ave.
Wilmore, KY 40390
http://place.asburyseminary.edu/firstfruits

Collins, Kenneth J.
A Wesley bibliography / by Kenneth J. Collins.
335 p.; 21 cm.
8th ed.
Wilmore, Ky.: First Fruits Press, c2019.
ISBN: 9781621719434 (pbk.)
1. Wesley, John, 1703-1791—Bibliography. 2. Methodism — Bibliography.
3. Methodist Church — Bibliography. I. Title.
Z8967 .C655 2019 263.092

Cover design by Jon Ramsay

asburyseminary.edu
800.2ASBURY
204 North Lexington Avenue
Wilmore, Kentucky 40390

First Fruits
THE ACADEMIC OPEN PRESS OF ASBURY SEMINARY

First Fruits Press
The Academic Open Press of Asbury Theological Seminary
859-858-2236
first.fruits@asburyseminary.edu
http://place.asburyseminary.edu/firstfruits

Asbury Theological Seminary
204 N. Lexington Ave., Wilmore, KY 40390
asburyseminary.edu
800-2ASBURY

Contents

Primary Sources:
Books Published....1

Primary Sources:
Books Unpublished at This Point....12

Secondary Sources:
Books....14

Chapters in Books....108

Articles....138

Dissertations....298

Primary Sources: Books Published

Albin, Thomas A., and Oliver A. Beckerlegge, eds. *Charles Wesley's Earliest Sermons.* London: Wesley Historical Society, 1987. Six unpublished manuscript sermons.

Baker, Frank, ed. *The Works of John Wesley.* Bicentennial ed. Vol. 25: Letters I. Nashville: Abingdon Press, 1980.

---. *The Works of John Wesley.* Bicentennial ed. Vol. 26: Letters II. Nashville: Abingdon Press, 1982.

---. *A Union Catalogue of the Publications of John and Charles Wesley.* Stone Mountain, GA: George Zimmerman, 1991. Reprint of the 1966 edition.

Burwash, Rev N., ed. *Wesley's Fifty Two Standard Sermons.* Salem, Ohio: Schmul Publishing Co., 1967.

Campbell, Ted A., ed. *The Works of John Wesley: Letters III 1756-1765.* Vol. 27 Nashville: Abingdon Press, 2015.

Chilcote, Paul Wesley, and Collins, Kenneth J. eds. *The Works of John Wesley: Doctrinal and Controversial Treatises II*. Vol. 13. Nashville: Abingdon Press, 2013.

Collins, Kenneth J. and Jason E. Vickers. eds. *The Sermons of John Wesley: A Collection for the Christian Journey*. Nashville: Abingdon Press, 2013.

Coke, Thomas, and Jason A. Vickers. *The Journals of Dr. Thomas Coke*. Nashville: Kingswood Books, 2005.

---. *The Letters of Dr. Thomas Coke*. Nashville: Kingswood Books, 2013.

Cragg, Gerald R., ed. *The Works of John Wesley.* Bicentennial ed. Vol. 11: The Appeals to Men of Reason and Religion and Certain Related Open Letters. Nashville: Abingdon Press, 1975.

Curnock, Nehemiah, ed. *The Journal of Rev. John Wesley.* 8 vols. London: Epworth Press, 1909-1916.

Davies, Rupert E., ed. *The Works of John Wesley.* Bicentennial ed. Vol. 9: The Methodist Societies, I: History, Nature and Design. Nashville: Abingdon Press, 1989.

Green, Richard. *The Works of John and Charles Wesley.* 2nd revised ed. New York: AMS Press, 1976. Reprint of the 1906 edition.

Harrison, W.P. Rev, ed. *The Wesleyan Standards: Sermons by the Rev. John Wesley, A.M.* Nashville, Tenn.: Publishing House of the Methodist Episcopal Church, South 1921.

Hildebrandt, Franz, and Oliver Beckerlegge, eds. *The Works of John Wesley.* Bicentennial ed. Vol. 7: A Collection of Hymns for the Use of the People Called Methodists. Nashville: Abingdon Press, 1983.

Idle, Christopher, ed. *The Journals of John Wesley.* Elgin, Illinois: Lion USA, 1996.

Jackson, Thomas, ed. *The Works of Rev. John Wesley.* 14 vols. London: Wesleyan Methodist Book Room, 1829-1831. Reprinted Grand Rapids, Michigan: Baker Book House, 1978.

---, ed. *The Journals of Rev. Charles Wesley.* 2 vols. London: John Mason, 1949. Reprinted Grand Rapids, Michigan: Baker Book House 1980.

Jarboe, Betty M. *John and Charles Wesley: A Bibliography.* Metuchen, New Jersey: Scarecrow Press, 1987.

Jarboe, Betty M., comp. *Wesley Quotations: Excerpts from the Writings of John Wesley and other Family Members.* Metuchen, New Jersey: Scarecrow Press, 1990.

Jay, Elisabeth, ed. *The Journal of John Wesley: A Selection.* New York: Oxford University Press, 1987.

Kimbrough, S.T., Jr., *A Song for the Poor: Hymns by Charles Wesley.* New York: Board of Global Ministry, 1993.

--- and Oliver A. Beckerlegge, eds. *The Unpublished Poetry of Charles Wesley.* Nashville: Abingdon Press, 1993.

---. *The Unpublished Poetical Writings of Charles Wesley.* 3 vols. Nashville: Kingswood Books, 1988-1992.

Kimbrough Jr., S. T., and Kenneth G. C. Newport, eds. *The Manuscript Journal of the Reverend Charles Wesley, M.A.* Vol. 1. Nashville: Kingswood Books, 2008.

---. *The Manuscript Journal of the Reverend Charles Wesley, M.A.* Vol. 2. Nashville: Kingswood Books, 2008.

Kinghorn, Kenneth C., ed. *A Plain Account of Christian Perfection as Believed and Taught by the Reverend Mr. John Wesley*. Lexington: Emeth Press, 2012.

Maddox, Randy L., ed. *The Works of John Wesley: Doctrinal and Controversial Treatises I*. Vol. 12. Nashville: Abingdon Press, 2012.

Maddox, Randy L., and James G. Donat, eds. The Works of John Wesley Volume 32: Medical Writings Vol. 32. Nashville: Kingswood Books, 2018.

Osborn, George, ed. *Poetical Works of John and Charles Wesley*. 13 vols. Salem, OH: Schmul Publishers, 1992.

Outler, Albert C., ed. *John Wesley*. The Library of Protestant Thought. New York: Oxford University Press, 1964.

---, ed. *The Works of John Wesley*. Bicentennial ed. Vol. 1-4: Sermons. Nashville: Abingdon Press, 1984-1987.

Outler, Albert C., and Richard P. Heitzenrater, eds. *John Wesley's Sermons: An Anthology*. Nashville: Abingdon Press, 1991.

Parker, Percy L. ed. *The Journal of John Wesley*. Chicago, Illinois: Moody, 1974.

Rack, Henry---. *The Works of John Wesley*. Bicentennial ed. Vol. 10: The Methodist Societies: The Conference. Nashville: Abingdon Press, 2011.

Rogal, Samuel J., and John Wesley. *A Detailed and Annotated Collection of John Wesley's Book Reviews, Readings, and Commentaries - Part I.* Lewiston, New York: The Edwin Mellen Press, 2016.

Sugden, Edward H., ed. *Wesley's Standard Sermons.* London: Epworth Press, 1951.

Telford, John, ed. *The Letters of the Rev. John Wesley.* 8 vols. London: Epworth Press, 1931.

---, ed. *Sayings and Portraits of John Wesley.* Salem, OH: Schmul Publishing Company, Incorporated, 1995.

Wainwright, Geoffrey, ed. *Hymns on the Lord's Supper.* Madison, New Jersey: Charles Wesley Society, 1995.

Ward, W. Reginald, and Richard P. Heitzenrater, eds. *The Works of John Wesley.* Bicentennial ed. Vol. 18: Journals and Diaries I. Nashville: Abingdon Press, 1988.

---. *The Works of John Wesley.* Bicentennial ed. Vol. 19: Journals and Diaries II. Nashville: Abingdon Press, 1990.

---. *The Works of John Wesley.* Bicentennial ed. Vol. 20: Journals and Diaries III. Nashville: Abingdon Press, 1991.

---. *The Works of John Wesley*. Bicentennial ed. Vol. 21: Journals and Diaries IV. Nashville: Abingdon Press, 1992.

---. *The Works of John Wesley.* Bicentennial ed. Vol. 22: Journals and Diaries V. Nashville: Abingdon Press, 1993.

---. *The Works of John Wesley*. Bicentennial ed. Vol. 23: Journals and Diaries VI. Nashville: Abington Press, 1995.

---. *The Works of John Wesley*. Bicentennial ed. Vol. 24: Journals and Diaries VII. Nashville: Abington Press, 2003.

Wesley, Charles. *The Journal of the Rev. Charles Wesley, M.A.* South Carolina: Methodist Reprint Society, 1977.

---. *The Journal Letters and Related Biographical Items of the Reverend Charles Wesley, Ma*, Edited by Frank Baker, Richard P. Heitzenrater and Randy L. Maddox. Nashville: Kingswood Books 2018.

Wesley, John. *Explanatory Notes upon the New Testament.* London: William Bowyer, 1755. Most recent reprint, Grand Rapids, Michigan: Baker Book House, 1987.

---. *Explanatory Notes upon the Old Testament.* 3 vols. Bristol: William Pine, 1765. Facsimile reprint, Salem, OH: Schmul Publishers, 1975.

---. *A Christian Library, Consisting of Extracts from and Abridgements of the Choicest Pieces of Practical Divinity which have been published in the English Tongue.* 30 vols. London: T. Blanshard, 1819-1827.

---. *Devotions and Prayers of John Wesley.* Grand Rapids, Michigan: Baker Book House, 1977.

--- and Charles Wesley. *Hymns and Sacred Poems.* London: William Strahan, 1739.

---. *John Wesley's Forty-Four Sermons.* London: Epworth Press, 1944.

---. *The Journal of John Wesley: A Selection.* New York: Oxford University Press, 1987.

---. *A Plain Account of Christian Perfection.* London: Epworth Press. Philadelphia: Trinity Press International, 1990.

---. *The Poetical Works of John and Charles Wesley.* London: Wesleyan Methodist Conference Office, 1868.

---. *The Sunday Service of the Methodists.* London: Strahan, 1784.

---. *Wesley's Forms of Prayers*. Library of Methodist Classics. Nashville: United Methodist Publishing House, 1992.

---. *A Plain Account of Genuine Christianity* Library of Methodist Classics. Nashville: United Methodist Publishing House, 1992.

---. *The Desideratum; or, Electricity Made Plain and Useful*. First ed. Library of Methodist Classics. Nashville: United Methodist Publishing House, 1992.

---. *Primitive Physic : An Easy and Natural Method of Curing Most Diseases by John Wesley* Library of Methodist Classics. Nashville: United Methodist Publishing House, 1992.

---. *A Collection of Forms of Prayer for Every Day in the Week*. The third ed. Library of Methodist Classics. Nashville: United Methodist Publishing House, 1992.

---. *The Dignity of Human Nature*. First ed. Nashville United Methodist Publishing House, 1992.

---. *Explanatory Notes Upon the New Testament*. Charleston: Forgotten Books, 2010.

---. *Christian Correspondence: Being a Collection of Letters Written by the Late Rev. John Wesley and Several Methodist Preachers in Connection with Him, to the Late Mrs. Eliza Bennis, with Her Answers, Chiefly Explaning and Enforcing the Doctrine of Sanctification.* Wilmore, KY: First Fruits Press, 2015.

Wesley, John, and Charles Wesley. *A New and Critical Edition of George Osborn's 'the Poetical Works of John and Charles Wesley' (1868-1872), with the Addition of Notes, Annotations, Biographical and Background Information.* Lewiston: Edwin Mellen Press, 2009.

Wesley, John, and Cary Balzer. *The Devotional Wesley: Inspirational Selections from John Wesley's Sermons.* Anderson, Ind.: Bristol House, Ltd., 2009.

Wesley, John, and Christopher Idle. *The Journal of John Wesley : A New Selection from Wesley's Own Account of His Life and Travels.* 2nd ed. Oxford: Lion, 2003.

Wesley, John, E.M. Bounds, Andrew Murray, and S.D. Gordon. *How to Live a Life of Prayer: Classic Christian Writers on the Divine Privilege of Prayer.* Uhrichsville, OH: Barbour Publishing, 2018.

Wesley, John, and Justo L. González. *Obras De Wesley*. 14 vols. Franklin, Tennessee.: Providence House, 1996.

Wesley, John, and Percy L. Parker. *The Heart of John Wesley's Journal*. Peabody, MA: Hendrickson Publishers, 2014.

Wesley, Samuel. *The Young Student's Library*. London: John Dunton, 1692.

---. *Advice to a Young Clergyman in a Letter to Him*. London: C. Rivington, 1735.

---. *Dissertationes in Librum Jobi*. London: William Boyer, 1736.

Wesley, Susanna. *The Prayers of Susanna Wesley*. Grand Rapids, Michigan: Zondervan Publishing House, 1984.

White, James F., ed. *John Wesley's Prayer Book : The Sunday Service of the Methodists in North America*. Cleveland, Ohio: OSL Publications, 1991.

Primary Sources: Books Unpublished at This Point

---. *The Works of John Wesley.* Bicentennial ed. Vol. 5-6: Explanatory Notes Upon the New Testament. Nashville: Abingdon Press, ?.

---. *The Works of John Wesley.* Bicentennial ed. Vol. 8: Worship and Prayer. Nashville: Abingdon Press, ?

---. *The Works of John Wesley.* Bicentennial ed. Vol. 14-15: Pastoral, Ethical, and Instructional Writings. Nashville: Abingdon Press, ?.

---. *The Works of John Wesley.* Bicentennial ed. Vol. 16: Natural Philosophy and Medicine. Nashville: Abingdon Press, ?.

---. *The Works of John Wesley.* Bicentennial ed. Vol. 17: Editorial Works. Nashville: Abingdon Press, ?.

---. *The Works of John Wesley.* Bicentennial ed. Vol. 33-34: A Description and Analytical Bibliography of the Publications of John and Charles Wesley. Nashville: Abingdon Press, ?.

---. *The Works of John Wesley.* Bicentennial ed. Vol. 35: General Index and Miscellanea. Nashville: Abingdon Press, ?.

Secondary Sources: Books

Abelove, Henry. *The Evangelist of Desire: John Wesley and the Methodists.* Stanford, California: Stanford University Press, 1990.

Abraham, William J. *Waking from Doctrinal Amnesia: The Healing of Doctrine in the United Methodist Church.* Nashville: Abingdon Press, 1995.

---. *Wesley for Armchair Theologians.* Louisville, Kentucky: Westminster John Knox Press, 2005.

---. *Aldersgate and Athens: John Wesley and the Foundations of Christian Belief.* Waco: Baylor University Press, 2009.

Abraham, William J. and James E. Kirby, eds., *The Oxford Handbook of Methodist Studies* Oxford: Oxford University Press, 2009.

Abraham, William J. and David F. Watson. *Key United Methodist Beliefs.* Nashville: Abingdon Press, 2013.

Acornley, John H. *A History of the Primitive Methodist Church in the United States of America.* Fall River, MA: N. W. Matthews, 1909.

Anderson, Neil D. *A Definitive Study of Evidence Concerning John Wesley's Appropriation of the Thought of Clement of Alexandria*. Lewiston, N.Y.: Edwin Mellen Press, 2004.

Armistead, M. Kathryn. *Wesleyan Theology and Social Science: The Dance of Practical Divinity and Discovery*. Newcastle: Cambridge Scholars, 2010.

---. *This We Believe: The Core of Wesleyan Faith and Practice: A Leader's Guide.* Nashville: Abingdon Press, 2010.

Armstrong, Anthony. *The Church of England, the Methodists and Society 1700-1850*. Totowa, New Jersey: Rowman and Littlefield, 1973.

Ayling, Stanley. *John Wesley.* New York: William Collins Publishers, 1979.

Baines-Griffiths. *Wesley the Anglican.* London: Macmillan and Co., Ltd., 1919.

Baker, Eric W. *A Herald of the Evangelical Revival: A Critical Inquiry into the Relationship between William Law and John Wesley and the Beginnings of Methodism.* London: Epworth Press, 1948.

---. *A Herald of the Evangelical Revival: A Critical Inquiry into the Relation of William Law to John Wesley and the Beginnings of Methodism*. Eugene: Wipf & Stock Publishers, 2016.

Baker, Frank. *Methodism and the Love Feast.* London, England: Epworth, 1957.

---. *A Union Catalogue of the Writings of John and Charles Wesley*. Durham, North Carolina: Duke University Press, 1966.

---. *John Wesley and the Church of England.* Nashville, Tennessee: Abingdon, 1970.

---, ed. *The Heart of True Spirituality: John Wesley's Own Choice.* 2 vols. Grand Rapids, Michigan: Francis Asbury Press of Zondervan Publishing House, 1985-1986.

---. *Charles Wesley's Verse: An Introduction.* 2nd ed. London: Epworth Press, 1988.

Barber, Frank Louis. *The Philosophy of John Wesley.* Toronto: Methodist Book and Publishing House, 1923.

Bartleman, Frank. *Azuza Street, 1907.* South Plainfield, NJ: Bridge Publications, 1980.

Bassett, Paul and William Greathouse. *Exploring Christian Holiness*, vol. 2. Kansas City, MO: Beacon Hill Press, 1985.

Beck, Brian. *Methodist Heritage and Identity* Routledge Methodist Studies Series. New York: Routledge, 2017.

Behney, J. Bruce and Paul H. Eller. *The History of the Evangelical United Brethren Church*. Nashville: Abingdon Press, 1979.

Bell, David. *How to Understand John Wesley's a Plain Account of Christian Perfection*. Auckland, N.Z.: AIM & Methodist Pub., 2008.

Bellon, Richard. *A Sincere and Teachable Heart: Self-Denying Virtue in British Intellectual Life, 1736-1859*. Leiden: Brill, 2015.

Benz, Ernst. *Die Protestantische Thebais: Zur Nachwirkung Makarios des Agypters im Protestantismus der 17. and 18. Jahrhunderts in Europa und Amerika*. Wiesbaden: Verlag der Academi der Wissenschaften und der Literatur in Mainz, 1963.

Berg, Johannes van den. *Het Christelijk Leven naar de Opvatting van John Wesley*. Kampen: J.H. Kok, 1959.

Berg, Johannes van den, and W. Stephen Gunter. *John Wesley and the Netherlands*. Nashville, Tenn.: Kingswood Books, 2002.

Berger, Teresa. *Theologie in Hymnen: Zum Verhaltnis von Theologie und Doxologie am Beispel des ‚Collection of Hymns for the Use of the People Called Methodists'.* Altenberge: Telos Verlag, 1989.

Best, Gary. *Charles Wesley: A Biography*. Peterborough, England: Epworth, 2006.

---. *The Cradle of Methodism, 1739-2017: A History of the New Room and of Methodism in Bristol and Kingswood in the Time of John and Charles Wesley and the Subsequent History of the Building.* Bristol: New Room Publications 2017.

Bett, Henry. *The Spirit of Methodism.* London: Epworth Press, 1938.

Bewes, Richard, ed. *John Wesley's England: A Nineteenth Century Pictorial History Based on an 18th Century Journal.* San Francisco: Harper, 1984.

Bevins, Winfield H. *Rediscovering John Wesley.* Cleveland: Pathway Press, 2004.

Birch, Bruce C., and Larry L. Rasmussen. *Bible and Ethics in Christian Life.* Revised and Expanded ed. Minneapolis: Augsburg, 1989.

Bird, Mark. *How Can You Be Sure? Charles Stanley and John Wesley Debate Salvation and Security.* Salem, Ohio: Schmul Publishing Co., 2004.

Bishop, John. *Methodist Worship in Relation to Free Church Worship.* New York: Scholars Studies, 1975.

Body, Alfred Harris. *John Wesley and Education.* London: Epworth, 1936.

Borgen, Ole E. *John Wesley on the Sacraments.* Grand Rapids, Michigan: Francis Asbury Press of Zondervan Publishing House, 1985.

Bowen, Marjorie. *Wrestling Jacob: A Study of the Life of John Wesley and Some Members of the Family.* London: W. Heineman Ltd., 1937.

Bowmer, John Coates. *The Sacrament of the Lord's Supper in Early Methodism.* London, England: Dacre Press, 1951.

---. *Pastor and People: A Study of Church and Ministry in Wesleyan Methodism.* London, England: Epworth, 1975.

Bowyer, O. Richard et al. *Prayer in the Black Tradition.* Nashville: Abingdon Press, 1986.

Boyd, Timothy L. *John Wesley's Christology: A Study in Its Practical Implications for Human Salvation, Transformation, and Its Influences for Preaching Christ.* Salem, Ohio: Allegheny Publishing, 2004.

Boyles, Helen. *Romanticism and Methodism: The Problem of Religious Enthusiasm* New York: Routledge, 2016.

Brailsford, Mabel Richmond, and D. Curtis Hale. *Head and Heart; the Dynamic Relationships of John and Charles Wesley*. Salem, Ohio: Schmul Publishing Co., 2006.

Brantley, Richard E. *Locke, Wesley and the Method of English Romanticism.* Gainesville, Florida: University Press of Florida, 1984.

Bready, J. Wesley. *Wesley and Democracy: A Series of Talks Given Over a National Network by the Canadian Broadcasting Corporation.* Toronto: Ryerson Press, 1939.

---. *The Freedom- Whence?* Winona Lake, Indiana: Light and Life Press, 1950.

---. *England Before and After Wesley: The Evangelical Revival and Social Reform.* London: Hodder and Stoughton, 1938.

Brendlinger, Irv A. *Social Justice through the Eyes of Wesley: John Wesley's Theological Challenge to Slavery*. Guelph, Ont.: Joshua Press, 2006.

Brittingham, John Thomas. *This Is My Body: Philosophical Reflections on Embodiment in a Wesleyan Spirit.* Eugene: Pickwick Publications, 2016.

Brown-Lawson, Albert. *John Wesley and the Anglican Evangelicals of the Eighteenth Century a Study in Cooperation and Separation with Special Reference to the Calvanistic Controversies.* Edinburgh: Pentland Press, 1994.

Brown, Earl Kent. *Women in Mr. Wesley's Methodism.* Lewiston, New York: Edwin Mellon, 1983.

Brown, Robert. *John Wesley's Theology: The Principle of its Vitality and its Progressive Stages of Development.* London: E. Stock, 1965.

---. *John Wesley or the Theology of Conscience.* 2nd ed. London: Elliot Stock, 1968.

Bruce, William. *Wesley and Swedenborg: A Review of the Rev. John Wesley's 'Thoughts on the Writings of Baron Swedenborg'.* London: J. Spears, 1877.

Brush, Robert L., and Vic Reasoner, eds. *The Wesley Workbook: A Brief Biography Plus Study Guide to the Standard Sermons.* Evansville, IN: Fundamental Wesleyan Publishers, 1996.

Bryant, Barry Edward. *John Wesley on the Origin of Evil.* Derbys, England: Moorley's Bookshop, 1992.

Bucke, Emory S., ed. *History of American Methodism.* 3 vols. Nashville: Abingdon Press, 1974.

Buckner, Richard. *30 Days with Wesley: A Prayer Book.* Kansas City: Beacon Hill Press, 2012.

Bullen, Donald A. *A Man of One Book? John Wesley's Interpretation and Use of the Bible*. Waynesboro, Georgia: Paternoster Publishing, 2007.

Burdon, Adrian. *Authority and Order: John Wesley and His Preachers*. Aldershot: Ashgate, 2006.

Burkhard, Johann Gottlieb. *Vollständige Geschichte Der Methodisten in England*. Stuttgart: Christliches Verlagshaus, 1995.

Burnett, Daniel L. *In the Shadow of Aldersgate: An Introduction to the Heritage and Faith of the Wesleyan Tradition*. Eugene: Cascade Books, 2006.

Burrows, Roland. *John Wesley in Reformation Tradition: The Protestant and Puritan Nature of Methodism Rediscovered*. Stoke-on-Trent: Tentmaker Publications, 2008.

Burrows, Roland. *How the Eighteenth Century Revival Saved Britain*. Stoke-on-Trent: Tentmaker Publications, 2012.

Burtner, Robert W., and Robert E. Chiles, eds. *John Wesley's Theology: A Collection from his Works*. Nashville: Abingdon Press, 1982.

Butler, David. *Methodists and Papists: John Wesley and the Catholic Church in the Eighteenth Century*. London: Darton, Longman & Todd, 1995.

Byrne, Herbert W. *John Wesley and Learning*. Salem, Ohio: Schmul Publishing. Co., 1997.

Calder, Sandy. *The Origins of Primitive Methodism*. Vol. 33 Studies in Modern British Religious History. Woodbridge, UK: The Boydell Press, 2016.

Caldwell, Wayne E., ed. *Reformers and Revivalists*. Wesleyan History series, Vol. 3. Indianapolis: Wesley Press, 1992.

Callen, Barry L. *God as Loving Grace*. Nappanee, Indiana: Evangel Publishing House, 1996.

Callen, Barry L., Kostlevy, William. *Heart of the Heritage: Core Themes of the Wesleyan/Holiness Tradition, as Highlighted by the Wesleyan Theological Society, 1965-2000*. Salem, Ohio: Schmul Publishing. Co., 2001.

Callen, Barry L., Richard P. Thompson, and Ted Ferguson. Reading the Bible in Wesleyan Ways. Kansas City, Missouri: Beacon Hill Press of Kansas City, 2003.

Campbell, Dennis M., William B. Lawrence, and Russell E. Richey, eds., *Doctrines & Discipline: Methodist Theology & Practice*, vol. 3, United Methodism & American Culture series. Nashville: Abingdon Press, US, 1999.

Campbell, Ted A. *John Wesley and Christian Antiquity: Religious Vision and Cultural Changes.* Nashville: Kingswood Books, 1991.

---. *Methodist Doctrine: The Essentials.* Nashville: Abingdon Press, 1999.

---. *Wesleyan Beliefs: Formal and Popular Expressions of the Core Beliefs of Wesleyan Communities.* Nashville: Kingswood Books, 2010.

Cannon, William R. *The Theology of John Wesley, with Special Reference to the Doctrine of Justification.* Lanham, Maryland: University Press of America, 1984. Reprint of the 1946 edition.

Carder, Kenneth L. *Sermons on United Methodist Beliefs.* Nashville: Abingdon Press, 1991.

Carder, Kenneth L., and Laceye Warner. *Grace to Lead: Practicing Leadership in the Wesleyan Tradition.* Nashville: General Board of Higher Education and Ministry, United Methodist Church, 2011.

Carole, Susan B. *Called into Communion: A Paradigm Shift in Holiness Theology*. Eugene, Or.: Pickwick, 2013.

Carpenter, William. *Wesleyana: A Selection of the Most Important Passages in the Writings of the Late Rev. John Wesley, A.M. Arranged to form a Complete Body of Divinity.* London: W. Booth, 1825.

Case, Riley B. *Evangelical and Methodist: A Popular History*. Nashville: Abingdon Press, 2004.

Castelo, Daniel. Embodying Wesley's Catholic Spirit. Eugene: Pickwick Publications, 2017.

Cataldo, Chet. *A Spiritual Portrait of a Believer: A Comparison between the Emphatic 'I' of Romans 7, Wesley and the Mystics*. Newcastle Upon Tyne: Cambridge Scholars, 2010.

Cell, George Croft. *John Wesley's New Testament Compared with the Authorized Version.* London: Lutterworth, 1938.

---. *The Rediscovery of John Wesley.* Lanham, Maryland: University Press of America, 1984. Reprint of the 1935 edition.

Chang, Kiyeong. *The Theologies of the Law in Martin Luther and John Wesley*. Lexington, KY: Emeth, 2014.

Chapell, Colin B. *Ye That Are Men Now Serve Him: Radical Holiness Theology and Gender in the South* Religion & American Culture. Chicago: University of Alabama Press, 2016.

Chapman, Daniel Pratt Morris. *Whither Methodist Theology Now? The Collapse of the 'Wesleyan Quadrilateral'*.Tiverton:Methodist Sacramental Fellowship 2010.

Cheek, H. Lee. *Confronting Modernity: Towards a Theology of Ministry in the Wesleyan Tradition.* Lake Junaluska: Wesley Studies Society, 2010.

Cheetham, J. Keith. *On the Trail of John Wesley.* Edinburgh: Luath, 2003.

Chilcote, Paul W. *John Wesley and the Women Preachers of Early Methodism.* Metuchen, New Jersey: Scarecrow, 1991.

---. *She Offered Them Christ: The Legacy of Women Preachers in Early Methodism.* Nashville: Abingdon Press, 1993.

---., ed. *The Wesleyan Tradition: A Paradigm for Renewal.* Nashville: Abingdon Press, 2002.

---. *Recapturing the Wesleys' Vision: An Introduction to the Faith of John and Charles Wesley.* Downers Grove, Illinois: InterVarsity Press, 2004.

---., ed. *Early Methodist Spirituality: Selected Women's Writings.* Nashville: Kingswood Books, 2007.

---. *John & Charles Wesley: Selections from Their Writings and Hymns Annotated and Explained.* Woodstock: SkyLight Paths 2011.

Chiles, Robert E. *Scriptural Christianity: A Call to John Wesley's Disciples.* Grand Rapids, Michigan: Francis Asbury Press of Zondervan Publishing House, 1984.

---. *Theological Transition in American Methodism, 1790-1935.* Lanham, Maryland: University Press of America, 1984. Reprint of the 1965 edition.

Christie, Thomas William. *Methodism: A Part of the Great Christian Apostasy.* London: Simpkin Marshall, 1881.

Church, Leslie. *Knight of the Burning Heart.* London: Epworth Press, 1938.

Clapper, Gregory S. *John Wesley on Religious Affections: His Views on Experience and Emotion and their Role in the Christian Life and Theology.* Metuchen, New Jersey: Scarecrow Press, 1989.

---. *As if the Heart Mattered: A Wesleyan Spirituality.* Nashville: Upper Room Books, 1997.

---. *The Renewal of the Heart Is the Mission of the Church: Wesley's Heart Religion in the Twenty-First Century*. Eugene, Oregon: Cascade Books, 2010.

Clarke, Martin V. British Methodist Hymnody: Theology, Heritage, and Experience Routledge Methodist Studies Series. New York: Routledge, 2017.

Clifford, Alan C. *Atonement and Justification. English Evangelical Theology, 1640-1790: An Evaluation.* Oxford: Clarendon Press, 1990.

Cobb, John B., Jr. *Grace and Responsibility: A Wesleyan Theology for Today.* Nashville: Abington Press, 1995.

Coe, Bufford W. *John Wesley and Marriage.* Cranbury, NJ: Lehigh University Press, 1996.

Coffey, John. *Heart Religion: Evangelical Piety in England & Ireland, 1690-1850.* New York: Oxford University Press, 2016.

Coke, Thomas, and Francis Asbury. *The Doctrines and Discipline of the Methodist Episcopal Church in America.* Philadelphia: Henry Tuckniss, 1798.

Coke, Thomas, and Henry Moore. *The Life of the Rev. John Wesley, A. M., Including an Account of the Great Revival of Religion in Europe and America, of Which He Was the First and Chief Instrument* Library of Methodist Classics. Nashville: United Methodist Publishing House, 1992.

Coleman, Robert E. *Nothing to do but Save Souls.. John Wesley: John Wesley's Charge to his Preachers.* Grand Rapids, Michigan: Zondervan, 1990.

Coleson, Joseph E. *Be Holy: God's Invitation to Understand, Declare, and Experience Holiness.* Indianapolis: Wesleyan Publishing House, 2008.

Collier, Frank Wilbur. *Back to Wesley.* New York: Methodist Book Concern, 1924.

---. *John Wesley Among the Scientists.* New York: Abingdon, 1928.

Collins, Kenneth J. and John H. Tyson. *Conversion in the Wesleyan Tradition.* Nashville, Tennessee: Abingdon Press, 2001.

Collins, Kenneth J. *Wesley on Salvation: A Study in the Standard Sermons.* Grand Rapids, Michigan: Francis Asbury Press of Zondervan Publishing House, 1989.

---. *A Faithful Witness: John Wesley's Homiletical Theology.* Wilmore, Kentucky: Wesley Heritage Press, 1993.

---. *The Scripture Way of Salvation: The Heart of John Wesley's Theology.* Nashville, Tennessee: Abingdon Press, 1997.

---.*A Real Christian: The Life of John Wesley.* Nashville, Tennessee: Abingdon Press, 1999.

---. *John Wesley: A Theological Journey*. Nashville, Tennessee: Abingdon Press, 2003.

---. *The Theology of John Wesley: Holy Love and the Shape of Grace*. Nashville: Abingdon Press, 2007.

---. *A Wesley Bibliography*. Wilmore, Kentucky: First Fruits Press, 2014.

---. *Soul Care: Deliverance and Renewal through the Christian Life*. Wilmore, Kentucky: First Fruits Press, 2014.

Colon-Emeric, Edgardo Antonio. *Wesley, Aquinas, and Christian Perfection: An Ecumenical Dialogue*. Waco, Tex.: Baylor University Press, 2009.

---. *Wesley, Aquinas, and Christian Perfection: An Ecumenical Dialogue*. Waco, Texas: Baylor University Press, 2018.

Coppedge, Allan. *John Wesley in Theological Debate.* Wilmore, KY: Wesley Heritage Press, 1988.

Cottret, Bernard. *Histoire De La Réforme Protestante: Luther, Calvin, Wesley, Xvie - Xviiie Siècles* Pour L'histoire. Paris: Perrin, 2001.

Cox, Leo George. *John Wesley's Concept of Perfection.* Kansas City, Missouri: Beacon Hill Press, 1964.

Coyner, Michael J. *A Year with John Wesley and Our Methodist Values.* Nashville: Discipleship Resources, 2007.

Cracknell, Kenneth, and Susan J. White. *An Introduction to World Methodism*. New York: Cambridge University Press, 2005.

Cragg, Gerald R. *The Church in the Age of Reason, 1648-1789*. Grand Rapids, Michigan: Wm. B. Eerdmans, 1960.

Crawford, Nathan, ed. *Continuing Relevance of Wesleyan Theology*. Eugene, Or.: Pickwick, 2011.

Creamer, David. *Methodist Hymnology Comprehending Notices of the Poetical Works of John and Charles Wesley*. New York: Self Published, 1848.

Crofford, James Gregory. *Streams of Mercy: Prevenient Grace in the Theology of John and Charles Wesley.* Lexington, Kentucky: Emeth Press, 2010.

Crutcher, Timothy J. *The Crucible of Life: The Role of Experience in John Wesley's Theological Method.* Lexington: Emeth Press, 2009.

---. *John Wesley: His Life and Thought*. Kansas City: Beacon Hill, 2015.

Cunha, Emma Salgard. *John Wesley, Practical Divinity, and the Defence of Literature* Routledge Methodist Studies Series. New York: Routledge, 2017.

Cunningham, Joseph W. *John Wesley's Pneumatology: Perceptible Inspiration.* Burlington: Ashgate, 2014.

Cushman, Robert E. *John Wesley's Experimental Divinity: Studies in Methodist Doctrinal Standards.* Nashville: Kingswood Books, 1989.

Dale, Alan T. *Study Notes on Christian Doctrine.* London: Epworth Press, 1952.

Dallimore, Arnold A. *Susanna Wesley: The Mother of John and Charles Wesley.* Grand Rapids, Michigan: Baker Book House, 1993.

Danker, Ryan N. *Wesley and the Anglicans: Political Division in Early Evangelicalism*. Downers Grove, Illinois: IVP Academic, 2016.

Davey, Cyril. *Horseman of the King (John Wesley).* Fort Washington, Pennsylvania: Christian Literature Crusade, 1964.

---. *John Wesley and the Methodists.* Nashville, Tennessee: Abingdon, 1986.

Davies, Horton. *Worship and Theology in England. Vol. III: From Watts and Wesley to Maurice, 1690-1850.* Princeton, New Jersey: Princeton University Press, 1961.

Davies, Rupert Eric. *Methodism.* London: Epworth, 1985.

Davison, Leslie. *Pathway to Power: The Charismatic Movement in Historical Perspective.* Watchung, New Jersey: Logos Books, 1972.

Day, Albert E. *Discipline and Discovery: Workbook Edition.* Nashville: The Upper Room, 1977.

Dayton, Donald W. *The Theological Roots of Pentecostalism.* Metuchen, New Jersey: Scarecrow Press, 1987.

---. *Discovering an Evangelical Heritage.* Peabody, MA: Hendrickson Publishers, 1988. Reprint of the 1976 edition.

Dean, Jonathan. *A Heart Strangely Warmed: John and Charles Wesley and Their Writings.* Norwich: Canterbury Press, 2014.

Dearing, Trevor. *Wesleyan and Tractarian Worship: An Ecumenical Study.* London: Epworth, 1966.

Deats, Paul, and Carol Robbs, eds. *The Boston Personalist Tradition in Philosophy, Social Ethics, and Theology.* Macon, GA: Mercer University Press, 1986.

Demaray, Donald E. *Devotions and Prayers of John Wesley.* Grand Rapids: Baker Book House, 1957.

Deschner, John. *Wesley's Christology: An Interpretation.* Dallas: Southern Methodist University Press, 1985. Reprint of 1960 edition with a new foreword by the author.

Derr, Colleen R. *John Wesley and the Faith Formation of Children: Lessons for the Church.* Lexington, Kentucky: Emeth Press, 2018.

Dewitt, John. *John Wesley and Premillenialism.* New York: Hunt and Eaton, 1894.

Dieter, Melvin E. *The Holiness Revival of the Nineteenth Century.* Metuchen, New Jersey: Scarecrow Press, 1980.

Dimond, Sydney George. *The Psychology of the Methodist Revival.* London: Humphrey Milford, 1926.

Dobree, Bonamy. *John Wesley.* Folcraft, PA: Folcroft Library Edition, 1974.

Dodge, Reginald. *Wesley and the Industrial Era.* London: Epworth Press, 1938.

Doughty, William Lamplough. *John Wesley: His Conferences and His Preachers.* London: Epworth, 1944.

---. *John Wesley: Preacher.* London: Epworth, 1955.

Dowley, T. E. *Through Wesley's England.* Nashville: Abingdon Press, 1988. Colorful Guide to Wesley's England.

Dreyer, Frederick A. *The Genesis of Methodism.* Bethlehem, New Jersey: Lehigh University Press, 1999.

Dunnam, Maxie D. *Going on to Salvation : A Study in the Wesleyan Tradition.* Nashville, Tennessee: Discipleship Resources, 1990.

---. *The Christian Way: A Wesleyan View of Spiritual Journey.* Grand Rapids: Francis Asbury Press, 1984.

---. *Going on to Salvation: A Study of Wesleyan Beliefs.* Nashville: Abingdon Press, 2008.

Dunning, H. Ray, and William M. Greathouse. *Introduction to Wesleyan Theology*. Kansas City: Beacon Hill Press, 1982.

Dunning, H. Ray. *The Second Coming : A Wesleyan Approach to the Doctrine of Last Things*. Kansas City, Missouri: Beacon Hill Press of Kansas City, 1995.

---. *Grace, Faith and Holiness.* Kansas City, Missouri: Beacon Hill, 1988.

---. *Reflecting the Divine Image: Christian Ethics in Wesleyan Perspective.* Downers Grove, Illinois: InterVarsity Press, 1998.

Eayrs, George. *John Wesley, Christian Philosopher and Church Founder.* London: Epworth, 1926.

Edwards, Clifford Walter, ed. *Japanese Contributions to the Study of John Wesley*. Macon, Georgia: Wesleyan College, 1967.

Edwards, Maldwyn. *John Wesley and the Eighteenth Century.* London: G. Allen and Unwin Ltd., 1953.

---. *Family Circle: A Study of the Epworth Household in Relation to John and Charles Wesley.* London: Epworth Press, 1961.

---. *John Wesley.* 4th ed. Madison, New Jersey: General Commission on Archives, 1987.

---. *Astonishing Youth: A Study of John Wesley as Men Saw Him*. Eugene, OR: Wipf & Stock Publishers, 2014.

Edwards, Rem Blanchard. *John Wesley's Values and Ours*. Lexington: Emeth Press, 2012.

Eli, R. George. *Social Holiness: John Wesley's Thinking on Christian Community and its Relationship to the Social Order.* New York: P Lang Publishers, 1993.

Ethridge, Willie S. *Strange Fires: The True Story of John Wesley's Love Affair in Georgia.* Birmingham, Alabama: Vanguard, 1971.

Ewbank, J. Robert. *John Wesley, Natural Man, and the "Isms"*. Eugene: Resource Publications, 2009.

---. *Wesley's Wars*. Bloomington, IN: WestBow Press, 2012.

Faulkner, John Alfred. *Wesley as a Churchman*. New York: Knickerbocker Press, 1897.

---. *The Socialism of John Wesley*. London: Robert Culley, 1908.

---. *Wesley as Sociologist, Theologian, Churchman.* New York: Methodist Book Concern, 1918.

Felleman, Laura. *The Form and Power of Religion: John Wesley on Methodist Vitality*. Eugene: Cascade Books, 2012.

Felton, Gayle C. *This Gift of Water: The Practice and Theology of Baptism Among Methodists in America.* Nashville: Abingdon, 1992.

Felton, Gayle C., ed. *How United Methodists Study Scripture*. Nashville: Abingdon Press, 1999.

Findlater, John. *Perfect Love: A Study of John Wesley's View of the Ideal Christian Life.* Edinburgh: Leith Printing and Publishing Co., 1914.

Fitchett, W.H. *Wesley and His Century: A Study in Spiritual Forces.* London: Smith, Elder, & Co., 1906

Flew, R. Newton. *The Idea of Perfection in Christian Theology.* London: Oxford University Press, 1934.

Foot, Isaac, and T. S. Gregory. *The City of the Living God: Studies of Wesley's Catholicity.* London: Epworth Press, 1932.

Forsaith, Peter S. *Image, Identity and John Wesley: A Study in Portraiture* Routledge Methodist Studies Series. New York: Routledge, 2017.

Frank, Thomas Edward. *Polity, Practice, and the Mission of The United Methodist Church.* Nashville: Abingdon Press, 1997.

Frost, Brian. *Living in Tension Between East and West.* London: New Word Publications, 1984.

Frost, Stanley B. *Die Autoritatslehre in den Werken John Wesleys.* Munich: Ernst Reinhardt, 1938.

Ganske, Karl Ludwig. *Religion of the Heart and Growth in Grace: John Wesley's Selection and Editing of Puritan Literature for a Christian Library.* Manchester University of Manchester, 2009.

Gibson, Stephen. *A Timeless Faith: John Wesley for the 21st Century.* Nappanee: Evangel Publishing House, 2006.

Gibson, William, Peter S. Forsaith, and Martin Wellings, eds. *The Ashgate Research Companion to World Methodism.* London/New York: Routledge, 2016.

Gill, Frederick C. *Charles Wesley, the First Methodist.* London: Lutterworth Press, 1964.

Wesley, John, and Justo L. González. *Obras De Wesley.* 14 vols. Franklin, Tennessee: Providence House, 1996.

Goodhead, Andrew. *A Crown and a Cross: The Rise, Development and Decline of the Methodist Class Meeting in Eighteenth Century England*. Eugene, Or.: Wipf & Stock Publishers, 2010.

Goodloe, Robert W. *The Sacraments in Methodism*. Nashville: Methodist Publishing House, 1943.

Gooch, John O. *John Wesley for the Twenty First Century: Set Apart for Social Witness*. Nashville: Discipleship Resources, 2006.

Gorveatte, Mark. *Lead Like Wesley: Help for Today's Ministry Servants*. Indianapolis: Wesleyan Publishing House, 2016.

Gounelle, Edmond. *John Wesley et le Reveil d'un Peuple Geneve.* : Labor et Fides, 1948.

Gramling, Roger, and Robert Spain. *John Wesley and the Beginnings of Methodism*. Columbia: Print Media Center, 2011.

Green, J. Brazier. *John Wesley and William Law.* London: Epworth Press, 1945.

Green, Joel B. *Reading Scripture as Wesleyans.* Nashville: Abingdon Press, 2010.

Green, Joel B., and David F. Watson. *Wesley, Wesleyans and Reading Bible as Scripture*. Waco: Baylor University Press, 2012.

Green, Richard. *The Works of John and Charles Wesley: A Bibliography*. London: Kelly, 1896.

Green, V. H. H. *The Young Mr. Wesley.* New York: St. Martin's Press Inc, 1961.

---. *John Wesley.* Lanham, Maryland: University Press of America, 1987. Reprint of 1964 edition.

Greenway, Jeffrey, and Joel B. Green. *Grace and Holiness in a Changing World: A Wesleyan Proposal for Postmodern Ministry*. Nashville: Abingdon Press, 2007.

Greet, Kenneth. *When the Spirit Moves.* London: Epworth Press, 1975.

Grider, Kenneth J. *A Wesleyan-Holiness Theology*. Kansas City: Beacon Hill Press, 1994.

Gross, John Owen. *John Wesley: Christian Educator.* Nashville, TN: The Board of Education, The Methodist Church, 1954.

Guerrant, William C. *Organic Wesley: A Christian Perspective on Food, Farming, and Faith.* Franklin, TN: Seedbed Publishing, 2015.

Gunter, W. Stephen. *The Limits of "Love Devine": John Wesley's Response to Antinomianism and Enthusiasm.* Nashville: Kingswood Books, 1989.

Gunter W. Stephen, Ted A. Campbell, Rebekah L. Miles, Randy L. Maddox, and Scott Jones. *Wesley and the Quadrilateral: Renewing the Conversation.* Nashville: Abingdon, 1997.

Gunter, W. Stephen and Elaine Robinson, eds. *Considering the Great Commission: Evangelism and Mission in the Wesleyan Spirit.* Nashville: Abingdon Press, 2005.

Gustafson, James. *Christ and Moral Life.* Chicago: University of Chicago Press, 1968.

Haddal, Ingvor. *John Wesley.* Nashville: Abingdon, 1961.

Haden, John. *The Wesleys of Epworth*. Hough-on-the-Hill, England: Barny Books, 2009.

Hagen, Odd. *Litt om Wesleys Laere om Kristleig Fullkommenheit* [Light on Wesley's Teaching on Christian Perfection]. Oslo: Methodismen, 1938.

Hall, Clarence and Samuel Brengle. *Portrait of a Prophet.* Atlanta, GA: The Salvation Army, 1933.

Hamilton, Barry W. *The Role of Richard Watson's Theological Institutes in the Development of Methodist after John Wesley*. Lewiston: The Edwin Mellen Press, 2014.

Hammond, Geordan. *John Wesley in America: Restoring Primitive Christianity*. New York: Oxford University Press, 2014.

Hammond, Geordan, and Peter Forsaith, eds. *Religion, Gender and Industry: Exploring Church and Methodism in a Local Setting*: Pickwick Publications, 2011.

Hammond, Geordan, and David Ceri Jones. *George Whitefield: Life, Context, Legacy*. New York: Oxford University Press, 2016.

Hanson, Jake. Crossing the Divide: John Wesley, the Fearless Evangelist. Uhrichsville, OH: Shiloh Run Press, 2016.

Harding, F. A. J. *The Social Impact of the Evangelical Revival*. London: Epworth Press, 1947.

Harkness, Georgia. *Prayer and the Common Life.* Nashville: Abingdon-Cokesbury, 1948.

Harmon, Mark A. *The Warmed Heart: A 30-day Journey in the Company of John Wesley*. Kansas City: Beacon Hill Press of Kansas City, 1995.

Harmon, Rebecca Lamar. *Susanna, Mother of the Wesleys.* Nashville: Abington Press, 1984.

Harnish, James A. *Simple Rules for Money: John Wesley on Earning, Saving and Giving*. Nashville: Abingdon Press, 2009.

Harnish, John E., ed. *The Orders of Ministry in The United Methodist Church.* Nashville: Abingdon Press, 2000.

Harper, Steve. *Devotional Life in the Wesleyan Tradition.* Nashville: The Upper Room, 1983.

---. *John Wesley's Message for Today.* Grand Rapids, Michigan: Zondervan, 1983.

---. *The Way to Heaven: The Gospel According to John Wesley*. Grand Rapids, MI: Zondervan Publishing House, 2003.

Harper, Steve and John Wesley. *Five Marks of a Methodist: The Fruit of a Living Faith.* Nashville: Abingdon Press, 2015.

Harrison, A. H. *The Separation of Methodism from the Church of England*. London: The Epworth Press, 1945.

Harrison, G. E. *Haworth Parsonage: Study of Wesley & the Brontes.* Folcroft, PA: Folcroft Press, 1937.

---. *Son of Susanna: The Private Life of John Wesley.* Baton Rouge, Louisiana: R West, 1937.

Harrison, Nick. *Best of All, God Is with Us: Heartwarming Devotions from the Life of John Wesley*. Indianapolis: Wesleyan Publishing House, 2005.

Hartley, John E., and R. L. Shelton, eds. *Salvation (Wesleyan Theological Perspective Ser, Vol. 1).* Anderson, Indiana: Warner Press, 1989.

Hattersley, Roy. *A Brand from the Burning: The Life of John Wesley*. New York: Doubleday, 2003.

Hauerwas, Stanley. *Character and the Christian Life: A Study in Theological Ethics.* San Antonio, TX: Trinity University Press, 1975.

---. *After Christendom: How the Church is to Behave if Freedom, Justice and a Christian Nation are Bad Ideas.* Nashville: Abingdon Press, 1991.

Hauerwas, Stanley and William H. Willimon. *Resident Aliens: Life in the Christian Colony.* Nashville: Abingdon Press, 1989.

Headley, Anthony J. *Family Crucible: The Influence of Family Dynamics in the Life and Ministry of John Wesley*. Eugene: Wipf & Stock Publishers, 2010.

---. *Getting It Right: Christian Perfection and Wesley's Purposeful List*. Lexington, KY: Emeth, 2013.

Heidinger, James V., ed. *Basic United Methodist Beliefs: An Evangelical View.* Wilmore, KY: Bristol Books, 1986.

Heitzenrater, Richard P. *The Elusive Mr. Wesley.* 2 vols. Nashville: Abingdon Press, 1984.

---. *Diary of an Oxford Methodist: Benjamin Ingham.* Durham, NC: Duke University Press, 1985.

---. *John Wesley and the Road to Aldersgate: The Oxford Years.* : Kentucky Methodist Center, 1973.

---. *Mirror and Memory: Reflections on Early Methodism.* Nashville: Kingswood Books, 1989.

---. *Wesley and the People Called Methodists.* Nashville: Abingdon Press, 1995.

---, ed. *The Poor and the People Called Methodists.* Nashville: Kingswood Books, 2002.

---, *The Elusive Mr. Wesley*. Second ed. Nashville: Abingdon Press, 2003.

---. *John Wesley und Der Frühe Methodismus*: Göttingen: Ruprecht, 2007.

---. *Wesley and the People Called Methodists*. Nashville: Abingdon Press, 2013.

---. *Exact Likeness: The Portraits of John Wesley.* Nashville: Abingdon Press, 2016.

Hempton, David Neil. *Methodism and Politics in British Society, 1750-1850.* Stanford, CA: Stanford University Press, 1984.

---, *Methodism: Empire of the Spirit.* New Haven: Yale University Press, 2005.

Henderson, D. Michael. *John Wesley's Class Meeting: A Model for Making Disciples.* Nappanee, Indiana: Evangel Publishing House, 1997.

Herbert, Thomas Walter. *John Wesley as Editor and Author.* Princeton, NJ: Princeton University Press, 1940.

Hildebrandt, Franz. *From Luther to Wesley.* London: Lutterworth, 1951.

---. *Christianity According to the Wesleys.* London: Epworth, 1956.

---. *I Offered Christ.* Philadelphia, Pennsylvania: Fortress, 1967.

---. *Christianity According to John Wesley.* Durham, NC: Labyrinth Press, 1992.

---. *Christianity According to the Wesleys.* Grand Rapids, MI: Baker Books, 1994.

Hillis, Newell D. *Great Men as Prophets of a New Era.* Manchester, New Hampshire: Ayer, 1968.

Hindmarsh, D. Bruce. *John Newton and the English Evangelical Tradition: Between the Conversions of Wesley and Wilberforce.* Pbk. ed. Grand Rapids, Michigan: William B. Eerdmans, 2001.

---. *The Evangelical Conversion Narrative: Spiritual Autobiography in Early Modern England*. Oxford: Oxford University Press, 2005.

Hockin, Frederick. *John Wesley and Modern Wesleyanism.* 3rd ed. London: J.T. Hayes, 1878.

Holden, Harrington William. *John Wesley in Company with High Churchmen.* London: Church Press, 1869.

Holifield, E. Brooks. *The Gentleman Theologians: American Theology in Southern Culture.* Durham, NC: Duke University Press, 1978. See especially 76-77, 140-143, 165-169, 186-202.

---. *Health and Medicine in the Methodist Tradition.* New York, New York: Crossroad, 1986.

Holland, Bernard G. *Baptism in Early Methodism.* London: Epworth, 1970.

Hong, John Sungschul. *John Wesley the Evangelist.* Lexington: Emeth Press, 2006.

Houghton, Edward. *The Handmaid of Piety and other papers on Charles Wesley's Hymns.* New York: Quack Books in association with the Wesley Fellowship, 1992.

Hulley, Leonard D. *Wesley: A Plain Man for Plain People.* Westville, South Africa: Methodist Church of South Africa, 1987.

---. *To Be and To Do: Exploring Wesley's Thought on Ethical Behavior.* Pretoria: University of South Africa, 1988.

Hunter, Fredrick. *John Wesley and the Coming Comprehensive Church.* Eugene: Wipf & Stock Publishers, 2016.

Hunter, George G., III. *To Spread the Power: Church Growth in the Wesleyan Spirit.* Nashville: Abingdon Press, 1987.

Hynson, Leon O. *To Reform the Nation: Theological Foundations of Wesley's Ethics.* Grand Rapids, Michigan: Zondervan, 1984.

Hynson, Leon O. *Through Faith to Understanding: Wesleyan Essays on Vital Christianity.* Lexington: Emeth, 2005.

Impeta, Christoffel Nicolaas. *De Leer der Heiliging en Volmaking bij Wesley en Fletcher* [The Doctrine of Sanctification and Perfection in Wesley and Fletcher]. Leiden: Mulder, 1913.

Jackson, Jack. *Offering Christ: John Wesley's Evangelistic Vision.* Nashville: Kingswood Books, 2017.

Jackson, Thomas. *The Life of the Rev. John Wesley: From Epworth to London.* Salem, Ohio: Schmul Publishing Co., 2002.

Jeffrey, Thomas Reed. *John Wesley's Religious Quest.* New York: Vantage Press, 1960.

Jennings, Theodore W., Jr. *Good News to the Poor: John Wesley's Evangelical Economics.* Nashville: Abingdon Press, 1990.

Job, Reuben. *A Wesleyan Spiritual Reader.* Nashville: Abingdon Press, 1997.

---. *Three Simple Rules That Will Change the World.* Nashville: Abingdon Press, 2009.

Johnson, Susanne. *Christian Spiritual Formation in the Church and Classroom.* Nashville: Abingdon Press, 1989.

Jones, Charles E. *A Guide to the Study of the Holiness Movement.* Metuchen, New Jersey: Scarecrow Press, 1974.

---. *Perfectionist Persuasion: The Holiness Movement and American Methodism, 1867-1936.* Metuchen, New Jersey: Scarecrow Press, 1974.

---. *A Guide to the Study of the Pentecostal Movement.* 2 vols. Metuchen, New Jersey: Scarecrow Press, 1983.

---. *The Charismatic Movement: A Guide to the Study of Neo-Pentecostalism with Emphasis on Anglo-American Sources.* Metuchen, New Jersey: Scarecrow Press, 1992.

Jones, Howard Watkins. *The Holy Spirit from Arminius to Wesley*. London: Epworth Press, 1929.

Jones, Ivor H., and Kenneth B. Wilson, eds. *Freedom and Grace.* London: Epworth Press, 1988.

Jones, Major J. *Christian Ethics for Black Theology.* Nashville: Abingdon Press, 1974.

Jones, Scott J. *John Wesley's Conception and Use of Scripture.* Nashville: Kingswood Books, 1995.

---. *Staying at the Table: The Gift of Unity for United Methodists.* Nashville: Abingdon Press, 2008.

---. *The Wesleyan Way: A Faith That Matters.* Nashville: Abingdon Press, 2013.

---. *The Once and Future Wesleyan Movement.* Nashville: Abingdon Press, 2016

Jones, Timothy K. and Keith Beasley-Topliffe, eds., *A Longing for Holiness: Selected Writings of John Wesley.* Nashville: Upper Room Books, 1997.

Kallstad, Thorvald. *John Wesley and the Bible: A Psychological Study.* Bjarnum, Sweden: Bjarnums Tyrckeri, 1974.

Kapic, Kelly M. *Sanctification: Explorations in Theology and Practice.* Downers Grove, Illinois: IVP Academic, 2014.

Keller, Rosemary Skinner, ed. *Spirituality & Social Responsibility: Vocational Vision of Women in the United Methodist Tradition.* Nashville: Abingdon Press, 1993.

Kent, John. *Wesley and the Wesleyans: Religion in Eighteenth Century Britain.* Cambridge: Cambridge University, 2002.

Kimbrough, S. T., Jr., ed. *Charles Wesley: Poet and Theologian.* Nashville: Kingswood Books, 1992.

---. *Methodism in Russia and the Baltic States: History and Renewal.* Nashville: Abingdon Press, 1995.

---. *Who are the People Called Methodist?* (Contribution by Kristin Markay and David Markay. Nashville: General Board of Global Ministries, The United Methodist Church, 1997.

---. *Resistless Love: Christian Witness in the New Millennium: A Wesleyan Perspective.* New York: GBGM Books, 2000.

---. ed., *Orthodox and Wesleyan Spirituality.* Crestwood, New York: St. Vladimir's Seminary Press, 2002.

---. ed., *Orthodox and Wesleyan Scriptural Understanding and Practice* Crestwood, New York: St. Vladimir's Seminary Press, 2005.

---. *Orthodox and Wesleyan Ecclesiology.* Crestwood, New York: St Vladimir's Seminary Press, 2007.

Kimbrough Jr., S. T., and Peter Bouteneff. *Partakers of the Life Divine: Participation in the Divine Nature in the Writings of Charles Wesley*. Eugene: Cascade Books, 2016.

Kinghorn, Kenneth C. *The Gospel of Grace: The Way of Salvation in the Wesleyan Tradition.* Nashville: Abingdon Press, 1992.

---. *The Heritage of American Methodism*. Strasbourg, France: Editions du Signe, 1999.

---, ed. *John Wesley on Christian Beliefs: The Standard Sermons in Modern English*. Vol. I, 1-20. Nashville, Tennessee: Abingdon Press, 2003.

---, ed. *John Wesley on the Sermon on the Mount: The Standard Sermons in Modern English*. Vol. II, 21-33. Nashville, Tennessee: Abingdon Press, 2003.

---, ed. *John Wesley on Christian Practice: The Standard Sermons in Modern English*. Vol. III, 34-53. Nashville, Tennessee: Abingdon Press, 2003.

---. *Wesley: A Heart Transformed Can Change the World. Study Guide*. Nashville: Abingdon Press, 2011.

---. *John Wesley on Methodism* Asbury Theological Seminary Series: The Study of World Christian Revitalization Movements in Pietist/Wesleyan Studies. Lexington: Emeth Press, 2014.

Kirby, James E. *The Episcopacy in American Methodism.* Nashville: Kingswood Books, 2000.

Kirkpatrick, Dow, ed. *Second, 1962: The Doctrine of the Church.* Nashville: Abingdon Press, 1964.

---, ed. *Third, 1965: The Finality of Christ.* Nashville: Abingdon Press, 1966.

---, ed. *Fourth, 1969: The Living God.* Nashville: Abingdon Press, 1971.

---, ed. *Fifth, 1973: The Holy Spirit.* Nashville: Tidings, 1974.

Kisker, Scott. *Mainline or Methodist: Discovering Our Evangelistic Mission.* Nashville: Discipleship Resources, 2008.

Kissack, Reginald. *Church or No Church? A Study of the Development of the Concept of Church in British Methodism.* London: Epworth, 1964.

Knight, Henry H. *The Presence of God in the Christian Life: John Wesley and the Means of Grace.* Metuchen, New Jersey: Scarecrow Press, 1992.

---. *From Aldersgate to Azusa Street: Wesleyan, Holiness, and Pentecostal Visions of the New Creation.* Eugene, OR: Pickwick Publications, 2010.

---. *Anticipating Heaven Below: Optimism of Grace from Wesley to the Pentecostals*. Eugene, OR: Cascade Books, 2014

---. *John Wesley: Optimist of Grace*. Eugene: Cascade Books, 2018.

Knight, Henry H. and Don E. Saliers. *The Conversation Matters: Why United Methodists Should Talk With One Another.* Nashville: Abingdon Press, 1999.

Knight, Henry H., and F. Powe. *Transforming Evangelism: The Wesleyan Way of Sharing Faith*. Nashville: Discipleship Resources, 2006.

---. *Transforming Community: The Wesleyan Way to Missional Congregations*. Nashville: Discipleship Resources, 2016.

Knox, Robert B. *James Ussher, Archbishop of Armagh: 1581-1656.* Atlantic Highlands, New Jersey: Humanities, 1968.

Knox, Ronald Arbuthnott. *Enthusiasm: A Chapter in the History with Special Reference to the XVII and XVIII Centuries.* Oxford: Clarendon, 1950.

Koerber, Carolo. *The Theology of Conversion According to John Wesley.* Rome: Neo-Eboraci, 1967.

Koskie, Steven Joe. *Reading the Way to Heaven: A Wesleyan Theological Hermeneutic of Scripture*. Winona Lake, Indiana: Eisenbrauns, 2013.

Kostlevy, William, ed. *Holiness Manuscripts: A Guide to Sources Documenting the Wesleyan Holiness Movement in the United States and Canada*. Metuchen, New Jersey: Scarecrow Press, 1994.

Kostlevy, William, and Wallace Thornton. *The Radical Holiness Movement in the Christian Tradition: A Festschrift for Larry D. Smith Studies* in World Christian History. Lexington, Kentucky: Emeth Press, 2016.

Kraft, Thomas. *Pietismus Und Methodismus: Sozialethik Und Reformprogramme Von August Hermann Francke (1663-1727) Und John Wesley (1703-1791) Im Vergleich* Beiträge Zur Geschichte Der Evangelisch-Methodistischen Kirche; 47. Stuttgart: Medienwerk der Evangelisch-methodistischen Kirch GmbH, 2001.

Kromrei, Gerhart. *John Wesley: Ein Erweis Gottlicher Gnade* [John Wesley: An Evidence of Divine Grace]. Munchen: Anker, 1948.

Kurewa, John Wesley Zwomunondiita. *The Church in Mission: A Short History of the United Methodist Church in Zimbabwe, 1897-1997*. Nashville: Abingdon Press, 1997.

LaGorre, Agnes de. *Maitre d'un Peuple*. Paris: A. Michel, 1965.

Lancaster, Sarah Heaner. *The Pursuit of Happiness*. Eugene: Wipf & Stock Publishers, 2011.

Langford, Thomas A. *Practical Divinity: Theology in the Wesleyan Tradition.* Nashville: Abingdon Press, 1983. The basic survey.

---, comp. *Wesleyan Theology: A Sourcebook.* Durham, NC: Labyrinth Press, 1984.

---, ed. *Doctrine and Theology in the United Methodist Church.* Nashville: Kingswood Books, 1990. Sets 1972 and 1988 doctrinal statements in historical context.

---. *God Made Known.* Nashville: Abingdon Press, 1992.

---. *Practical Divinity, Volume I: Theology in the Wesleyan Tradition.* Nashville: Abingdon Press, 1998.

---. *Practical Divinity, Volume II: Readings in the Wesleyan Tradition.* Nashville: Abingdon Press, 1998.

Langford, Thomas A., Robert K. Johnston, L. Gregory Jones, and Jonathan R. Wilson. *Grace Upon Grace : Essays in Honor of Thomas A. Langford.* Nashville: Abingdon Press, 1999.

Laver, James. *Wesley.* Baton Rouge, Louisiana: R West, 1933.

Lawrence, William B. *Methodism in Recovery: Renewing Mission, Reclaiming History, Restoring Health*. Nashville: Abingdon Press, 2008.

Lawson, Albert B. *John Wesley and the Christian Ministry*. London: SPCK, 1963.

Lawson, Arvest N. *John Wesley and the Holy Spirit*. New York: Vantage Press, Inc., 1996.

Lawson, John. *Methodism and Catholicism*. London: S.P.C.K., 1954.

---. *Selections from John Wesley's Notes on the New Testament, Systematically Arranged with Explanatory Comments*. London: Epworth, 1955.

---. *Notes on Wesley's Forty-Four Sermons*. London: Epworth Press, 1964.

---. *The Wesley Hymns: As a Guide to Scriptural Teachings*. Grand Rapids, Michigan: Zondervan, 1988.

Lawton, George. *John Wesley's English: A Study of His Literary Style*. London: Allen and Unwin, 1962.

Lean, Garth. *John Wesley*. London: Blandford Press, 1964.

---. *Strangely Warmed*. Wheaton, Illinois: Tyndale, 1979.

---. *John Wesley: Revolution ohne Gewalt.* Griessen: Brunner Verlag, 1982.

Leclerc, Diane. *Discovering Christian Holiness: The Heart of Wesleyan-Holiness Theology*. Kansas City: Beacon Hill Press of Kansas City, 2010.

Leclerc, Diane and Mark A. Maddix. *Pastoral Practices: A Wesleyan Paradigm*. Kansas City: Beacon Hill, 2013.

Lee, Umphrey. *Historical Backgrounds of Early Methodist Enthusiasm.* New York: AMS Press, 1931.

---. *John Wesley and Modern Religion.* Nashville: Abingdon-Cokesbury, 1936.

---. *The Lord's Horseman: John Wesley the Man..* New York: Abingdon Press, 1928.

Leger, Augustin. *L'Angleterre religieuse et les Origins du Methodisme au xviiie Siecle.* Paris: Hatchette, 1910.

Lenton, John H. *My Sons in the Gospel: An Analysis of Wesley's Itinerant Preachers.* Loughborough, England: Wesley Historical Society, 2000.

---. *John Wesley's Preachers: A Social and Statistical Analysis of the British and Irish Preachers Who Entered the Methodist Itinerancy before 1791.* Colorado Springs: Paternoster Publishing, 2009.

Lelievre, Mateo. *Juan Wesley - Su Vida y Su Obra: The Life & Work of John Wesley.* Fort Lauderdale, Florida: TSELF, --.

Lelievre, Matthieu. *John Wesley: His Life and Works.* Charleston: BiblioLife, 2009

Lewis, Jayne Elizabeth, ed. Religion in Enlightenment England, 1660-1750: An Anthology of Primary Sources Documents of Anglophone Christianity Waco: Baylor University Press, 2017.

Lindsay, Gordon. *John Wesley and William Carey.* Vol. 4. 7 vols. Dallas, Texas: Christ Nations, 1979.

Lindstrom, Harald. *Wesley and Sanctification: A Study in the Doctrine of Salvation.* Grand Rapids, Michigan: Francis Asbury Press of Zondervan Publishing House, 1982. Reprint of 1950 edition.

Lipsky, Abram. *John Wesley: A Portrait.* New York: AMS Press, 1928.

Lischer, Richard. *The Company of Preachers : Wisdom on Preaching, Augustine to the Present.* Grand Rapids, MI: W.B. Eerdmans, 2002.

Little, Arthur Wilde. *The Times and Teachings of John Wesley.* Milwaukee, Wisconsin: The Young Churchman Co., 1905.

Lloyd, Gareth. *Charles Wesley and the Struggle for Methodist Identity*. Oxford: Oxford University Press, 2007.

Lockyer, Thomas F. *Paul, Luther, Wesley: A Study in Religious Experience as Illustrative of the Ethic of Christianity*. London: Epworth Press, 1922.

Lodahl, Michael. *The Story of God: Wesleyan Theology and Biblical Narrative.* Kansas City, Missouri: Beacon Hill Press, 1994.

---. God of Nature and of Grace: Reading the World in a Wesleyan Way. Nashville: Kingswood Books, 2003.

Logan, James C. *Theology and Evangelism in the Wesleyan Heritage*. Nashville, Tennessee: Kingswood Books, 1993.

Long, D. Stephen. *John Wesley's Moral Theology: The Quest for God and Goodness*. Nashville: Abingdon Press, 2005.

Long, D. Stephen, and George Kalantzis. *The Sovereignty of God Debate*. Eugene, Or.: Cascade Books, 2009.

Long, John Dixon, John Wesley, Richard Watson, University of North Carolina at Chapel Hill. Documenting the American South (Project), and University of North Carolina at Chapel Hill. Library. *Pictures of Slavery in Church and State Including Personal Reminiscences, Biographical Sketches, Anecdotes, Etc. Etc. : With an Appendix, Containing the Views of John Wesley and Richard Watson on Slavery*. Electronic ed. [Chapel Hill, N.C.]: Academic Affairs Library University of North Carolina at Chapel Hill, 2000.

Lowery, Kevin Twain. *Salvaging Wesley's Agenda: A New Paradigm for Wesleyan Virtue Ethics.* Eugene: Pickwick Publications, 2008.

Loyer, Kenneth. *God's Love through the Spirit: The Holy Spirit in Thomas Aquinas & John Wesley.* Washington, DC: The Catholic University Press, 2014.

Luby, Daniel Joseph. *The Perceptibility of Grace in the Theology of John Wesley. A Roman Catholic Consideration.* Rome: Pontificia Studiorum Universitas A.S. Thomas Aquinas in Urbe, 1994.

Luckock, Herbert Mortimer. *John Wesley's Churchmanship*. London: Longmans, Green and Co., 1891.

Lunn, Arnold. *John Wesley.* New York: The Dial Press, 1929.

Maas, Robin. *Crucified Love: The Practice of Christian Perfection.* Nashville: Abingdon Press, 1989.

MacArthur, Kathleen Walker. *The Economic Ethics of John Wesley.* New York: Abingdon-Cokesbury, 1936.

MacDonald, James A. *Wesley's Revision of the Shorter Catechism.* Edinburgh: George A. Morton, 1906.

Macquiban, Tim. *Pure, Universal Love: Reflections on the Wesleys and Inter-Faith Dialogue* Westminster Wesley Series No. 3. Oxford: Applied Theology Press, 1995.

---. *Issues in Education: Some Methodist Perspectives* Westminster Wesley Series No. 4. Oxford: Applied Theology Press, 1996.

Madden, Deborah. *A Cheap, Safe and Natural Medicine: Religion, Medicine and Culture in John Wesley's Primitive Physic.* Amsterdam, New York: Rodopi, 2007.

---. *Inward and Outward Health: John Wesley's Holistic Concept of Medical Science, the Environment and Holy Living.* Eugene, Or.: Wipf & Stock Publishers, 2012.

Maddock, Ian J. *Men of One Book: A Comparison of Two Methodist Preachers, John Wesley and George Whitefield.* Eugene: Pickwick Publications, 2011.

Maddock, Ian J., and David F. Wells. *Wesley and Whitefield?: Wesley Versus Whitefield?* Eugene, Oregon: Pickwick Publications, 2018.

Maddox, Randy L., ed. *Aldersgate Reconsidered.* Nashville: Kingswood Books, 1990.

---. *Responsible Grace: John Wesley's Practical Theology.* Nashville, Tennessee: Kingswood Books, 1994.

---. *Rethinking Wesley's Theology for Contemporary Methodism* Nashville, Tennessee: Kingswood Books, 1998.

Maddox, Randy L., and Jason E. Vickers. *The Cambridge Companion to John Wesley.* Cambridge: Cambridge University Press, 2010.

Malony, H. Newton. *The Amazing John Wesley: An Unusual Look at an Uncommon Life.* Colorado Springs: Biblica, 2010.

Marquardt, Manfred. *Praxis und Principien det SozialethikJohn Wesleys.* Gottingen: Vandenhoeck und Ruprecht, 1977.

---. *John Wesley's Social Ethics: Praxis and Principles.* Nashville: Abingdon Press, 1992.

---. *Praxis and Prinzipien Der Sozialethik John Wesleys.* Gottingen: Ruprecht, 2008.

Marston, Leslie Ray. *From Age to Age, A Living Witness: A Historical Interpretation of Free Methodism's First Hundred Years.* Winona Lake, IN: Light and Life Press, 1960.

Martin, Sydney. *John Wesley and the Witness of the Spirit.* Derbys, England: Morley's Bookshop, 1990.

Mathews, Donald G. *Slavery and Methodism.* Princeton, New Jersey: Princeton University Press, 2016.

Matthaei, Sondra. *Making Disciples: Faith Formation in the Wesleyan Tradition.* Nashville: Abingdon Press, 2000.

McClendon, James W., Jr. *Ethics: Systematic Theology I.* Nashville: Abingdon Press, 1987.

McConnell, Francis J. *John Wesley.* New York: Abingdon Press, 1939.

McCown, Wayne, and James Massey, eds. *God's Word for Today.* Anderson, Indiana: Warner Press, 1989.

McCormick, K. Steve. *Triune Love: John Wesley's Theology*. Nashville: Abingdon Press, 2018.

McDonald, Hugh Dermot. *Ideas of Revelation, Chapter IX.* London: MacMillan, 1959.

McDonald, Rev W. *John Wesley and his Doctrine.* Titusville, Pennsylvania: The Allegheny Wesleyan Methodist Connection, 1893.

McDonald, William. *John Wesley and His Doctrine*. Boston: McDonald and Gill Co., 1893.

McDonnell, Kilian, ed. *Presence, Power, Praise: Documents on the Charismatic Renewal.* Collegeville, MN: Liturgical Press, 1980.

McEllhenney, John G., ed. *United Methodism in America: A Compact History.* Nashville: Abingdon Press, 1992.

---. *John Wesley*, 4th ed. General Commission on Archives & History, United Methodist Church, 1996.

McEwan, David B. *Wesley as a Pastoral Theologian: Theological Methodology in John Wesley's Doctrine of Christian Perfection*. Colorado Springs: Paternoster Publishing, 2011.

---. *The Life of God in the Soul: The Integration of Love, Holiness, and Happiness in the Thought of John Wesley.* Milton Keynes: Paternoster Publishing, 2015.

---. *Exploring a Wesleyan Theology*. Lenexa, Kansas Global Nazarene Publications, 2017.

McGonigle, Herbert. *The Arminianism of John Wesley.* Derby's, England: Moorley's Bookshop, 1988.

---. *John Wesley's Doctrine of Prevenient Grace.* Derby's, London: Moorley's Bookshop, 1995.

---. *Sufficient Saving Grace: John Wesley's Evangelical Arminianism.* Carlisle, Cumbria UK: Paternoster Publishing, 2001.

---. *John Wesley: Exemplar of the Catholic Spirit.* Ilkeston: Moorley's Print & Publishing, 2014.

---. *John Wesley: The Death of Christ.* Ilkeston: Moorley's Print & Publishing, 2014.

---. *Epworth: The Cradle of Methodism.* Ilkeston: Moorley's Print & Publishing, 2014.

---. *John Wesley: Doctrine of Final Judgment.* Ilkeston: Moorley's Print & Publishing, 2015.

---. *The Methodist Pentecost, 1758-1763.* Ilkeston: Moorley's Print & Publishing, 2016.

---. John Wesley on the Great Salvation. Ilkeston: Moorley's Print & Publishing, 2017.

McGonigle, Herbert, Joseph Cunningham, and David Rainey. *The Path of Holiness: Perspectives in Wesleyan Thought in Honor of Herbert B. McGonigle.* Lexington: Emeth Press, 2014.

McKenna, David L. *Wesleyan Leadership in Troubled Times: Confronting the Culture, Challenging the Church*. Kansas City, Missouri: Beacon Hill Press of Kansas City, 2002.

McLeister, Ira Ford. *Conscience and Commitment: The History of the Wesleyan Methodist Church of America.* Wesleyan History series, Vol. 1. 4th revised ed. Marion, IN: Wesley Press, 1976.

McNeer, May, and Lynd Ward. *John Wesley.* Nashville, Tennessee: Abingdon, 1957.

McPheeters, J.C. *John Wesley's Heart-Warming Religion*. Nicholasville: Schmul Publishing Co., 2010.

McPherson, Joseph D. *Just as New as Christianity: An Early Methodist Critique of Modern Holiness Teaching*. Evansville, Illinois: Fundamental Wesleyan Publishers, 2016.

Meadows, Philip Roger. *The Wesleyan DNA of Discipleship: Fresh Expressions of Discipleship For the 21st-Century Church*. Cambridge, England: Grove Books, 2013.

Meeks, M. Douglas, ed. *The Future of the Methodist Theological Traditions.* Nashville: Abingdon Press, 1985.

---, ed. *What Should Methodists Teach? Wesleyan Tradition and Modern Diversity.* Nashville: Kingswood Books, 1990.

---, ed. *The Portion of the Poor: Good News to the Poor in the Wesleyan Tradition.* Nashville: Kingswood Books, 1995.

---. *Trinity, Community, and Power: Mapping Trajectories in Wesleyan Theology.* Nashville: Kingswood Books, 2000.

Meistad, Tore. *Martin Luther and John Wesley on the Sermon on the Mount.* Pietist and Wesleyan Studies, vol. 10. Metuchen, N.J.: Scarecrow Press, US, 1999.

Mercer, Jerry. *Being Christian: A United Methodist Vision for the Christian Life: Based on John Wesley's Original Tract, "The Character of a Methodist".* Nashville, Tennessee: Discipleship Resources, 1993.

Messer, Donald E., and William J. Abraham. *Unity, Liberty, and Charity: Building Bridges Under Icy Waters.* Nashville: Abingdon Press, 1996.

Methodist Episcopal Church., Thomas Coke, and John Wesley. *A Form of Discipline for the Ministers, Preachers, and Members of the Methodist Episcopal Church in America* Library of Methodist Classics. Nashville: United Methodist Publishing House, 1992.

Methodist Episcopal Church., and John Wesley. *The Sunday Service of the Methodists in North America. With Other Occasional Services* Library of Methodist Classics. Nashville: Methodist Publishing House, 1992.

Mickey, Paul A. *Essentials of Wesleyan Theology.* Grand Rapids, Michigan: The Francis Asbury Press of Zondervan Publishing House, 1980.

Milburn, G. E., and Wesley Historical Society. North East Branch. *The Travelling Preacher : John Wesley in the North-East of England 1742-1790 : With Details Also of the Work of Charles Wesley and Other Early Methodist Preachers.* Rev. ed. [Great Britain]: Wesley Historical Society North-East Branch, 2003.

Miller, Basil. *John Wesley.* Minneapolis, Minnesota: Bethany House, 1969.

---. *John Wesley.* Minneapolis, Minnesota: Edit Betania, 1983.

Miller, William C. *Holiness Works: A Bibliography.* Revised ed. Kansas City, MO: Beacon Hill Press, 1986.

Mitchell, Frank N. *The Writings of John Wesley: A Man for All Ages.* New York: Vantage Press, 1997.

Mitton, Charles Leslie. *A Clue to Wesley's Sermons.* London: Epworth Press, 1951.

Moede, Gerald F. *The Office of Bishop in Methodism: Its History and Development.* Nashville: Abingdon Press, 1964.

Monk, Robert C. *John Wesley: His Puritan Heritage.* Nashville: Abingdon Press, 1966.

---. John Wesley: His Puritan Heritage. 2nd ed. Pietist and Wesleyan Studies No. 11. Lanham, Maryland: Scarecrow Press, 1999.

Montgomery, Brint, Thomas Jay Oord, and others, eds. *Relational Theology: A Contemporary Introduction.* Eugene: Wipf & Stock Publishers, 2012.

Moore, Mary Elizabeth Mullino. "A Living Tradition: Critical Recovery and Reconstruction of Wesleyan Heritage." Nashville, Tennessee: Kingswood Books, 2013.

Moore, Robert L. *John Wesley and Authority: A Psychological Perspective.* Missoula, Montana: Scholars Press, 1979.

Morton, Harold Christopherson. *Messages that Made the Revival: Being a Presentation of the Main Teachings of Wesley and His Helpers.* London: Epworth Press, 1920.

Murray, Iain H. *Wesley and Men Who Followed.* Carlisle, PA: Banner of Truth Trust, 2003.

Naglee, David I. *From Font to Faith: John Wesley on Infant Baptism and the Nurture of Children.* New York: Peter Lang, 1987.

---. *From Everlasting to Everlasting: John Wesley on Eternity and Time.* 2 vols. New York: Peter Lang, 1991-1992.

Newton, John A. *Methodism and the Puritans.* London: Dr. William's Library Trust, 1964.

---. *Susanna Wesley and the Puritan Tradition in Methodism*. London: Epworth Press, 1968.

---. *John and Charles Wesley: Brothers in Arms.* Truro, England: Cornish Methodist Historical Association, 2004.

---. *Faith Working by Love: The Methodist Tradition.* Maryknoll, New York: Orbis Books, 2007.

Noppen, J. P. van. *Transforming Words : The Early Methodist Revival from a Discourse Perspective* Religions and Discourse, V. 3. Bern ; New York: Peter Lang, 1999.

Norris, Clive Murray. The Financing of John Wesley's Methodism C.1740-1800 Oxford; New York: Oxford University Press, 2017.

Norwood, Frederick A. *The Story of American Methodism: A History of the United Methodists and Their Relations.* Nashville: Abingdon Press, 1974.

---, ed. *The Methodist Discipline of 1798, including the annotations of Thomas Coke and Francis Asbury.* Rutland, VT: Academy Books, 1979.

---, ed. *Sourcebook of American Methodism.* Nashville: Abingdon Press, 1983.

Nuelsen, John Lewis. *Die Ordination in Methodismus: Beitrag zur Entstehungsgeschichte der kirkliche Selbstandigkeit der Methodistenkirche* [Ordination in Methodism]. Bremen: Verlagshaus der Methodistenkirche, 1935.

---. *Das Heilserlebnis im Methodismus* [The Experience of Salvation in Methodism]. Zurich: Christliche Vereinsbuchandlung, 1938.

O'Brien, Glen, and Hilary M Carey. *Methodism in Australia: A History Ashgate* Methodist Studies. London: Routledge, 2016.

Oden, Thomas C. *Doctrinal Standards in the Wesleyan Tradition.* Grand Rapids, Michigan: Francis Asbury Press of Zondervan Publishing House, 1988.

---. *John Wesley's Scriptural Christianity: A Plain Exposition of His Teaching on Christian Doctrine.* Grand Rapids, Michigan: Zondervan Publishing House, 1994.

---. and Leicester, eds. *The Wesleyan Theological Heritage: Essays of Albert C. Outler.* Grand Rapids, Michigan: Zondervan, 1991.

Oden, Thomas C. *Classic Christianity: A Systematic Theology*. New York: HarperOne, 1992.

---. *John Wesley's Teachings: God and Providence*. Vol. 1. 4 vols. Grand Rapids: Zondervan, 2012.

---. *John Wesley's Teachings: Christ and Salvation*. Vol. 2. 4 vols. Grand Rapids: Zondervan, 2012.

---. *John Wesley's Teachings: Pastoral Theology*. Vol. 3. 4 vols. Grand Rapids: Zondervan, 2013.

---. *John Wesley's Teachings: Ethics and Society*. Vol. 4. 4 vols. Grand Rapids: Zondervan, 2014.

Ogletree, Thomas W. *The Use of the Bible in Christian Ethics: A Constructive Essay.* Philadelphia: Fortress Press, 1983.

Oh, Gwang Seok. *John Wesley's Ecclesiology: A Study in Its Sources and Development*. Lanham, Maryland: Scarecrow Press, 2008.

Olson, Mark Jeffrey. *Wesley and Aldersgate: Interpreting Conversion Narratives*. Oxon; New York: Abingdon; Routledge, 2019.

Olson, Mark K. *John Wesley's Theology of Christian Perfection: Developments in Doctrine & Theological System*. Fenwick, MI: Truth in Heart, 2007.

O'Malley, J. Steven, and Jason A. Vickers, eds. *Methodist and Pietist: Retrieving the Evangelical United Brethren Tradition*. Nashville: Kingswood Books, 2011.

Oord, Thomas Jay. *Divine Grace and Emerging Creation: Wesleyan Forays in Science and Theology of Creation*. Eugene: Pickwick Publications, 2009.

---. and Michael Lodahl. *Relational Holiness: Responding to the Call of Love*. Kansas City, Missouri: Beacon Hill Press, 2005.

Outler, Albert C. *Evangelism in the Wesleyan Spirit.* Nashville: Tidings, 1971. See especially Chapter 3, "A Third Great Awakening?".

---. *Theology in the Wesleyan Spirit.* Nashville: Discipleship Resources, 1975.

Overton, J. H. *John Wesley.* London: Methuen and Co., 1891.

Owen, Christopher H. *The Sacred Flame of Love: Methodism & Society in Nineteenth-Century Georgia*. Athens, GA: University of Georgia Press, 1998.

Padgett, Alan G. *The Mission of the Church in Methodist Perspective : The World Is My Parish* Studies in the History of Missions V.10. Lewiston, New York: E. Mellen Press, 1992.

Page, Isaac E. *Scriptural Holiness as Taught by John Wesley*. London: Charles H. Kelly, 1891.

Palmer, Phoebe. *Phoebe Palmer: Selected Writings.* New York: Paulist Press, 1987.

Park, John Sungmin, ed. *Holiness as a Root of Morality: Essays on Wesleyan Ethics: Essays in Honor of Lane A. Scott.* Lewiston, N.Y.: Edwin Mellen Press, 2006.

Parris, John R. *John Wesley's Doctrine of the Sacraments.* London: Epworth Press, 1963.

Pasquarello, Michael. *John Wesley: A Preaching Life.* Nashville: Abingdon Press, 2010.

Payk, Christopher. *Grace First: Christian Mission and Prevenient Grace in John Wesley*. Toronto: Clements Academic, 2013.

Pellowe, Susan, ed. *A Wesley Family Book of Days.* Aurora, IL: Renard Productions, 1994.

Pellowe, William Charles Smithson. *John Wesley, Master in Religion: A Study in Methods and Attitudes.* Nashville: Methodist Episcopal Church, South, 1939.

Peters, John L. *Christian Perfection and American Methodism.* Grand Rapids, Michigan: Francis Asbury Press of Zondervan Publishing House, 1985. Reprint of the 1956 edition with a new foreword by Albert C. Outler.

Piccirilli, Agnostino. *I Valori Spirituali Wesleyani.* Salerno: Linotypographia M. Spadafora, 1938.

Pierce, T. R. *The Intellectual Side of John Wesley.* Nashville: Methodist Episcopal Church, South, 1897.

Piette, Maximin. *John Wesley in the Evolution of Protestantism.* London: Sheed and Ward, 1938.

Plumb, J.H. *England in the Eighteenth Century.* Harmondsworth, England: Penguin Books, 1950.

Podmore, Colin. *The Moravian Church in England 1728-1760.* Oxford: Clarendon Press, 1998.

Pollock, John. *John Wesley.* Oxford, England: Lion Publishing, 1989.

---. *John Wesley.* : Harold Shaw Publishers (North Wind Books), 1995.

---. *Wesley the Preacher*. Eastbourne, UK: Kingsway Publications, 2008.

Pool, Thomas E. *John Wesley the Soul Winner.* Salem, Ohio: Schmul Pub Co, 1979.

Price, Lynne. *Interfaith Encounter and Dialogue : A Methodist Pilgrimage*. Frankfurt am Main ; Bern ; New York: Lang, 1991.

Pritchard, John. *Methodists and Their Missionary Societies 1760-1900*. Burlington, VT: Ashgate Publishing Company, 2013.

--. *Methodists and Their Missionary Societies 1900-1996*. Burlington, VT: Ashgate, 2014.

---. *Methodists and Their Missionary Societies 1760-1900* Ashgate Methodist Studies. London: Routledge, 2016.

Prince, John Wesley. *Wesley on Religious Education.* New York: Methodist Book Concern, 1926.

Pucelik, Thomas M. *Christian Perfection According to John Wesley.* Rome: Officium Libri Catholici, 1963.

Pudney, John. *John Wesley and His World.* New York: Charles Scribner's Sons, 1978. Readable text, plus 125 excellent illustrations.

Pyke, Richard. *Dawn of American Methodism*. Eugene: Wipf & Stock Publishers, 2016.

Rack, Henry D. *The Future of John Wesley's Methodism.* Richmond, VA: John Knox, 1965.

---. *Reasonable Enthusiast: John Wesley and the Rise of Methodism.* London: Epworth Press, 1989.

---. *Reasonable Enthusiast : John Wesley and the Rise of Methodism*. 2nd ed. Nashville: Abingdon Press, 1993.

---. *The Methodist Societies: The Minutes of Conference.* Nashville: Abingdon Press, 2011.

Rack, Henry D., and Robert Webster. *Perfecting Perfection: Essays in Honour of Henry D Rack.* Cambridge: James Clarke & Co, 2016.

Raedel, Christoph, ed. *Methodismus Und Charismatische Bewegung*, Reutlinger Theologische Studien Band 2. Göttingen: Edition Ruprecht, 2007.

Rataboul, Louis J. *John Wesley, Un Anglican Sans Frontières: 1703-1791*. Nancy: Presses Universitaires de Nancy, 1991.

Rattenbury, J. Earnest. *Wesley's Legacy to the World: Six Studies in the Permanent Values of the Evangelical Revival.* London: Epworth Press, 1928.

---. *The Conversion of the Wesleys: A Critical Study.* London: Epworth Press, 1938.

---. *The Evangelical Doctrines of Charles Wesley.* London: Epworth, 1941.

---. *John Wesley and Social Service.* London: C. H. Kelley, 1943.

---. *The Eucharistic Hymns of John and Charles Wesley.* London: Epworth, 1948.

---. Timothy J. Crouch, ed. *The Eucharistic Hymns of John and Charles Wesley*, 2d ed. Akron, OH: Order of Saint Luke Publications, 1996.

---. *Eucharistic Hymns of John and Charles Wesley: To Which Is Appended Wesley's Preface Extracted... From Brevint's Christian Sacraments and Sacrifice.* Eugene, Or.: Wipf & Stock Publishers, 2014.

Rattenbury, John Ernest, John Wesley, Charles Wesley, and Timothy J. Crouch. *The Eucharistic Hymns of John and Charles Wesley : To Which Is Appended Wesley's Preface Extracted from Brevint's Christian Sacrament and Sacrifice Together with Hymns on the Lord's Supper.* American ed. Cleveland, Ohio: OSL Publications, 1990.

Ratnayka, Shanta. *Two Ways of Perfection: Buddhist and Christian.* Columbo: Lake House Investments, 1978.

Reasoner, Vic. *The Importance of Inerrancy: How Scriptural Authority Has Eroded in Modern Wesleyan Theology*. Evansville, IN: Fundamental Wesleyan Publishers, 2013.

Reasoner, Victor P. and Robert L. Brush, eds. *The Wesley Workbook: A Brief Biography Plus a Study Guide to the Standard Sermons* Evansville, IN: Fundamental Wesleyan Publishers, 1996.

Redwell, Randall. *May I Quote You, John Wesley*. : Cool Springs Press, 1996.

Renders, Helmut. *John Wesley Als Apologet: Systematisch-Theologische Hintergründe Und Praxis Wesleyanischer Apologetik Und Ihre Missionarische Bedeutung* Beiträge Zur Geschichte Der Evangelisch-Methodistischen Kirche 38. Stuttgart: Christliches Verlagshaus, 1990.

Richey, Russell E. *The Methodist Conference in America: A History*. Nashville: Abingdon Press, 1996.

---. *Extension Ministers: Mr. Wesley's True Heirs*. Nashville: United Methodist Church, General Board of Higher Education and Ministry, 2008.

---. *Methodism in the American Forest*. New York: Oxford University Press, 2015.

Richey, Russell, Dennis M. Campbell, and William B. Lawrence. *Marks of Methodism: Theology in Ecclesial Practice*. Nashville: Abingdon Press, 2005.

Richey, Russell E., Kenneth E. Rowe, and Jean Miller Schmidt, eds. *Perspectives on American Methodism: Interpretive Essays*. Nashville: Abingdon Press, 1993.

---, ed. *The Methodist Experience in America Sourcebook*. Nashville: Abingdon Press, 2000.

---. *American Methodism: A Compact History*. Nashville: Abingdon Press, 2012.

Rieger, Joerg, and John J. Vincent, eds. *Methodist and Radical: Rejuvenating a Tradition*. Nashville: Abingdon Press, 2003.

Rigg, James Harrison. *The Relations of John Wesley and Wesleyan Methodism to the Church of England Investigated and Determined*. London: Longmans, Green and Company Ltd., 1871.

---. *John Wesley, the Church of England, and Wesleyan Methodism: Their Relation to Each Other Clearly and Fully Explained*. London: Wesleyan Methodist Book Room, 1883.

---. *The Churchmanship of John Wesley and the Relations of Wesleyan Methodism to the Church of England.* London: Wesleyan Methodist Book Room, 1886.

---. *Oxford High Anglicanism and Its Chief Leaders.* London: C.H. Kelly, 1895.

Rightmire, David. *Sacraments and the Salvation Army: Pneumatological Foundations.* Studies in Evangelicalism ed. Metuchen, New Jersey: Scarecrow Press, 1990.

---. *Sanctified Sanity: The Life and Teaching of Samuel Logan Brengle.* Alexandria, Virginia: Crest Books, 2003.

Rodes, Stanley J. *From Faith to Faith: John Wesley's Covenant Theology and the Way of Salvation.* Cambridge: James Clarke & Co, 2014.

---. and Thomas A. Noble. From Faith to Faith: John Wesley's Covenant Theology and the Way of Salvation. Eugene: Pickwick, 2013.

Rogal, Samuel J. *John and Charles Wesley.* New York, New York: Macmillan, 1983.

---. *John Wesley's London: A Guidebook.* Lewiston, New York: E Mellen, 1988.

---. *John Wesley's Mission to Scotland.* Lewiston, New York: E Mellen, 1988.

---. *John Wesley in Ireland, 1747-1789.* Vol. 2 pts. Lewiston, New York: E Mellen, 1993.

---. *John Wesley in Wales, 1739-1790: Lions & Lambs.* Lewiston, New York: E Mellen, 1993.

---. *A Biographical Dictionary of 18th Century Methodism: P-Q,* vol. V., Lewiston, New York: E. Mellen Research University Press, 1998.

---. *The Financial Aspects of John Wesley's British Methodism.* Lewiston, N.Y.: Edwin Mellen Press, 2002.

---. *The Historical, Biographical, and Artistic Background of Extant Portrait Paintings and Engravings of John Wesley, (1742-1951)* Studies in Art and Religious Interpretation ; V. 30. Lewiston, N.Y.: Edwin Mellen Press, 2003.

---. *Bibliographical Survey of the Published Works of Eighteenth-Century Wesleys (Samuel the Elder, Samuel the Younger, Mehetabel, John, and Charles).* Lewiston: Edwin Mellen Press, 2008.

--. *The Literary Influence of Shakespeare Upon Charles and John Wesley.* Lewiston: The Edwin Mellen Press, 2015.

--. *The Wesleys in Cornwall, 1743-1789: A Record of Their Activities Town by Town.* Jefferson, NC: McFarland & Company, 2015.

Rogal, Samuel J., and Leslie Stephen. *Methodism through Victorian Eyes: Leslie Stephen, W.E.H. Lecky, and Woodrow Wilson.* Lewiston, N.Y.: Edwin Mellen Press, 2006.

Ross, Roger. *Meet the Goodpeople: Wesley's 7 Ways to Share Faith.* Nashville: Abingdon Press, 2015.

Routley, Erik R. *The Musical Wesleys.* New York: Oxford University Press, 1968.

Roux, Theophile. *La Conversion Evangelique de Wesley.* Paris: Depot des Publications Methodistes, 1938?

Rowe, Kenneth E., ed. *The Place of Wesley in the Christian Tradition.* Revised ed. Metuchen, New Jersey: Scarecrow Press, 1980. Reissue of 1976 edition with updated bibliography.

---. *United Methodist Studies: Basic Bibliographies, Fourth Edition.* Nashville: Abingdon Press, 1998.

Runyon, Theodore H., ed. *Sanctification and Liberation: A Reexamination in the Light of the Wesleyan Tradition.* Nashville: Abingdon Press, 1981.

---, ed. *Wesleyan Theology Today: A Bicentennial Theological Consultation.* Nashville: Kingswood Books, 1985.

---. *The New Creation: John Wesley's Theology Today.* Nashville: Abingdon Press, 1998.

---. *Exploring the Range of Theology*. Eugene, Or.: Wipf & Stock Publishers, 2012.

Rupp, E. Gordon. *Principalities and Powers.* London: Epworth, 1952.

---. *Methodism in Relation to the Protestant Tradition.* London: Epworth Press, 1954.

---. *Religion and England, 1688-1791.* Oxford: Clarendon, 1986.

Ruth, Lester. *A Little Heaven Below: Worship at Early Methodist Quarterly Meetings.* Nashville: Kingswood Books, 2000.

---., ed. *Early Methodist Life and Spirituality: A Reader.* Nashville: Kingswood Books, 2005.

Ryan, Linda Ann. *John Wesley and the Education of Children: Gender, Class and Piety* Routledge Methodist Studies Series. New York: Routledge, 2017.

Saliers, Don E. *Worship and Spirituality.* Philadelphia: Westminster Press, 1985.

---. *The Soul in Paraphrase: Prayer and the Religious Affections.* Cleveland: Order of Saint Luke Publications, 1992.

Sample, Tex. *The Future of John Wesley's Theology.* Eugene, Oregon: Cascade Books, 2012.

Sanders, Fred. *Wesley on the Christian Life: The Heart Renewed in Love.* Wheaton, Illinois: Crossway, 2013.

Sanderson, Joseph E. *The First Century of Methodism in Canada.* 2 vols. Toronto: William Briggs, 1908.

Sangster, William E. *The Path to Perfection: An Examination and Restatement of John Wesley's Doctrine of Christian Perfection.* London: Epworth Press, 1984. Reprint of 1943 edition.

Sargent, George Etell. *Oxford Methodist: Or, the Early Life of John Wesley.* [S.I.]: General Books, 2010.

Schempp, Johannes. *Seelsorge und Seelenfurhung bei John Wesley* [Spiritual Care and Spiritual Direction According to John Wesley]. Stuttgart: Christliches Verlaghaus, 1949.

Schilling, Sylvester Paul. *Methodism and Society in Theological Perspective.* Nashville: Abingdon, 1960.

Schlenther, Boyd S. *Queen of the Methodists: The Countess of Huntingdon & the Eighteenth-Century Crisis of Faith & Society.* Durham: Durham Academic Press, 1997.

Schmidt, Darren. *The Pattern of Revival: John Wesley's Vision of "Iniquity" and "Godliness" in Church History.* Woodbridge, UK: Boydell Press for the Ecclesiastical History Society, 2008.

Schmidt, Jean Miller. *Grace Sufficient.* Nashville: Abingdon Press, 1999.

Schmidt, Martin. *Die Bedeutung Luthers fur John Wesleys Bekerhung* [The Significance of Luther for the Conversion of John Wesley]. Bremen, 1938.

---. *The Young Wesley: Missionary and Theologian of Missions.* London: Epworth, 1958.

---. *John Wesley: A Theological Biography.* 2 vols. Nashville: Abingdon Press, 1962-1973.

---. *John Wesley: A Theological Biography*. Eugene: Wipf & Stock Publishers, 2016.

Schneider, A. Gregory. *The Way of the Cross Leads Home: Social Religion and Domestic Ideology in 19th Century Methodist Evangelicalism.* Bloomington, IN: Indiana University Press, 1992.

Schoenhals, G. Roger. *Wesley's Notes on the Bible.* Grand Rapids, Michigan: Zondervan, 1987.

Schwartz, William Andrew, John M. Bechtold, and Michael Lodahl. *Embracing the Past -- Forging the Future: A New Generation of Wesleyan Theology.* Eugene, OR: Pickwick Publications, 2015.

Schwenk, James L. *Catholic Spirit: Wesley, Whitefield, and the Quest for Evangelical Unity in Eighteenth-Century British Methodism.* Lanham, Maryland: Scarecrow Press, 2008.

Scott, Sir Percy. *John Wesleys Lehre von der Heiligung vergleichen mit einen lutherish-pietistischen Beispel* [John Wesley's Doctrine of Salvation compared with a Lutheran-pietistic Example]. Berlin: Alfred Topelman, 1939.

Seamands, Steve A. *Holiness of Heart and Life.* Nashville: Abingdon Press, 1991.

Seifert, Harvey. *What on Earth? Making Personal Decisions on Controversial Issues.* Nashville: Discipleship Resources for Church and Society, 1991.

Semmel, Bernard. *The Methodist Revolution.* New York: Basic Books, 1972.

Shelton, W. Brian. *Prevenient Grace: God's Provision for Fallen Humanity.* Anderson, Indiana: Warner Press, Inc., 2014.

Shephard, Thomas B. *Methodism and the Literature of the 18th Century.* New York: Haskell House, 1966.

---. *Methodism & the Literature of the 18th Century.* Brooklyn, New York: M S G Haskell House, 1969.

Shepherd, Victor A. *Mercy Immense and Free: Essays on Wesley and Wesleyan Theology*. Toronto: Clements Academic 2010.

---. *Mercy Immense and Free: Essays on Wesley and Wesleyan Theology*. Toronto: BPS Books, 2016.

Short, L. Faye, and Kathryn D. Kiser. *Reclaiming the Wesleyan Social Witness: Offering Christ*. Franklin, Tennessee.: Providence House, 2008.

Simon, John S. *John Wesley and the Advance of Methodism*. London: The Epworth Press, 1925.

---. *John Wesley and the Religious Societies*. London: Epworth Press, 1955.

---. *John Wesley: The Last Phase*. Eugene: Wipf & Stock Publishers, 2016.

Slaatte, Howard. *Fire in the Brand: An Introduction to the Creative Work and Theology of John Wesley*. Lanham, Maryland: University Press of America, 1983.

---. *A Purview of Wesley's Theology*. Lanham, Maryland: University Press of America, 2000.

Slater, William Fletcher. *Methodism in the Light of the Early Church*. London: T. Woolmer, 1885.

Smith, Timothy L. *Called Unto Holiness: The Story of the Nazarenes, the Formative Years.* Kansas City: Nazarene Publishing House, 1962.

---. *Revivalism and Social Reform: American Protestantism on the Eve of the Civil War.* New York: Peter Smith, 1976. Reprint of 1957 edition.

---. *Whitefield and Wesley on the New Birth.* Grand Rapids, Michigan: Francis Asbury Press of Zondervan Publishing House, 1986.

Smith, Warren T. *John Wesley and Slavery.* Nashville: Abingdon, 1986.

Snell, F. J. *Wesley and Methodism.* New York: Scribner, 1900.

Snyder, Howard A. *The Radical Wesley and Patterns for Church Renewal.* Downers Grove, Illinois: Inter-Varsity Press, 1980.

---. *The Radical Wesley: Pattern for Church Renewal.* Grand Rapids, Michigan: Zondervan Publishing House, 1987.

---. *Sign of the Spirit: How God Reshapes the Church.* Grand Rapids, Michigan: Zondervan, 1989.

---. *Yes in Christ: Wesleyan Reflections on Gospel, Mission and Culture.* Toronto: Clements Academic, 2010.

Snyder, Howard A., and Daniel V. Runyon. *The Divided Flame: Wesleyans and the Charismatic Renewal.* Grand Rapids, Michigan: Francis Asbury Press of Zondervan Publishing House, 1986.

Sommer, Johann Willhelm Ernst. *John Wesley und die soziale Frage Mit einem Bericht uber den Verein fur Geschichte des Methodismus von Theopil Mann.* Bremen: Verlagshaus der Methodistenkirche, 1930.

Southey, Robert. *The Life of Wesley; and Rise and Progress of Methodism.* Vol. 1. London: Longman, Brown, Green, and Longmans, 1846.

Spurgeon, C. H. *The Two Wesleys.* Pasadena, Texas: Pilgrim Publishers, 1975.

---. *The Two Wesleys: On John and Charles Wesley.* Eugene: Wipf & Stock Publishers, 2014.

Stacey, John, ed. *John Wesley: Contemporary Perspectives.* Valley Forge, Pennsylvania: Epworth Press, 1988.

Stanglin, Keith D., Mark G. Bilby, and Mark H. Mann, eds. *Reconsidering Arminius: Beyond the Reformed and Wesleyan Divide.* Nashville: Abingdon Press, 2014.

Staples, Rob L. *Outward Sign and Inward Grace: The Place of Sacraments in Wesleyan Spirituality.* Kansas City, Missouri: Beacon Hill, 1991.

Starkey, Lycurgus M. *The Work of the Holy Spirit: A Study in Wesleyan Theology.* Nashville: Abingdon Press, 1962.

Steele, Richard B. *Gracious Affection & True Virtue According to Jonathan Edwards & John Wesley.* Metuchen, New Jersey: Scarecrow Press, 1994.

Stephen, Leslie. *History of English Thought in the Eighteenth Century*. London: Smith, Elder and Co., 1881.

Stokes, Mack B. *The Holy Spirit in the Wesleyan Heritage.* Nashville: Graded Press, 1985.

---. *The Bible in the Wesleyan Heritage*. Nashville: Abingdon Press, 1981.

Stone, Bryan P., and Thomas Jay Oord, eds. *Thy Name and Thy Nature Is Love: Wesleyan and Process Theologies in Dialogue*. Nashville: Kingswood Books, 2001.

Stone, Ronald H. *John Wesley's Life & Ethics*. Nashville, Tennessee: Abingdon Press, 2001.

Strong, Douglas M. *Reclaiming the Wesleyan Tradition: John Wesley's Sermons for Today*. Nashville: Discipleship Resources, 2007.

Stuart, James. *The John Wesley Code: Finding a Faith That Matters*. Wellington, N.Z.: Philip Garside, 2008.

Sturm, Roy A. *Sociological Reflections on John Wesley and Methodism.* Indianapolis, Indiana: Central Publishing, 1982.

Suray, Joseph Basappa. *Towards a Theology of Universality: John Wesley's Socio-Economic, Political & Moral Insights on British Class & Indian Caste Distinctions.* New Delhi: Christian World Imprints, 2015.

Sweet, Leonard I., ed. *The Evangelical Tradition in America.* Macon, GA: Mercer University Press, 1984.

---. *11 Genetic Gateways to Spiritual Awakening.* Nashville: Abingdon Press, 1998.

Sweet, William W. *Methodism in American History.* Revised ed. Nashville: Abingdon Press, 1953.

---. *Religion of the American Frontier, 1783-1940: The Methodists, a Collection of Source Materials.* New York: Cooper Square, 1964.

Synan, Vinson. *The Holiness-Pentecostal Movement.* Grand Rapids, Michigan: Wm. B. Eerdmans, 1972.

Tabraham, Barrie W. *The Making of Methodism.* London: Epworth Press, 1995.

Taylor, Blaine. *John Wesley: A Blueprint for Church Renewal.* Urbana, Illinois: C-Four Res., 1984.

Taylor, E.R. *Methodism and Politics*. Cambridge: Cambridge University Press, 2016.

Taylor, Isaac. *Wesley and Methodism*. London: Longman, Brown, Green and Longmans, 1852.

Taylor, Richard S. *A Right Conception of Sin*. Kansas City: Beacon Hill Press, 1939.

Telford, John. *The Life of John Wesley.* London: Wesleyan Methodist Book Room, 1899.

Temperley, Nicholas. *Music and the Wesleys*. Urbana: University of Illinois Press, 2010.

Thomas, Paul W. *The Days of our Pilgrimage: The History of the Pilgrim Holiness Church.* Wesleyan History series, Vol. 2. Marion, IN: Wesley Press, 1976.

Thompson, D. D. *John Wesley and George Whitefield in Scotland: Or, the Influence of the Oxford Methodists on Scottish Religion*. London: Blackwood and Sons, 1898.

---. *John Wesley as a Social Reformer.* Manchester, New Hampshire: Ayer, 1898.

Thompson, Edgar W. *Wesley: Apostolic Man: Some Reflections on Wesley's Consecration of Dr. Thomas Coke*. London: Epworth Press, 1957.

Thompson, Matthew. *Kingdom Come: Revisioning Pentecostal Eschatology*. Blandform Forum, Dorset, U.K.: Deo Pub., 2010.

Thorsen, Donald A. *The Wesleyan Quadrilateral: Scripture, Tradition, Reason & Experience as a Model of Evangelical Theology.* Grand Rapids, Michigan: Francis Asbury Press of Zondervan Publishing House, 1990.

---. *Calvin Vs Wesley: Bringing Belief in Line with Practice*. Nashville: Abingdon Press, 2013.

Todd, John M. *John Wesley and the Catholic Church.* London: Hodder and Stoughton, 1958.

Tolar Burton, Vicki. *Spiritual Literacy in John Wesley's Methodism: Reading, Writing, and Speaking to Believe*. Waco, Tex.: Baylor University, 2008.

Tomkins, Stephen. *John Wesley: A Biography*. Grand Rapids, Michigan: William B. Eerdmans, 2003.

Tooley, Mark. *Methodism and Politics in the Twentieth Century*. Fort Valley, Georgia: Bristol House, 2011.

Towlson, Clifford W. *Moravian and Methodist: Relationships and Influences in the Eighteenth Century.* London: Epworth Press, 1957.

Tripp, David H. *The Renewal of the Covenant in the Methodist Tradition.* London: Epworth, 1969.

Truesdale, Albert L., and Keri Mitchell. *With Cords of Love: A Wesleyan Response to Religious Pluralism*. Kansas City: Beacon Hill Press of Kansas City, 2006.

Truesdale, Albert L., and Henry H. Knight, et. al. *Global Wesleyan Dictionary of Theology*. Kansas City: Beacon Hill Press, 2013.

Tucker, Karen B. Westerfield. *The Sunday Service of the Methodists: Twentieth-Century Worship in Worldwide Methodism.* Nashville: Abingdon Press, 1996.

Tuell, Jack M. *The Organization of the United Methodist Church.* Nashville: Abingdon Press, 1997.

Turner, George Allen. *The More Excellent Way.* Winona Lake, IN: Light and Life Press, 1952.

---. *The Vision That Transforms: Is Christian Perfection Scriptural?* Kansas City, Missouri: Beacon Hill Press of Kansas City, 1964.

Turner, John M. *Conflict and Reconciliation: Studies in Methodism and Ecumenism in England, 1740-1982.* London: Epworth, 1985.

---. John Wesley: The Evangelical Revival and the Rise of Methodism in England. Peterborough: Epworth Press, 2002.

Tuttle, Robert G., Jr. *John Wesley: His Life and Theology.* Grand Rapids, Michigan: Zondervan, 1982.

---. *Mysticism in the Wesleyan Tradition.* Grand Rapids, Michigan: Francis Asbury Press of Zondervan Publishing House, 1989.

Tyerman, L. *The Life and Times of the Rev. John Wesley, M.A.* Vol. 3 vols. New York: Burt Franklin, 1872.

---. *The Life and Times of Samuel Wesley, M.A., Rector of Epworth and Father of the Revs. John and Charles, the Founders of the Methodists.* London: Simpkin and Marshall, 1866.

---. *The Life and Times of the Rev. John Wesley, M.A., Founder of the Methodists.* London: Hodder and Stoughton, 2009.

Tyson, John R. *Charles Wesley on Sanctification: A Biographical and Theological Study.* Grand Rapids, Michigan: Francis Asbury Press of Zondervan Publishing House, 1986.

---. comp. Charles Wesley: A Reader. New York: Oxford University Press, 1989.

---. *Assist Me to Proclaim: The Life and Hymns of Charles Wesley*. Grand Rapids, Michigan: William B. Eerdmans, 2007.

---. *The Way of the Wesleys: A Short Introduction.* Grand Rapids: William B. Eerdmans, 2014.

United Methodist Church. *Guidelines: The United Methodist Church and the Charismatic Renewal.* Nashville: Discipleship Resources, 1976.

---. *Foundations for Teaching and Learning in the United Methodist Church.* Nashville: Discipleship Resources, 1979.

---. *Wesleyan Spirituality in Contemporary Theological Education: A Consultation held October 17-19, 1987.* Nashville: Division of Ordained Ministry, General Board of Higher Education and Ministry, United Methodist Church, 1987.

---. *Faith, Doubt, and Courage in Fifteen Great People of Faith and What We Can Learn from Them.* Nashville: Abingdon Press, 2008.

Urlin, Richard Denny. *John Wesley's Place in Church History.* London: Rivington's, 1870.

---. *The Churchman's Life of Wesley.* London: SPCK, 1880.

Urwin, Evelyn Clifford, and Douglas Wollen. *John Wesley--Christian Citizen: Selections From His Social Teaching.* London: Epworth Press, 1937.

Vallins, George Henry. *The Wesley's and the English Language.* London: Epworth, 1957.

van Noppen, Jean-Pierre. *Transforming Words: The Early Methodist Revival From a Discourse Perspective.* Bern: Peter Lang (Religion and Discourse, 3), 1999.

---. *Critical Theolinguistics: Methodism, its Discourse and its Work Ethic.* Duisburg, Germany: Linguistic Agency of the University of Duisburg, 1996.

Verhalen, Phillipo A. *The Proclamation of the Word in the Writings of John Wesley.* Rome: Pontificia Universitas Gregoriana, 1969.

Vernon, Louise. *A Heart Strangely Warmed: The Life of John Wesley.* Pasadena: Greenleaf Press, 1994.

Vickers, Jason E. *Wesley: A Guide for the Perplexed.* London: T & T Clark, 2009.

Vickers, John. *John Wesley.* Fort Washington, PA: Christian Literature Crusade, 1977.

---. *Myths of Methodism*. Oxford: Wesley Historical Society, 2008.

Vincent, John J. *OK, Let's Be Methodist.* London: Epworth, 1984.

Vulliamy, C. E. *John Wesley.* Westwood, New Jersey: Barbour and Company, 1985.

Wainwright, Geoffrey. *Doxology: A Systematic Theology*. New York: Oxford University Press, 1984.

---. *Geoffrey Wainwright on Wesley and Calvin: Sources for Theology, Liturgy and Spirituality.* Melbourne: Uniting Church Press, 1987.

---. *Methodists in Dialog.* Nashville, TN: Kingswood Books, 1995.

Wakefield, Gordon. *Methodist Devotions: The Spiritual Life in the Methodist Tradition, 1791-1945.* London: Epworth Press, 1966.

---, ed. *The Fire of Love: The Spirituality of John Wesley.* London: Darton,Longman and Todd, 1976.

Waldo, Beach, and H. Richard Niebuhr, eds. *Christian Ethics.* New York: Roland Press, 1955. See "John Wesley," 353-365.

Waller, Ralph. *John Wesley : A Personal Portrait.* New York: Continuum, 2003.

Walls, Francine E. *The Free Methodist Church: A Bibliography.* Winona Lake, IN: Free Methodist Historical Center, 1977.

Warner, Wellman J. *Wesleyan Movement in the Industrial Revolution.* Berkeley, California: Russell, 1967.

Watson, David L. *The Early Methodist Class Meeting: Its Origins and Significance.* Nashville: Discipleship Resources, 1985.

---. *Class Leaders: Recovering a Tradition.* Nashville: Discipleship Resources, 1991.

---. *Covenant Discipleship: Christian Formation Through Mutual Accountability.* Nashville: Discipleship Resources, 1991.

---. *Forming Christian Disciples: The Role of Covenant Discipleship and Class Leaders in the Congregation.* Nashville: Discipleship Resources, 1991.

Watson, Kevin M. *A Blueprint for Discipleship: Wesley's General Rules as a Guide for Christian Living.* Nashville: Discipleship Resources, 2009.

---. *Pursuing Social Holiness: The Band Meeting in Wesley's Thought and Popular Methodist Practice.* New York: Oxford University Press, 2013.

---. *The Class Meeting: Reclaiming a Forgotten (and Essential) Small Group Experience.* Wilmore, Kentucky: Seedbed Publishing, 2014.

Watson, Pauline. 'Two Scrubby Travellers': A Psychoanalytic View of Flourishing and Constraint in Religion through the Lives of John and Charles Wesley. London: Taylor and Francis, 2018.

Watson, Philip S., ed. *The Message of the Wesleys: A Reader of Instruction and Devotion.* Grand Rapids, Michigan: Zondervan Publishing House, 1984. Reprint of 1964 edition.

---. *Anatomy of a Conversion.* Grand Rapids, Michigan: Zondervan, 1990.

Watson, Richard. *The Life of the Rev. John Wesley.* S. Hoyt & Co.: New York, 1831.

Webb, Todd. *Transatlantic Methodists: British Wesleyanism and the Formation of an Evangelical Culture in Nineteenth-Century Ontario and Quebec*. Montreal: McGill-Queen's University Press, 2013.

Weber, Theodore R. *Politics and the Order of Salvation: Transforming Wesleyan Political Ethics.* Nashville: Kingswood Books, 1998.

Webster, Robert. *Methodism and the Miraculous: John Wesley's Idea of the Supernatural and the Identification of Methodists in the Eighteenth-Century*. Lexington: Emeth Press, 2012.

Webster, Robert and Henry Rack. *Perfecting Perfection: Essays in Honor of Henry D. Rack.* Eugene, OR: Pickwick Publications, 2015.

Weems, Jr. Lovett H. *Leadership in the Wesleyan Spirit.* Nashville: Abingdon Press, 1999.

---. *John Wesley's Message Today.* Nashville: Abingdon Press, 1991.

Weeter, Mark L. *John Wesley's View and Use of Scripture.* Eugene: Wipf & Stock Publishers, 2007.

Weissbach, Jurgen. *Der neu Mensch in theologischen Denken John Wesleys* [The New Humanity in the Theological Thought of John Wesley]. Stuttgart: Christliches Verlaghaus, 1970.

Wellman, Sam. *John Wesley*, (Heroes of the Faith series). New Jersey: Barbour Publishing, 1997.

---. *John Wesley: Founder of the Methodist Church*, (Heroes of the Faith series). : Chelsea House Publishers, 1999.

Wesley, John, and Dave Armstrong. *The Quotable Wesley*. Kansas City: Beacon Hill, 2014.

Weston, Frank. *The Teaching of John Wesley as Gathered from His Writings*. London: Society for Promoting Christian Knowledge, 1912.

Weyer, Michel. *Die Bedeutung von Wesleys Lehrpredigten fur die Methodisten.* Stuttgart: Christliches Verlagshaus, 1987.

Whaling, Frank, ed. *John and Charles Wesley: Selected Prayers, Hymns, Journal Notes, Sermons, Letters and Treatises.* Classics of Western Spirituality. New York: Paulist Press, 1981.

---, ed. *John and Charles Wesley: Selected Writings and Hymns.* Mahwah, New Jersey: Paulist Press, 1981.

Whiteman, Darrell L. *World Mission in the Wesleyan Spirit.* Franklin, Tn.: Providence House Publishers, 2009.

Wigger, John H. *Taking Heaven by Storm: Methodism & the Popularization of American Christianity, 1770-1820.* (Religion in America series). New York: Oxford University Press, 1998.

---. American Saint: Francis Asbury and the Methodists. Oxford: Oxford University Press, 2009.

Wiley, H. Orton. *Christian Theology, Vol 1.* Kansas City: Beacon Hill Press, 1940-1943.

---. *Christian Theology,* Vol 2. Kansas City: Beacon Hill Press, 1940-1943.

---. *Christian Theology,* Vol 3. Kansas City: Beacon Hill Press, 1960.

Wiley, H. Orton, and Paul T. Culbertson. *Introduction to Christian Theology*. Kansas City, Missouri: Beacon Hill Press of Kansas City, 1946.

Williams, Colin. *John Wesley's Theology Today.* Nashville: Abingdon Press, 1960.

Williamson, Mark. *A Blueprint for Revival: A New Biography: Lessons from the Life of John Wesley.* Milton Keynes: Authentic, 2011.

Willimon, William H. *Why I Am a United Methodist.* Nashville: Abingdon Press, 1990.

--- . *This We Believe: The Core of Wesleyan Faith and Practice.* Nashville: Abingdon Press, 2010.

Wilmoth, Rodney E. *How United Methodists Share Their Faith.* Nashville: Abingdon Press, 1999.

Wilson, Charles Randall. *The Correlation of Love and Law in the Theology of John Wesley.* Ann Arbor, Michigan: University Microfilms International, 1959.

Wilson, David D. *Many Waters Cannot Quench: A Study of the Sufferings of Eighteenth-century Methodism and their Significance for John Wesley and the First Methodists.* London: Epworth, 1969.

Wilson, David. *Church and Chapel in Industrializing Society: Anglican Ministry and Methodism in Shropshire, 1760-1785* American University Stuides: Theology and Religion. New York: Peter Lang Publishing 2016.

Wilson, Julian. *The Wesleys.* Milton Keynes: Authentic Publishers, 2016.

Wimberly, Edward P. *No Shame in Wesley's Gospel: A Twenty-First Century Pastoral Theology.* Eugene: Wipf & Stock Publishers, 2011.

Witherington, Ben. *The Problem with Evangelical Theology: Testing the Exegetical Foundations of Calvinism, Dispensationalism, Wesleyanism, and Penecostalism.* Waco: Baylor University Press, 2016.

Wogaman, J. Philip. *Christian Moral Judgement.* Philadelphia: Westminster Press, 1989.

---. *Making Moral Decisions.* Nashville: Abingdon Press, 1990.

Wood, A. Skevington. *The Burning Heart: John Wesley, Evangelist.* Minneapolis, MN: Bethany House, 1978.

---. *Love Excluding Sin: Wesley's Doctrine of Sanctification.* Derbys, England: Moorley's Bookshop, 1986.

---. *Revelation and Reason: Wesleyan Responses to Eighteenth-Century Rationalism.* Bulkington: The Wesley Fellowship, 1992.

Wood, Laurence W. *The Meaning of Pentecost in Early Methodism, Rediscovering John Fletcher as John Wesley's Vindicator and Designated Successor.* Lanham, Maryland: Scarecrow Press, 2002.

Workman, Herbert Brook. *The Place of Methodism in the Catholic Church.* London: Hodder and Stoughton, 1921.

---. *Methodism.* Cambridge: Cambridge University Press, 2012.

Wynkoop, Mildred Bangs. *Foundations of Wesleyan-Arminian Theology*. Kansas City, MO: Beacon Hill Press, 1967.

---. *John Wesley, Christian Revolutionary*. Kansas City: Beacon Hill, 1970.

---. *A Theology of Love.* Kansas City, Missouri: Beacon Hill Press, 1972.

Yates, Arthur S. *The Doctrine of Assurance: With Special Reference to John Wesley.* London: Epworth Press, 1952.

Yoo, Joseph Chang Hyung. *A Reformed Doctrine of Sanctification for the Korean Context: The Critical Analysis of Calvin, Wesleyan and Barth on Sanctification and It's Application to the Korean Context.* Saarbrucken, Germany: VDM Verlag Dr. Muller Aktiengesellschaft & Co. KG 2009.

Young, Carlton. *Music of the Heart: John and Charles Wesley on Music and Musicians - An Anthology.* Introduction by S.T. Kimbrough, Jr. Birmingham, AL: Hope Publishing Company, 1995.

Yrigoyen, Charles. *T & T Clark Companion to Methodism.* New York: T & T Clark, 2010.

Yrigoyen, Charles and Warrick, Susan E. *Historical Dictionary of Methodism.* London: The Scarecrow Press, 1996.

Yrigoyen, Charles Jr. and Ruth A. Daugherty. *John Wesley: Holiness of Heart and Life.* Nashville: Abingdon Press, 1999.

Yrigoyen, Charles, John G. McEllhenney, and Kenneth A. Rowe. *United Methodism at Forty: Looking Back Looking Forward.* Nashville: Abingdon Press, 2008.

Chapters in Books

Abelove, Henry Diamond. "The Sexual Politics of Early Wesleyan Methodism." In *Disciplines of Faith.*, edited by Jim Obelkevich, 86-99. London: Routledge & Kegan Paul, 1987.

Abraham, William James. "Inspiration in the Classical Wesleyan Tradition." In *A Celebration of Ministry: Essays in Honor of Frank Bateman Stanger.*, edited by Kenneth C. Kinghorn, 33-47. Wilmore, Kentucky: Francis Asbury Press, 1982.

---. "The Wesleyan Quadrilateral." In *Wesleyan Theology Today.*, edited by Theodore H. Runyon, 119-26. Nashville: Kingswood, 1985.

Allchin, Arthur MacDonald. "Our Life in Christ, in John Wesley and the Eastern Fathers." In *We Belong to One Another: Methodist, Anglican and Orthodox.*, edited by Arthur MacDonald Allchin, 62-78. London: Epworth, 1965.

Arias, Mortimer. "Methodist Societies in the Eighteenth Century and Christian Base Communities in the Twentieth Century." In *Wesleyan Theology Today.*, edited by Theodore H. Runyon, 227-39. Nashville: Kingswood Books, 1985.

---. "Distortions in the Transmission of the Original Legacy of Wesley." In *Faith Born in the Struggle for Life.*, edited by Dow Kirkpatrick, 229-43. Grand Rapids, MI: Eerdmans, 1988.

Assmann, Hugo. "Is `Social Holiness' Enough? A Catholic Reading." In *Faith Born in the Struggle for Life.*, edited by Dow Kirkpatrick, 26-37. Grand Rapids, Michigan: Eerdmans, 1988.

Baker, Frank. "The Doctrines in the Discipline." In *From Wesley to Asbury: Studies in Early American Methodism.*, edited by Frank Baker, 162-82. Durham, NC: Duke University Press, 1976.

Barratt, Thomas H. "The Lord's Supper in Early Methodism." *In Methodism: Its Present Responsibilities, The Proceedings of the Methodist Church Conference, Bristol,* 71-81. London: Epworth Press, 1929.

Bence, Clarence Luther. "Salvation and the Church: The Ecclesiology of John Wesley." In *The Church.*, edited by Melvin Dieter and Daniel Berg, 297-317. Anderson, Indiana: Warner, 1984.

Berg, Daniel. "The Marks of the Church in the Theology of John Wesley." In *The Church.*, edited by Melvin Dieter and Daniel Berg, 319-31. Anderson, Indiana: Warner, 1984.

Berger, Teresa. "Charles Wesley: A Literary Overview." In *Charles Wesley: Poet and Theologian.*, edited by S. T. Kimbrough, Jr., 21-29. Nashville: Kingswood Books, 1988.

Bouyer, Louis. "John Wesley and Methodism." In *Orthodox Spirituality & Protestant and Anglican Spirituality.*, 187-93. New York, New York: Desclee, 1965.

Brown, Earl Kent. "Feminist Theology and the Women of Mr. Wesley's Methodism." In *Wesleyan Theology Today.*, edited by Theodore H. Runyon, 143-50. Nashville: Kingswood, 1985.

Burrows, Aelred. "Wesley the Catholic." In *John Wesley: Contemporary Perspectives.*, edited by John Stacey, 54-66. London, England: Epworth, 1988.

Campbell, Ted Allen. "John Wesley on the Mission of Church." In *The Mission of the Church in Methodist Perspective.*, edited by Alan Padgett, 45-62. Lewiston, New York: Edwin Mellen, 1992.

Chandler, Douglas R. "John Wesley and the Uses of the Past." In *The 1972 Wilson Lectures.*, 27-37. Washington, DC: Wesley Theological Seminary, 1972.

Christensen, Michael J. "John Wesley: Christian Perfection as Faith Filled with the Energy of Love." In *Partakers of the Divine Nature*. Grand Rapids, MI: Baker Academic, 2008.

Cho, John Chongnahm. "John Wesley's View of Fallen Man." In *Spectrum of Thought.*, edited by Michael Peterson, 67-77. Wilmore, KY: Francis Asbury Press, 1982.

Collins, Kenneth J. "The Conversion of John Wesley: A Transformation to Power," in *Conversion.* Edited by John S. Hong. Bucheon City, Kyungki-Do, South Korea: Seoul Theological University, 1993. Published in Korean.

---. "A Reconfiguration of Power: The Basic Trajectory in John Wesley's Practical Theology," in *Heart of the Heritage: Core Themes of the Wesleyan/ Holiness Tradition,* pp. 131-150. Edited by Barry L Callen and William C. Kostlevy. Salem, Ohio: Schmul Publishing Company, 2001.

---. "The Doctrine of Justification: Historic Wesleyan and Contemporary Understandings." In *Justification: What's at Stake in the Current Debate,* ed. Mark Husbands and Daniel J. Treier, 177-204. Downers Grove, Illinois: InterVarsity Press, 2004.

---. "John Wesley." In *The Encyclopedia of Christianity,* ed. Jaroslav Pelikan, 5, 727-29. Grand Rapids, Michigan: William B. Eerdmans, 2008.

---. "Atonement," "Misunderstandings of Perfection," "Forgiveness," "Christian Perfection," "Evil Speaking," "Altogether/Real Christian," "Going on to Perfection." In *The Wesley Study Bible* ed. Joel B. Green and William H. Willimon, p. 142, 230, 423, 479, 676, 1472, and 1488. Nashville, Abingdon Press, 2009.

---. "Wesley's Life and Ministry." In *The Cambridge Companion to John Wesley*, ed. Randy. L. Maddox and J. A. Vickers, 43-59. Cambridge: Cambridge University Press, 2010.

---. "Assurance." In *The Oxford Handbook of Methodist Studies*, ed. William J. Abraham and James E. Kirby, 602-617. Oxford: Oxford University Press, 2009.

---. "Scripture as a Means of Grace." In *Wesley, Wesleyans, and Reading Bible as Scripture*, 19-32. Waco, Texas: Baylor University Press, 2012.

---. "John Wesley's Engagement with Islam: Exploring the Soteriological Possibilities in Light of a Diversity of Graces and Theological Frameworks." In *The Path of Holiness: Perspectives in Wesleyan Thought in Honor of Herbert B. McGonigle*, edited by Joseph Cunningham and David Rainey, 172-193. Wilmore, Kentucky: Emeth Press, 2014.

Cooper, Austin. "John Wesley." In *John Wesley, 1703-1791: A Commemorative Symposium.*, edited by W. A. Whitehouse, 10-19. Victoria, Australia: Uniting Church Historical Society, 1991.

Coppedge, Allan. "How Wesleyans Do Theology." In *Doing Theology in Today's World.*, edited by John Woodbridge and Thomas McComiskey, 267-89. Grand Rapids, Michigan: Zondervan, 1991.

Couture, Pamela D. "Sexuality, Economics, and the Wesleyan Alternative." In *Blessed are the Poor? Women's Poverty, Family Policy, and Practical Theology.*, 119-34. Nashville: Abingdon, 1991.

Cubie, David Livingstone. "Separation or Unity? Sanctification and Love in Wesley's Doctrine of the Church." In *The Church.*, edited by Melvin Dieter and Daniel Berg, 333-95. Anderson, Indiana: Warner, 1984.

---. "Eschatology from a Theological and Historical Perspective." In *The Spirit and the New Age.*, edited by R. L. Shelton and A. R. G. Deasley, 357-414. Anderson, Indiana: Warner, 1986.

Cuninggim, Jesse L. "John Wesley: Evangelical Arminianism." In *The Theology of Methodism: A Defense of the Rev. John Wesley.* Baltimore: Joseph Robinson, 1860.

Cushman, Robert Earl. "Salvation for All: John Wesley and Calvinism." In *Methodism.*, edited by W. K. Anderson, 103-15. New York, New York: Methodist Publishing House, 1947.

---. "Baptism and the Family of God." In *The Doctrine of the Church.*, edited by Dow Kirkpatrick, 79-102. New York: Abingdon, 1964.

Davaney, Sheila Greeve. "Feminism, Process Thought and the Wesleyan Tradition." In *Wesleyan Theology Today.*, edited by Theodore H. Runyon, 105-16. Nashville: Kingswood Books, 1985.

Dayton, Wilber. "Infallibility, Wesley and British Wesleyanism." In *Inerrancy and the Church.*, edited by John D. Hannah, 223-54.

Davies, Horton. "Charles Wesley and the Calvinist Tradition." In *Charles Wesley: Poet and Theologian.*, edited by S. T. Kimbrough, Jr., 186-203. Nashville: Kingswood Books, 1992.

Davies, Rupert Eric. "Justification, Sanctification, and the Liberation of the Person." In *Sanctification and Liberation.*, edited by Theodore H. Runyon, 64-82. Nashville, Tennessee: Abingdon, 1981.

Dayton, Donald W. "The Use of Scripture in the Wesleyan Tradition." In *The Use of the Bible in Theology.*, edited by Robert K. Johnston, 121-36. Atlanta, Georgia: John Knox, 1985.

---. "Preneumatological Issues in the Holiness Movement." In *Spirit of Truth: Ecumenical Perspectives on the Holy Spirit.*, edited by T. Stylianopoulos and S. Mark Heim, 131-57. Brookline, MA: Holy Cross Orthodox Press, 1986.

---. "`Good News for the Poor': The Methodist Experience After Wesley." In *The Portion of the Poor.*, edited by M. Douglas Meeks, . Nashville: Kingswood, 1994.

Dayton, Wilber T. "Infallibility, Wesley, and British Methodism." In *Inerrancy and the Church.*, 223-54. Chicago, Illinois: Moody, 1984.

Dieter, Melvin E. "The Wesleyan Perspective." In *Five Views of Sanctification.*, edited by Melvin E. Dieter, 11-46. Grand Rapids, Michigan: Zondervan, 1987.

---. "Wesleyan Theology." In *John Wesley: Contemporary Perspectives.*, edited by John Stacey, 162-75. London: Epworth, 1988.

Downey, James. "John Wesley." In *The Eighteenth Century Pulpit.*, 189-225. Oxford: Clarendon, 1969.

Dreyer, Frederick. "Edmund Burke and John Wesley: The Legacy of Locke." In *Religion, Secularization and Political Thought.*, edited by James E. Crimmins, 111-29. London: Routledge, 1989.

Duffy, Eamon. "Primitive Christianity Revived: Religious Renewal in Augustan England." *In Renaissance and Renewal in Church History.*, 287-300. Oxford: Basil Blackwell, 1977.

---. "Wesley and the Counter-Reformation." In *Revival and Religion Since 1700.*, edited by Jane Garnett and Colin Matthew, 1-19. London: Hambledon, 1993.

Elliot, Charles Middleton. "The Ideology of Economic Growth: A Case Study." In *Land, Labor and Population in the Industrial Revolution.*, edited by E. Jones and G. Minggay, 75-99. New York: Barnes & Noble, 1967.

Faulkner, John Alfred. "The Socialism of John Wesley." In *Social Ideals.*, 103-24. London: Robert Culley, 1909.

Flew, R. Newton. "Methodism and the Catholic Tradition." In *Northern Catholicism.*, edited by N. Williams, 515-30. New York: Macmillan, 1933.

Foster, Durwood. "Wesleyan Theology: Heritage and Task." In *Wesleyan Theology Today.*, edited by Theodore H. Runyon, 31-37. Nashville: Kingswood Books, 1985.

Fowler, James Wiley. "John Wesley's Development in Faith." In *The Future of the Methodist Theological Traditions.*, edited by M. Douglas Meeks, 172-92. Nashville, TN: Abingdon, 1985.

George, A. Raymond "The Lord's Supper." In *The Doctrine of the Church.*, edited by Dow Kirkpatrick, 140-60. New York: Abingdon, 1964.

---."Ordination [18th Century]." *In A History of the Methodist Church in Great Britain.*, edited by W. Reginald Ward . London: Epworth Press, 1965.

Gill, Frederick Cyril. "Introduction." In *John Wesley's Prayers.*, edited by Fredrick Cyril Gill, 9-17. London: Epworth, 1951.

Gordon, James M. "John and Charles Wesley." In *Evangelical Spirituality.*, 11-40. London: SPCK, 1991.

Greathouse, William M. "John Wesley's View of the Last Things." In *The Second Coming: A Wesleyan Approach to the Doctrine of the Last Thing.*, edited by H. Ray Dunning, 139-60. Kansas City, MO: Beacon Hill, 1995.

Hall, Thor. "Tradition Criticism: A New View of Wesley." In *Inaugurating the Leroy A. Martin Distinguished Professorship of Religious Studies.*, 6-23. : The University of Tennessee Chattanooga, 1987.

Hammond, Geordan. "The Revival of Practical Christianity: The Society for Promoting Christian Knowledge, Samuel Wesley, and the Clerical Society Movement." In *Revival and Resurgence in Christian History, Studies in Church History 44*, ed. Kate Cooper and Jeremy Gregory, 116-27. Woodbridge, UK: Boydell and Brewer, 2008.

---. "John Wesley's Relations with the Lutheran Pietist Clergy in Georgia." In *The Pietist Impulse in Christianity*, edited by Christian T. et. al. Collins: Pickwick Publications, 2011.

Hauerwas, Stanley M. "Christianizing Perfection: Second Thoughts on Character and Sanctification." In *Wesleyan Theology Today.*, edited by Theodore C. Runyon, 251-63. New York: AMS Press, 1976.

---. "Characterizing Perfection: Second Thoughts on Character and Sanctification." In *Wesleyan Theology Today.*, edited by Theodore H. Runyon, 251-63. Nashville: Kingswood, 1985.

Heitzenrater, Richard P. "Wesley and His Diary." In *John Wesley: Contemporary Perspectives.*, edited by John Stacey, 11-22. London: Epworth, 1988.

---. "At Full Liberty: Doctrinal Standards in Early American Methodism." In *Mirror and Memory: Reflections on Early Methodism.*, edited by Richard P. Heitzenrater, 189-204. Nashville: Kingswood Books, 1989.

---. "The Imiatio Christi and the Great Commandment: Virtue and Obligation in Wesley's Ministry with the Poor." In *The Portion of the Poor.*, edited by M. Douglas Meeks. Nashville, Tennessee: Kingswood, 1994.

Hempton, David Neil. "John Wesley and England's `Ancien Regime'." In *Modern Religious Beliefs.*, edited by Stuart Mews, 36-55. London: Epworth, 1993.

Hodges, Herbert Arthur, and Archibald Macdonald Allchin. "Introduction." In *A Rapture of Praise: Hymns of John and Charles Wesley.*, edited by Herbert Arthur Hodges and Archibald Macdonald Allchin, 19-50. London: Hodder and Soughton, 1966.

Hurley, Michael. "Salvation Today and Wesley Today." In *The Place of Wesley in the Christian Tradition.*, edited by Kenneth A. Rowe, 94-116. Metuchen, New Jersey: Scarecrow, 1976.

---. "Introduction." In *John Wesley's Letters to a Roman Catholic.*, edited by Micheal Hurley, 22-47. Nashville: Abingdon, 1968.

Hynson, Leon O. "The Ordered State and Christian Responsibility." In *Christian Ethics: An Inquiry into Christian Ethics from a Biblical Theological Perspective.*, edited by Leon O. Hynson and Lane W. Scott, 255-94. Anderson, Indiana: Warner Press, 1983.

---. "Implications of Wesley's Ethical Method and Political Thought." In *Wesleyan Theology Today.*, edited by Theodore H. Runyon, 373-88. Nashville, Tennessee: Kingswood, 1985.

Johnson, Susanne. "John Wesley on the Duty of Constant Communion: The Eucharist as a Means of Grace for Today." In *Wesleyan Spirituality in Contemporary Theological Education.*, 25-46. Nashville: General Board of Higher Education and Ministry, United Methodist Church, 1987.

Jones, W. Paul. "The Wesleyan Means of Grace." In *Wesleyan Spirituality in Contemporary Theological Education.*, 11-15. Nashville: General Board of Higher Education and Ministry, United Methodist Church, 1987.

Joy, Donald M. "Toward Christian Holiness: John Wesley's Faith Pilgrimage." In *Moral Development Foundations.*, edited by D. M. Joy, 207-32. Nashville: Abingdon, 1983.

Kimbrough, S. T. Jr. "Charles Wesley and Biblical Interpretation." In *Charles Wesley: Poet and Theologian.*, edited by S. T. Jr. Kimbrough, 106-36. Nashville: Kingswood Book, 1992.

---. "Charles Wesley and the Poor." In *The Portion of the Poor.*, edited by M. Douglas Meeks, 147-67. Nashville: Kingswood Books, 1995.

Langford, Thomas Anderson. "Constructive Theology in the Wesleyan Tradition." In *Wesleyan Theology Today.*, edited by Theodore H. Runyon, 56-61. Nashville: Kingswood, 1985.

Langford, Thomas. "Charles Wesley as Theologian." In *Charles Wesley: Poet and Theologian.*, edited by S. T. Kimbrough, Jr., 97-105. Nashville: Kingswood Books, 1992.

Lee, Hoo-Jung. "John Wesley and Early Eastern Spirituality." In *Religious Pluralism and Korean Theology.* Seoul: Korean Institute of Theology Press, 1992.

---. "Experiencing the Spirit in Wesley and Macarius." In *Rethinking Wesley's Theology for Contemporary Methodism.*, ed. Randy Maddox., 197-212. Nashville: Abingdon Press, 1998.

Leland, Scott. "The Concern for Systematic Theology, 1840-1870." In *History of American Methodism.*, edited by Emory S. Bucke, 2:380-390. Nashville: Abingdon Press, 1974.

---. "The Message of Early American Methodism." In *History of American Methodism.*, edited by Emory S. Bucke, 1:291-359. Nashville: Abingdon Press, 1974.

Logan, James "Baptism: The Ecumenical Sacrament and the Wesleyan Tradition." In *Wesleyan Theology Today: A Bicentennial Theological Consultation.*, edited by Theodore Runyon, 323-29. Nashville: Kingswood Books, 1985.

---. "Toward a Wesleyan Social Ethic." In *Wesleyan Theology Today.*, edited by Theodore H. Runyon, 361-72. Nashville: Kingswood, 1985.

Lovin, Robin W. "The Physics of True Virtue." In *Wesleyan Theology Today.*, edited by Theodore H. Runyon, 264-72. Nashville: Kingswood, 1985.

Macquiban, Tim. "Dialogue with the Wesleys: Remembering Origins." In *Unmasking Methodist Theology*, 17-28. New York: Continuum, 2004.

---. "Imprisonment and Release in the Writings of the Wesleys." In *Retribution, Repentance, and Reconciliation*, 240-252. Rochester: Boydell Pr., 2004.

Madron, Thomas W. "John Wesley on Economics." In *Sanctification and Liberation.*, edited by Theodore Runyon, 102-15. Nashville: Abingdon, 1981.

Marquardt, Manfred. John Wesley's ‚Synergismus'." In *Die Einheit der Kirche: Dimensionen ihrer Heiligkeit Katholizitat und Apostolizitat: Festgabe Peter Hein.*, 96-102. Weisbaden: Steiner Verlag, 1977.

Mass, Robin. "Wesleyan Spirituality: Accountable Discipleship." In *Spiritual Traditions for the Contemporary Church.*, edited by Robin Mass and Gabriel O'Donnell O.P., 303-31. Nashville: Abingdon Press, 1990.

Matthews, Rex D. "With the Eyes of Faith': Spiritual Experience and the Knowledge of God in the Theology of John Wesley." In *Wesleyan Theology Today.*, edited by Theodore Runyon, 406-15. Nashville, Tennessee: Kingswood, 1985.

McCulloh, Gerald O. "The Discipline of Life in Early Methodism through Preaching and Other Means of Grace." In *The Doctrine of the Church.*, edited by Dow Kirkpatrick, 161-81. New York: Abingdon, 1964.

McCutcheon, William J. "American Methodist Thought and Theology, 1919-1960." In *History of American Methodism.*, edited by Emory S. Bucke, 3:261-327. Nashville: Abingdon Press, 1974.

McIntosh, Lawrence D. "The Place of John Wesley in the Christian Tradition: A Selected Bibliography." In *The Place of Wesley in the Christian Tradition*, edited by Kenneth E. Rowe, 134-59. Metuchen, New Jersey: Scarecrow Press, 1976.

McNeall, Rodney. "Pastoral Response." In *From Aldersgate to Azusa Street*, 45-47. Eugene: Pickwick, 2010.

Meeks, Merrill D. "The Future of the Methodist Theological Traditions." In *The Future of the Methodist Theological Traditions*, edited by Merrill D. Meeks, 13-33. Nashville: Abingdon, 1985.

---. "John Wesley's Heritage and the Future of Systematic Theology." In *Wesleyan Theology Today*, edited by Theodore H. Runyon, 38-46. Nashville: Kingswood, 1985.

Meistad, Tore. "Martin Luther and John Wesley on the Sermon on the Mount." In *Context: Essays in Honour of Peder Borgen.*, edited by P. W. Bockmann and R. Kristiansen, 137-51. Trondheim, Norway: Tapir, 1987.

Mercer, Jerry Lee. "Counterforce: A Review of Wesley's Ethics." In *Christian Ethics: An Inquiry into Christian Ethics from a Biblical Theological Perspective.*, edited by Leon O. Hynson and Lane W. Scott, 77-95. Anderson, Indiana: Warner Press, 1983.

Michaelson, Carl. "The Hermeneutics of Holiness in Wesley." In *The Heritage of Christian Thought: Essays in Honor of Robert Lowry Calhoun.*, edited by Robert Cushman and Egil Grislis, 127-41. New York: Harper and Row, 1965.

---. "The Hermeneutics of Holiness in Wesley." In *God's Word for Today.*, edited by Wayne McCown and James E. Massey, 31-52. Anderson, IN: Warner, 1982.

Miguez Bonino, Jose. "Wesley's Doctrine of Sanctification From a Liberationist Perspective." In *Sanctification and Liberation.*, edited by Theodore H. Runyon, 49-63. Nashville: Abingdon, 1981.

Nelson, James D. "Christian Conference." In *Wesleyan Spirituality in Contemporary Theological Education.*, 47-53. Nashville, Tennessee: General Board of Higher Education and Ministry, United Methodist Church, 1987.

Nettles, Thomas J. "John Wesley's Contention with Calvinism: Interactions Then and Now." In *The Grace of God, the Bondage of the Will.*, edited by T. R. Schreiner and B. A. Ware. Vol. 2, 297-332. Grand Rapids, Michigan: Baker, 1995.

Newton, John A. "The Theology of the Wesleys." In *The Methodist Heritage.*, edited by D. Milbank, 1-10. London: Southlands College, 1984.

Nutall, Geoffrey F. "Continental Pietism and the Evangelical Movement in Britain." In *Pietismus und Reveil: Referate der internationalen Tagung der Pietismus in der Niederlanden und seiner internationalen Beziehungen.*, edited by J. Van den Berg and J. P. Van Doreen, 74ff. : Zist, no date.

O'Brien, Glen. "Reading Wesley's Sermons in Edwardian Melbourne." In *The Master: Life and Times of Edward Sugden*, 109-124. Melbourne: Uniting Academic Press, 2009.

Oord, Thomas Jay. "Prevenient Grace and Nonsensory Perception of God in a Postmodern Wesleyan Philosophy." In *Between Nature and Grace: Mapping the Interface of Wesleyan Theology and Psychology*, ed. Bryan P. Stone and Thomas Jay Oord. San Diego, California: Point Loma Press, 2000.

---. "A Process Wesleyan Theodicy: Freedom, Embodiment, and the Almighty God." In *Thy Name and Nature Is Love: Wesleyan and Process Theologies in Dialogue*, ed. Bryan P. Stone and Thomas Jay Oord, 193-216. Nashville: Kingswood Books, 2001.

---. "Wesleyan Theology, Boston Personalism, and Process Thought." In *Thy Name and Nature Is Love: Wesleyan and Process Theologies in Dialogue*, ed. Bryan P. Stone and Thomas Jay Oord, 379-392. Nashville: Kingswood Books, 2001.

Orcibal, Jean. "The Theological Originality of John Wesley and Continental Spirituality." In *A History of the Methodist Church in Great Britain, Vol. I.*, edited by R. E. Davies and E. G. Rupp, 83-111. London, England: Epworth, 1965.

Outler, Albert C. "Do Methodists Have a Doctrine of the Church?" *In The Doctrine of the Church.*, edited by Dow Kirkpatrick, 11-28. New York: Abingdon Press, 1964.

---. "The Current Theological Scene: A View from the Beach at Ebb Tide." In *Proceedings.*, edited by Anonymous, 157-66. Nashville: World Methodist Council, 1966.

---. "The Place of Wesley in Christian Tradition." In *The Place of Wesley in Christian Tradition.*, edited by Kenneth E. Rowe, 11-38. Metuchen, NJ: Scarecrow, 1976.

---. "How to Run a Conservative Revolution and Get No Thanks for It." In *Albert Outler: The Churchman.*, edited by Bob W. Parrott, 397-416. Anderson, IN: Bristol House, 1985.

---. "Pietism and Enlightenment: Alternatives to Tradition." In *Christian Spirituality III.*, edited by Louis Dupre and Don Saliers, 240-56. New York: Crossroad, 1989.

---. "Methodists in Search of Consensus." In *What Should Methodists Teach?*, edited by M. Douglas Meeks, 23-38. Nashville: Kingswood, 1990.

---. "'Biblical Primitivism' in Early American Methodism." In *The Wesleyan Theological Heritage: Essays of Albert C. Outler.*, edited by Thomas C. Oden and Leicester R. Longden, 145-58. Grand Rapids, Michigan: Zondervan, 1991.

---. "Do Methodists Have a Doctrine of the Church?" In *The Wesleyan Theological Heritage: Essays of Albert C. Outler.*, edited by Thomas C. Oden and Leicester R. Longden, 211-26. Grand Rapids, Michigan: Zondervan, 1991.

---. "A Focus of the Holy Spirit: Spirit and Spirituality in John Wesley." In *The Wesleyan Theological Heritage: Essays of Albert C. Outler.*, edited by Thomas C. Oden and Leicester R. Longden, 159-74. Grand Rapids, Michigan: Zondervan, 1991.

---. "John Wesley as Theologian--Then and Now." In *The Wesleyan Theological Heritage: Essays of Albert C. Outler.*, edited by Thomas C. Oden and Leicester R. Longden, 55-74. Grand Rapids, Michigan: Zondervan, 1991.

---. "John Wesley: Folk-Theologian." In *The Wesleyan Theological Heritage: Essays of Albert C. Outler.*, edited by Thomas C. Oden and Leicester R. Longden, 111-24. Grand Rapids, Michigan: Zondervan, 1991.

---. "John Wesley's Interests in the Early Fathers of the Church." In *The Wesleyan Theological Heritage: Essays of Albert C. Outler.*, edited by Thomas C. Oden and Leicester R. Longden, 97-110. Grand Rapids, Michigan: Zondervan, 1991.

---. "Methodism in the World Christian Community." In *The Wesleyan Theological Heritage: Essays of Albert C. Outler.*, edited by Thomas C. Oden and Leicester R. Longden, 241-52. Grand Rapids, Michigan: Zondervan, 1991.

---. "Methodism's Theological Heritage: A Study in Perspective." In *The Wesleyan Theological Heritage: Essays of Albert C. Outler.*, edited by Thomas C. Oden and Leicester R. Longden, 189-210. Grand Rapids, Michigan: Zondervan, 1991.

---. "The Mingling of Ministries." In *The Wesleyan Theological Heritage: Essays of Albert C. Outler.*, edited by Thomas C. Oden and Leicester R. Longden, 227-40. Grand Rapids, Michigan: Zondervan, 1991.

---. "A New Future for Wesley Studies: An Agenda for "Phase III"." In *The Wesleyan Theological Heritage: Essays of Albert C. Outler.*, edited by Thomas C. Oden and Leicester R. Longden, 125-44. Grand Rapids, Michigan: Zondervan, 1991.

---. "Pastoral Care in the Wesleyan Spirit." In *The Wesleyan Theological Heritage: Essays of Albert C. Outler.*, edited by Thomas C. Oden and Leicester R. Longden, 175-88. Grand Rapids, Michigan: Zondervan, 1991.

---. "The Place of Wesley in the Christian Tradition." In *The Wesleyan Theological Heritage: Essays of Albert C. Outler.*, edited by Thomas C. Oden and Leicester R. Longden, 75-96. Grand Rapids, Michigan: Zondervan, 1991.

---. "Towards a Re-Appraisal of John Wesley as a Theologian." In *The Wesleyan Theological Heritage: Essays of Albert C. Outler.*, edited by Thomas C. Oden and Leicester R. Longden, 39-54. Grand Rapids, Michigan: Zondervan, 1991.

---. "Visions and Dreams; the Unfinished Business of an Unfinished Church." In *The Wesleyan Theological Heritage: Essays of Albert C. Outler.*, edited by Thomas C. Oden and Leicester R. Longden, 253-62. Grand Rapids, Michigan: Zondervan, 1991.

---. "The Wesleyan Quadrilateral in John Wesley." In *The Wesleyan Theological Heritage: Essays of Albert C. Outler.*, edited by Thomas C. Oden and Leicester R. Longden, 21-38. Grand Rapids, Michigan: Zondervan, 1991.

Paulson, Ross. "On the Meaning of Faith in the Great Awakening and the Methodist Revival." *In The Immigration of Ideas.*, edited by J. I. Dowie and J. T. Treadway, 1-13. :, 1968.

Rack, Henry D. "Doctors, Demons and Early Methodist Healing." In *The Church and Healing.*, edited by William Sheils, 137-52. : The Ecclesiastical History Society, 1982.

Rankin, Stephen W. "The People Called Methodists." In *From Aldersgate to Azusa Street.* Eugene: Pickwick Publications, 2010.

---. "A Theological Interpretation." In *From Aldersgate to Azusa Street* Eugene: Pickwick Publications, 2010.

Rall, Harris F. "Was John Wesley a Premillenialist?" In *Modern Premillenialism and the Christian Hope.*, 245-53. New York: Abingdon, 1920.

Rivers, Isabel. "Dissenting and Methodist Books of Practical Divinity." In *Books and their Readers in Eighteenth Century England.*, edited by Isabel Rivers, 127-64. New York: St. Martins, 1982.

Rowe, Kenneth E. "The Search for the Historical Wesley." In *The Place of Wesley in the Christian Tradition.*, edited by Kenneth E. Rowe, 11-38. Metuchen, NJ: Scarecrow, 1976.

Runyon, Theodore H. "Wesley and the Theologies of Liberation." In *Sanctification and Liberation: Liberation in the Light of the Wesleyan Tradition.*, edited by Theodore H. Runyon, 9-48. Nashville: Abingdon, 1981.

---. "What is Methodism's Theological Contribution Today?" In *Wesleyan Theology Today.*, edited by Theodore H. Runyon, 7-13. Nashville: Kingswood Books, 1985.

---. "The Importance of Experience for Faith." In *Aldersgate Reconsidered.*, edited by Randy Maddox, 93-107. Nashville: Kingswood, 1990.

Rupp, E. Gordon. "Methodism in Relation to Protestant Tradition." In *Proceedings of the Eighth Ecumenical Methodist Conference.*, 93-106. London: Epworth, 1952.

---. "Methodists, Anglicans, and Orthodox." In *We Belong to One Another: Methodist, Anglican and Orthodox.*, edited by A. M. Allchin, 13-29. London: Epworth, 1965.

---. "Paul and Wesley." In *De Dertende Apostel en het Elfde Gebod.*, edited by G. C. Berkouwer and H. A. Oberman, 102-10. Kampen: K.H. Kok, 1971.

---. "Son to Samuel: John Wesley, Church of England Man." *In The Place of Wesley in the Christian Tradition.*, edited by Kenneth E. Rowe, 39-66. Metuchen, New Jersey: Scarecrow Press, 1976.

Schmidt, Martin. "Wesley's Place in Church History." In *The Place of Wesley in the Christian Tradition.*, edited by Kenneth A. Rowe, 67-93. Metuchen, NJ: Scarecrow, 1976.

Shipley, David C. "The Ministry in Methodism in the Eighteenth Century." In *The Ministry in the Methodist Heritage.*, edited by Gerald McCulloh, 11-31. Nashville: Department of Ministerial Education, 1960.

Smith, Timothy L. "The Holiness Crusade." In *History of American Methodism.*, edited by Emory S. Bucke, 2:608-627. Nashville: Abingdon Press, 1974.

Speaks, Reuben L. "Christian Perfection and Human Liberation: the Wesleyan Synthesis." *In The People Called Methodists.*, edited by Gordon Rupp, Rosemary S. Keller, and Reuben L. Speaks, 13-30. Nashville: Discipleship Resources, 1984.

Stephens, W. P. "Wesley and the Moravians." In *John Wesley: Contemporary Perspectives.*, edited by John Stacey, 23-36. London: Epworth, 1988.

Stoeffler, F. Ernest. "Pietism, the Wesleys and Methodist Beginnings in America." In *Continental Pietism and Early American Christianity.*, edited by F. Ernest Stoeffler, 184-221. Grand Rapids, Michigan: Wm. B. Eerdmans, 1976.

---. "Tradition and Renewal in the Ecclesiology of John Wesley." In Traditio - Krisis - Renovatio aus theologischer Sicht., edited by B. Jaspert and R. Mohr, 298-316. Marburg: Elwert, 1976.

Tamez, Elsa. "Wesley as Read by the Poor." In *The Future of the Methodist Theological Traditions.*, edited by M. Douglas Meeks, 67-84. Nashville: Abingdon, 1985.

Thompson, Matthew K. "Eschatology as Soteriology: The Cosmic Full Gospel." In *Perspectives in Pentecostal Eschatologies*, 189-204. Eugene: Pickwick, 2010.

Trickett, David. "Spiritual Vision and Discipline in the Early Wesleyan Movement." In *Christian Spirituality: Post-Reformation and Modern.*, edited by Louis Dupre and Don E. Saliers, 354-71. New York: Crossroad, 1989.

Turner, George Allen. "John Wesley as an Interpreter of Scripture." In *Inspiration and Interpretation.*, edited by John F. Walvoord, 156-78. Grand Rapids, Michigan: Eerdmans, 1957.

Van Noppen, Jean-Pierre. "Beruf, Calling and the Methodist Work Ethic." In *Wahlverwandtschaften in Sprache, Malerei, Literatur, Geschichte..*, edited by Heidelberger-Leonard and M. Tabash , 69-78. Stuttgart: Verlag Hans-Dieter Heinz, 2000.

Villa-Vicencio, Charles M. L. "The Origins and Witness of Methodism." In *Denominationalism - Its Sources and Implications.*, edited by W. S. Vorster, 64-94. Pretoria: University of South Africa, 1982.

Wainwright, Geoffrey. "Schisms, Heresies, and the Gospel: Wesleyan Reflections on Evangelical Truth and Ecclesial Unity." In *Ancient and Postmodern Christianity*, 183-198. Downers Grove, Illinois: InterVarsity Press, 2002.

---. "A Primatial Ministry of Unity in a Conciliar and Synodical Context." In *How Can the Petrine Ministry Be a Service to the Unity of the Universal Church?*, 284-309. Grand Rapids: William B. Eerdmans, 2010.

Wakefield, Gordon S. "The Virgin Mary in Methodism." In *Mary's Place in Christian Dialogue*, edited by Aberic Staacpole, 151-157. Wilton, Connecticut: Morehouse-Barlow Co, 1983.

---. "'A Mystical Substitute for the Glorious Gospel'? A Methodist Critique of Tractarianism." In *Tradition Renewed.*, edited by Geoffrey Rowell, 185-98. Allison Park, PA: Pickwick, 1986.

Walsh, John. "Origins of the Evangelical Revival." In *Essays in Modern English Church History.*, edited by G. V. Bennett and J. D. Walsh, 132-62. New York: Oxford University Press, 1966.

---. "John Wesley and The Community of Goods." In *Protestant Evangelicalism.*, edited by Keith Robbins, 25-50. Oxford: Blackwell, 1990.

Watson, David L. "Methodist Spirituality." In *Protestant Spiritual Traditions.*, edited by Frank Senn, 217-73. New York: Paulist, 1986.

---. "Aldersgate Street and the General Rules: The Form and the Power of Methodist Discipleship." In *Aldersgate Reconsidered.*, edited by R. L. Maddox, 33-47. Nashville, Tennessee: Kingswood, 1990.

Watson, J. Richard. "Charles Wesley's Hymns and the Book of Common Prayer." In *Crammer: A Living Influence for 500 Years.*, edited by Margot Johnson, 204-28. Durham, England: Turnstone Ventures, 1990.

---. "The Presentation of Holiness and the Concept of Christian Perfection in the Sermons and Hymns of the Wesleys." In Transforming Holiness: Representations of Holiness in English and American Literary Texts, ed. Irene Visser, and Wilcox, Helen, 81-94. Dudley, Massachusetts: Peeters, 2006.

Wesley, John. "Cautions and Directions Given to the Greatest Professors in the Methodist Societies." In *John Wesley.*, edited by Albert C. Outler, 298-305. New York: Oxford University Press, 1964.

---. "A Collection of Forms of Prayer for Every Day in the Week." In *The Works of John Wesley.*, edited by Thomas Jackson, 11:203-259. Grand Rapids, Michigan: Baker Book House, 1978.

---. "A Collection of Prayers for Families." In *The Works of John Wesley.*, edited by Thomas Jackson, 11:237-259. Grand Rapids, Michigan: Baker Book House, 1978.

---. "A Scheme of Self-Examination used by the First Methodists in Oxford." In *The Works of John Wesley.*, edited by Thomas Jackson, 11:521-523. Grand Rapids, Michigan: Baker Book House, 1978.

---. "The Witness of the Spirit, Discourses I and II." In *The Works of John Wesley: Sermons I.* Bicentennial ed., edited by Albert C. Outler, 267-98. Nashville: Abingdon Press, 1984.

---. "The Nature of Enthusiasm." In *The Works of John Wesley: Sermons II.* Bicentennial ed., edited by Albert C. Outler, 44-60. Nashville: Abingdon Press, 1985.

---. "The Nature, Design, and General Rules of the United Societies." In *The Works of John Wesley: The Methodist Societies: History, Nature, and Design.* Bicentennial ed., edited by Rupert E. Davies. Vol. 9, 77-79. Nashville: Abingdon Press, 1989.

---. "A Plain Account of the People Called Methodists." In *The Works of John Wesley: The Methodist Societies: History, Nature, and Design.* Bicentennial ed., edited by Rupert E. Davies. Vol. 9, 253-80. Nashville: Abingdon Press, 1989.

White, James Floyd. "Introduction." In *John Wesley's Sunday Service of the Methodist in North America.*, edited by James Floyd White, 9-21. Nashville: United Methodist Publishing House & United Methodist Board of Higher Education and Ministry, 1984.

Wigger, John H. "Where Have All the Asburys Gone? Francis Asbury and Leadership in the Wesleyan, Holiness, and Pentecostal Traditions." In *From Aldersgate to Azusa Street.* Eugene: Pickwick Publications, 2010.

Wilson, Kenneth. "The Methodist Idea of Covenant." In *Anglician Covenant,* ed. Mark D. Chapman. London: Mowbray, 2008.

Witherington, Ben. "The Study of Scripture in Early Methodism." In *How United Methodists Study Scripture,* edited by Gayle C. Felton. Nashville: Abingdon Press, 1999.

Wood, A. Skevington. "The Contribution of John Wesley to the Theology of Grace." In *Grace Unlimited.*, edited by Clark Pinnock, 209-22. Minneapolis,Minnesota: Bethany Fellowship, 1975.

Young, Frances. "The Significance of John Wesley's Conversion Experience." In *John Wesley: Contemporary Perspectives.*, edited by John Stacy, 37-46. London: Epworth, 1988.

Articles

Abelove, Henry. "George Berkeley's Attitude to John Wesley: The Evidence of a Lost Letter." *Harvard Theological Review* 70 (January-April 1977): 175-76.

Abraham, William J. "On How to Dismantle the Wesleyan Quadrilateral: A study in the Thought of Albert C Knudson." *Wesleyan Theological Journal* 20, no. 1 (Spring 1985): 34-44.

---. "Redeeming the Evangelical Experiment." *TSF Bulletin* 8, no. 3 (January-February 1985): 11-13.

---. "Saving Souls in the Twenty-First Century: A Missiological Midrash on John Wesley." *Wesleyan Theological Journal* 38, no. 1 (2003): 7-20.

---. "The End of Wesleyan Theology." *Wesleyan Theological Journal* 40 (2005): 7-25.

---. "Whose Wesley? Which Wesleyan Tradition." *Wesleyan Theological Journal* 46, no. 2 (2011): 142-149.

---. "Smoky the Cow Horse and Wesleyan Understanding of Scripture." *Wesleyan Theological Journal* 51, no. 2 (2016): 7-25.

Adamo, David Tuesday. "Soteriological Dialogue Between Wesleyan Christians and Pure Land Sect Buddhism." *Journal of Dharma: An International Quarterly of World Religions* 14 (October-December 1989): 366-75.

Adamthwaite, Murray. "Charles Wesley: Musician and Seeker for Perfection." *Reformed Theological Review* 74, no. 2 (2015): 94-108.

Affleck, Bert. "John Wesley's Spiritual Disciplines for Today's Pastor." *Perkins Journal* 40 (January 1987): 1-8.

Agnew Cochran, Elizabeth. "Christian Perfection and Moral Reasoning: A Wesleyan Challenge to Dilemmas in Bioethics." *Wesleyan Theological Journal* 44, no. 1 (2009): 104-117.

Alexander, Estrelda Y. "Liturgy in Non-Liturgical Holiness-Penticostalism." *Wesleyan Theological Journal* 32, no. 2 (Fall 1997): 158-93.

Allison, Christopher. "The Methodist Edwards: John Wesley's Abridgement of the Selected Works of Jonathan Edwards." *Methodist History* 50, no. 3 (2012): 144-160.

Anderson, E. Byron. "Day of New Beginnings: Wesleyan Theologies of the New Birth." *Wesleyan Theological Journal* 38, no. 2 (2003): 230-250.

---. "Reform, Participation, and Mission: "To Derive the True Christian Spirit"." *Worship* 88, no. 3 (2014): 218-239.

Andrews, Stuart. "John Wesley and the Age of Reason." *History Today* 19 (January 1969): 25-32.

Anonymous. "John Wesley and Premillenarianism." *Christian Workers Magazine* (1916).

Armistead, M. Kathryn. "Empathy and Healing in a Methodist Ecclesial Context." *Journal of Spirituality in Mental Health* 9, no. 2 (2007).

Arnett, William M. "Current Theological Emphases in the American Holiness Tradition." *The Mennonite Quarterly Review* 35 (April 1961): 120-29.

---. "John Wesley and the Bible." *Wesleyan Theological Journal* 3 (1968).

---. "Study in John Wesley's Explanatory notes upon the Old Testament." *Wesleyan Theological Journal* 8 (Spring 1973): 14-32.

---. "John Wesley and the Law." *Asbury Seminary Journal* 34 (1979): 22-31.

---. "The Role of the Holy Spirit in Entire Sanctification in the Writings of John Wesley." *Wesleyan Theological Journal* 14, no. 2 (Fall 1979): 15-30.

Ashley, Sir William. "Wesley's Influence on Christian Thought." *Methodist Magazine* 150 (1927): 3-6.

Atherstone, Andrew. "Honouring George Whitefield: Funeral Eulogies and Elegies in England and America." *Churchman* 130, no. 2 (2016): 127-143.

Aukema Cieslukowski, Corrie M., and Elmer M. Colyer. "Wesley's Trinitarian Ordo Salutis." *Reformation and Revival* 14 (2005): 105-131.

Ayers, Jeremy. "John Wesley's Therapeutic Understanding of Salvation." *Encounter* 63, no. 3 (2002): 263-297.

Baker, Frank. "John Wesley and the Imitatio Christi." *London Quarterly & Holborn Review* 166 (1941): 74-87.

---.. "A Study of John Wesley's Readings." London Quarterly & Holborn Review 168 (1943): 140-45; 234-42.

---. "Beginnings of the Methodist Covenant Service." *London Quarterly & Holborn Review* 180 (July 1955): 215-20.

---. "Erskines and the Methodists." *London Quarterly & Holborn Review* 183 (January 1958): 36-45.

---. "John Wesley's Churchmanship." *London Quarterly & Holborn Review* 185 (July 1960): 210-15.

---. "John Wesley's Churchmanship." *London Quarterly & Holborn Review* 185 (October 1960): 269-74.

---. "Wesley's Puritan Ancestry." *London Quarterly & Holborn Review* 187 (July 1962): 180-86.

---. "Aldersgate 1738-1963; The Challenge of Aldersgate [Address]." *Duke Divinity School Bulletin* 28 (May 1963): 67-80.

---. "Early American Methodism; A Key Document." *Methodist History* 3 (January 1965): 3-15.

---. "Aldersgate and Wesley's Editors." *London Quarterly & Holborn Review* 191 (October 1966): 310-19.

---. "John Wesley's First Marriage." *Duke Divinity School Bulletin* 31 (Autumn 1966): 175-88.

---. "John Wesley's First Marriage [reprint]." *London Quarterly & Holborn Review* 192 (October 1967): 305-15.

---. "Birth of John Wesley's Journal." *Methodist History* 8 (January 1970): 25-32.

---. "Oxford Edition of Wesley's Works." *Methodist History* 8 (July 1970): 41-48.

---. "Whitefield's Break with the Wesleys." *Church Quarterly Review* 3 (October 1970): 103-13.

---. "Oxford Edition of Wesley's Works." *Duke Divinity School Bulletin* 36 (Spring 1971): 87-99.

---. "John Wesley and Cokesbury College's First President." *Methodist History* 11 (January 1973): 54-59.

---. "The Real John Wesley." *Methodist History* 12 (July 1974): 183-97.

---. "Shaping of John Wesley's "Calm Address" [1775]." *Methodist History* 14 (October 1975): 3-12.

---. "Unfolding John Wesley: A Survey of Twenty Years Study in Wesley's Thought." *Quarterly Review* 1, no. 1 (Fall 1980): 44-58.

---. "The Origins, Character, and Influence of John Wesley's Thoughts Upon Slavery." *Methodist History* 22, no. 2 (January 1984): 75-86.

---. "Riding Around with John Wesley." *Methodist History* 23, no. 3 (April 1985): 163-67.

---. "John Wesley and Practical Divinity." *Wesleyan Theological Journal* 22, no. 1 (1987): 7-15.

---. "Practical Divinity - John Wesley's Doctrinal Agenda for Methodism." *Wesleyan Theological Journal* 22, no. 1 (Spring 1987): 7-16.

---. "Investigating Wesley Family Traditions [genealogical table]." *Methodist History* 26, no. 3 (April 1988): 154-62.

---. "John Wesley's Publishing Apprenticeship." *Bulletin of the John Rylands University Library of Manchester* 70 (Spring 1988): 71-80.

---. "John Wesley, Biblical Commentator." *Bulletin of the John Rylands University Library of Manchester* 71 (Spring 1989): 110-20.

---. "Eye-witnesses to Early Methodism [representative extracts from John Wesley, 1725-1785]." *Methodist History* 28, no. 2 (January 1990): 92-103.

---, ed. "John Wesley and Miss Mary Clark of Worcester [text of letters]." *Methodist History* 10 (January 1972): 45-51.

Baker, Josiah. "Reassessing the Viability of Wesley as a Bridge in Orthodox-Pentecostal Dialogue." *International Journal of Orthodox Theology* 9, no. 1 (2018): 160-186.

Baldwin, Lewis V. "Sources and Ideas for the Study of John Wesley and Africa [2pts]." *The AME Zion Quarterly Review* 95, no. 3 (October 1983): 25-29.

---. "Sources and Ideas for the Study of John Wesley and Africa [2pts]." *The AME Zion Quarterly Review* 96, no. 2 (July 1984): 24-28.

Ball-Kilbourne, Gary L. "The Christian as Steward in John Wesley's Theological Ethics." *Quarterly Review* 4 (Spring 1984): 43-54.

Bangs, Carl O. "Historical Theology in the Wesleyan Mode [reply, L O Hynson]." *Wesleyan Theological Journal* 17, no. 1 (Spring 1982): 85-92.

Barratt, Thomas H. "The Place of the Lord's Supper in Early Methodism." *London Quarterly Review* 140 (1923): 56-73.

Bartels, Laura. "John Wesley and Dr. George Cheyne on the Spiritual Senses." *Wesleyan Theological Journal* 39, no. 1 (2004): 163-172.

Barton, J. Hamby. "Double Letter John Wesley and Thomas Coke to Freeborn Garrettson." *Methodist History* 17 (October 1978): 59-63.

---. "The Two Versions of the First Edition of John Wesley's 'The Sunday Service of the Methodists in North America'" [bibliog]. *Methodist History* 23, no. 3 (April 1985): 153-62.

Bassett, Paul M. "Conservative Wesleyan Theology and the Challenge of Secular Humanism." *Wesleyan Theological Journal* 8 (Spring 1973): 73-82.

---. "The Holiness Movement and the Protestant Principle." *Wesleyan Theological Journal* 18, no. 1 (Spring 1983): 7-29.

---. "Finding the Real John Wesley [bibliog essay; por; il]." *Christianity Today* 28, no. 16 (9 November 1984): 86-88.

---. "Wesleyan Words in the Nineteenth-Century World: "Sin," a Case Study." *Evangelical Journal* 8 (Spring 1990): 15-40.

---, ed. "[John Wesley's Aldersgate Experience]." *Wesleyan Theological Journal* 24 (1989): 7-73.

Bates, E. Ralph. "Methodist Legend of the South Leigh: In Celebration of the 250th Anniversary of the Ordination of John Wesley, S 19, 1725." *Methodist History* 13 (July 1975): 18-24.

Beals, J. D. "John Wesley's Concept of the Church." *Wesleyan Theological Journal* 9 (Spring 1974): 28-37.

Beckerlegge, Oliver A. "Wesley and Toplady." *Epworth Review* 17 (May 1990): 48-53.

Beeson, Trevor. "Reopening of Wesley's Chapel: An Act of Faith." *The Christian Century* 95 (22 November 1978): 1125-26.

Bell, Richard J. "Our People Die Well: Deathbed Scenes in John Wesley's Arminian Magazine." *Mortality* 10, no. 3 (2005): 210-223.

Bence, Clarence L. "Processive Eschatology: A Wesleyan Alternative." *Wesleyan Theological Journal* 14, no. 1 (Spring 1979): 45-59.

Bennett, David. "How Arminian was John Wesley?" *The Evangelical Quarterly* 72, no. 3 (July 2000): 237-48.

Berg, Daniel N. "The Theological Context of American Wesleyanism." *Wesleyan Theological Journal* 20, no. 1 (Spring 1985): 45-60.

Bernhardt, W. H. "Was John Wesley a Pacifist?" *Methodist Review* 108 (1925): 551-60.

Brewer, Kenneth W. "Rob Bell and John Wesley on the Fate of the Lost and Those Who Never Heard the Gospel." *Wesleyan Theological Journal* 48, no. 1 (2013): 117-134.

Bertucci, Paola. "Revealing Sparks: John Wesley and the Religious Utility of Electrical Healing." *The British Journal for the History of Science* 39, no. 3 (2006): 341-362.

Bett, Henry. "The Wesleys and the English Bible." *Methodist Recorder* 52, no. 2 (1911): 256-57.

Bevins, Winfield H. "Wesley and the Pentecostals." *Pneuma Review* 8, no. 3 (2005): 10-17.

---. "Pentecostal Appropriation of the Wesleyan Quadrilateral." *Journal of Pentecostal Theology* 14, no. 2 (2006): 229-246.

---. "The Historical Development of Wesley's Doctrine of the Spirit." *Wesleyan Theological Journal* 41, no. 2 (2006): 161-181.

Bible, Ken. "The Wesley's Hymns on Full Redemption and Pentecost: A Brief Comparison." *Wesleyan Theological Journal* 17, no. 2 (Fall 1982): 79-87.

Black, Jeremy. "John Wesley and History." Wesley and Methodist Studies 9, no. 1 (2017): 1-17.

Blakemore, G. Stephen. "By the Spirit Through the Water: John Wesley's 'Evangelical' Theology of Infant Baptism." *Wesleyan Theological Journal* 31, no. 2 (Fall 1996): 167-91.

Blanchette, Kyle. "A Brief Look at Methodology and Grace in Wesleyan Theology." *Asbury Journal* 66, no. 1 (2011): 105-118.

Blankenship, Paul Freeman. "The Significance of John Wesley's Abridgement of the Thirty-Nine Articles as Seen from His Deletions." *Methodist History* 2, no. 3 (1964): 35-47.

Blevins, Dean G. "Means of Grace: Towards a Wesleyan Praxis of Spiritual Formation." *Wesleyan Theological Journal* 32, no. 1 (Spring 1997): 69-84.

---. "A Wesleyan View of the Liturgical Construction of the Self." *Wesleyan Theological Journal* 38, no. 2 (2003): 7-29.

---. "Holy Church, Holy People: A Wesleyan Exploration in Congregational Holiness and Personal Testament." *Wesleyan Theological Journal* 39, no. 2 (2004): 54-73.

---. "To Be a Means of Grace: A Wesleyan Perspective on Christian Practices and the Lives of Children." *Wesleyan Theological Journal* 43 (2008): 47-67.

---. "Neuroscience, John Wesley and the Christian Life." *Wesleyan Theological Journal* 44, no. 1 (2009): 219-247.

Bloor, Joshua D. "Revisiting Wesley's Ethics and His Ministry to the Poor: Social, Economical, and Medical Solutions." *Wesleyan Theological Journal* 50, no. 2 (2015): 80-95.

Boeckel, Peter. "The Polyvalence of Atonement in the Old Testament: A Wesleyan Reflection on Leviticus and Jonah." *Wesleyan Theological Journal* 50, no. 1 (2015): 116-133.

Boetcher, Jim. "Our Personal Core Identity: A Wesleyan Perspective." *Asbury Theological Journal* 65, no. 1 (2010): 6-29.

Boggan, Ashley. "A God-Sent Movement: Methodism, Contraception, and the Protection of the Methodist Family." *Methodist History* 53, no. 2 (2015): 68-84.

Bolster, George Reed. "Wesley's Doctrine of Sanctification." *The Evangelical Quarterly* 24 (1952): 144-55.

Bondi, Roberta C. "The Role of the Holy Spirit from the United Methodist Perspective." *Greek Orthodox Theological Review* 31, no. 3-4 (1986): 351-60.

Borgen, Ole E. "John Wesley on the Sacraments; A Theological Study [precis of dissertation]." *The Drew Gateway* 40 (Spring 1970): 160-61.

---. "Baptism, Confirmation, and Church Membership in the Methodist Church Before the Union of 1968: A Historical and Theological Study." *Methodist History* 27 (1989): 89-109, 163-81.

---. "No End Without the Means: John Wesley and the Sacraments." *The Asbury Theological Journal* 46, no. 1 (Spring 1991): 63-85.

---. "John Wesley and Early Swedish Pietism: Carl Magnus Wrangel and Johan Hinric Liden." *Methodist History* 38, no. 2 (January 2000): 82-103.

Boshears, Onva K. "The Books in John Wesley's Life." Wesleyan Theological Journal 3, no. 1 (Spring 1967): 66-81.

Bowmer, John C. "The Sacrament of the Lord's Supper in Early Methodism." *London Quarterly & Holborn Review* 175 (October 1950): 338-45.

---. "Wesley's Revision of the Communion Service in The Sunday Service of the Methodists." *London Quarterly & Holborn Review* 176 (July 1951): 230-37.

---. "The History of Holy Communion in Methodism." *London Quarterly & Holborn Review* 184 (1959): 97-102.

---. "John Wesley's Philosophy of Suffering." *London Quarterly & Holborn Review* 184 (January 1959): 60-66.

---. "A Converting Ordinance and The Open Table." *The Proceedings of the Wesley Historical Society* 34 (1964): 109-13.

---. "The Wesleyan Conception of Ministry." *Religion in Life* 40 (Spring 1971): 85-96.

Braisdell, Sarah. "Transforming the World from the Kitchen?: The Story of Women Working Together in British Methodism." *Methodist History* 54, no. 3 (2016): 202-215.

Brantley, Richard. "Charles Wesley's Experimental Art." *Eighteenth Century Life* 11 (May 1987): 1-11.

Brantley, Richard Estes. "The Common Ground of Wesley and Edwards." *Harvard Theological Review* 83 (1990): 271-303.

Brendlinger, Irv A. "John Wesley and Slavery: Myth and Reality." *Wesleyan Theological Journal* 41, no. 1 (2006): 223-243.

Brendlinger, Irv A., and Mueller, Eric E. "Psychological Implications of the Doctrine of Christian Perfection with Special Reference to John Wesley's View." *Journal of Pastoral Care and Counseling* 160, no. 3 (2006): 275-286.

Brewer, Brian C. "Evangelical Anglicanism: John Wesley's Dialectical Theology of Baptism." *Evangelical Quarterly* 83, no. 2 (2011): 107-132.

Brian, Rustin E. "Kneeling, Sharia Law, and the Sermon on the Mount: The Peculiar Moral Vision of John Wesley's Methodist Ecclesiology". *Wesleyan Theological Journal* 53, no. 1 (2018): 161-174.

Brigden, Thomas E. "Wesley on the Ethics of Dress." *Wesleyan Methodist Magazine* 127 (1904): 41-45; 128-34; 190-95.

---. "The Wesleys and Islam." *The Proceedings of the Wesley Historical Society* 8 (1912): 91-94.

---. "Wesley and the Slave Trade: Benezet and Clarkson." *The Proceedings of the Wesley Historical Society* 12 (1920): 132-34.

---. "Wesley and the Conference on Wigs, Hair Powder, Curls and Barbers." *The Proceedings of the Wesley Historical Society* 13 (1922): 138-41.

Bridges-Johns, Cheryl. "From Strength to Strength: Neglected Role of Crisis in Wesleyan and Pentecostal Discipleship." *Wesleyan Theological Journal* 39, no. 1 (2004): 137-153.

Briggs, John P., and John Briggs. "Unholy Desires, Inordinate Affections: A Psychodynamic Inquiry into John Wesley's Relationship with Women [bibliog, pors]." *Connecticut Review* 13 (Spring 1991): 1-18.

Brittain, John N. "Theological Foundations for Spiritual Care [5 Wesleyan tenets for nurses]." *Journal of Religion and Health* 25, no. 2 (Summer 1986): 107-21.

Brockwell, Charles W. "John Wesley's Doctrine of Justification [bibliog]." *Wesleyan Theological Journal* 18, no. 2 (Fall 1983): 18-32.

---. "Wesleyan Spirituality: A Methodist/Anglican Nexus [Bibliog]." *Mid-Stream: An Ecumenical Journal* 29 (April 1990): 140-52.

Broholm, Richard R. "Evangelical Community and Social Transformation." *Foundations* 20 (October-December 1977): 352-61.

---. "Personal Piety and Social Transformation: Learning from the Past [the "class meetings" of John Wesley]." *The Other Side* 18, no. 4 (April 1982): 14-15.

Brown, Dale W. "The Wesleyan Revival From a Pietist Perspective." *Wesleyan Theological Journal* 24 (1989): 7-17.

Brown, Kenneth D. "John Wesley: Post or Premillennialist?" *Methodist History* 28, no. 1 (October 1989): 33-41.

Brown, R. H. "The Brownate of Truths: In Contradiction of John Wesley." *Methodist Recorder* 61 (1920): 9.

Bryant, Barry Edward. "Trinity and Hymnody: The Doctrine of the Trinity in the Hymns of Charles Wesley." *Wesleyan Theological Journal* 25, no. 2 (Fall 1990): 64-73.

Bryant, Barry E. "Molina, Arminius, Plaifere, Goad, and Wesley on Human Free-will, Divine Omniscience, and Middle Knowledge." *Wesleyan Theological Journal* 27 (Spring-Fall 1992): 93-103.

---. "John Wesley on the Origins of Evil." *Wesleyan Theological Journal* 30, no. 1 (Spring 1995): 111-33.

Bryne, Brendan. "Ignatius Loyola and John Wesley: Experience and Strategies of Conversion." *Colloquium: The Australian and New Zealand Theological Review* 19, no. 1 (October 1986): 54-66.

Bundy, David. "Christian Virtue: John Wesley and the Alexandrian Tradition." *Wesleyan Theological Journal* 26, no. 1 (1991): 139-63.

---. "Visions of Sanctification: Themes of Orthodoxy in the Methodist, Holiness, and Pentecostal Traditions." *Wesleyan Theological Journal* 39, no. 1 (2004): 104-136.

---. "The African and Caribbean Origins of Methodism in the Bahamas." Methodist History 53, no. 3 (2015): 173-183.

Bunton, Peter. "300 Years of Small Groups: The European Church from Luther to Wesley." *Christian Education Journal* 11 (2014): 88-106.

Burdon, Adrian. "Ordination in British Methodism." *Studia Liturgica: An International Ecumenical Review for Liturgical Research and Renewal* 25, no. 2 (1995): 151-73.

---. "Wesleyan Models for Liturgical Theology." *Worship* 71 (July 1997): 309-17.

Burgess, Harold W. "A Wesleyan Theology of Ministry [reply, D N Berg]." *Wesleyan Theological Journal* 18, no. 1 (Spring 1983): 30-43.

Burnett, Ivan. "Methodist Origins: John Wesley And Alcohol." *Methodist History* 13 (July 1975): 3-17.

Burris, Christopher T., and Raluca Petrican. "Hearts Strangely Warmed (and Cooled): Emotional Experience in Religious and Atheistic Individuals." *International Journal for the Psychology of Religion* 21, no. 3 (2011): 183-197.

Burroughs, Presian. "Wesley's Representation of Salvation in 'the Scripture Way of Salvation': A Pauline Assessment." *Wesleyan Theological Journal* 51, no. 1 (2016): 203-208.

Butler, David. "Good News to the London Poor: A Comparison of the Philanthropy of John Wesley and Richard Chailoner (1691-1781), Vicar Apostolic of the London District." *Epworth Review* 21 (January 1994): 109-17.

---. ""Look for the Mother to Find the Son": The Influence of Susanna Wesley On Her Son John." *Epworth Review* 25 (October 1998): 90-100.

Byassee, Jason, and L. Gregory Jones. "Methodists & Microcredit." *First Things: A Monthly Journal of Religion & Public Life*, no. 197 (2009): 20-22.

Byrne, Brendan. "Ignatius Loyola and John Wesley: Experience and Strategies of Conversion." *Colloquium: The Australian and New Zealand Theological Review* 19, no. 1 (1986): 54-66.

Callaway, Clifford Wayne. "John Wesley's Primative Physick: An Essay in Appreciation." *Proceedings of the Mayo Clinic* 49 (1974): 318-24.

Campbell, Ted A. "Exploring Methodist Theology after John Wesley [review article]." *Books and Religion* 14, no. 3 (March 1986): 6.

---. "John Wesley and Conyers Middleton on Divine Intervention in History." *Church History* 55, no. 1 (March 1986): 39-49.

---. "The "Wesleyan Quadrilateral": The Story of a Modern Methodist Myth." *Methodist History* 29, no. 2 (January 1991): 87-95.

---. "The Wesleys' New Denomination: How a Revival Became an Institution." *Christianity Today* 35 (11 March 1991): 33-35.

---. "Christian Tradition, John Wesley, and Evangelicalism [his view of apostolic and Anglican traditions]." *Anglican Theological Review* 74 (Winter 1992): 54-67.

---. "John Wesley and the Asian Roots of the Christianity." *Asia Journal of Theology* 8 (October 1994): 281-94.

---. "Wesley's Use of the Church Fathers." *Asbury Theological Journal* 50-52, no. 2-1 (Fall-Spring 1995-1996): 57-70.

---. "Wesleyan Quest for Ancient Roots: The 1980's." *Wesleyan Theological Journal* 32, no. 1 (Spring 1997): 5-16.

---. "The "Way of Salvation" and the Methodist Ethos Beyond John Wesley: A Study in Formal Consensus and Popular Reception." *Asbury Journal* 63 (2008): 53-31.

---. "Crisis, John Wesley's Intimate Disconnections 1755-1764." *Methodist History* 51, no. 3 (2013): 185-200.

Cannon, William R. "Perfection." *London Quarterly & Holborn Review* 184 (1959): 213-17.

---. "John Wesley's Doctrine of Sanctification and Perfection." *The Mennonite Quarterly Review* 35 (April 1961): 91-95.

---. "The Holy Spirit in Vatican II and in the Writings of Wesley." *Religion in Life* 37 (1968): 440-53.

---. "Meaning of the Ministry in Methodism." *Methodist History* 8 (October 1969): 3-19.

---. "Salvation in the Theology of John Wesley." *Methodist History* 9 (October 1970): 3-12.

---. "Methodism in a Philosophy of History." *Methodist History* 12 (July 1974): 27-43.

---. "Methodism - Our Theology." *Asbury Seminary Journal* 40, no. 2 (Winter 1985): 3-9.

Carder, Kenneth L. "Doctrinal/Theological Themes for Preaching: John Wesley and the Galatian and Colossian Letters." *Quarterly Review* 12 (Summer 1992): 103-19.

Carey, Jonathan Sinclair. "Wesley, Methodism and the Unitarians [Christology and Ethics]." *Faith and Freedom: A Journal of Progressive Religion* 45 (Autumn 1992): 102-12.

Carile, Sergio. "Il Metodismo: Espressione Teologicamente Significativa [faith, action in Wesley and followers]." *Protestantesimo* 43, no. 3-4 (1988): 130-36.

Carrier, E. Theodore. "Wesley's Views on Prayers for the Dead." *The Proceedings of the Wesley Historical Society* 1 (1898): 123-25.

Carroll, Michael. "Comment on Keith Haartman's 'Religious Ecstasy and Personality Transformation in John Wesley's Methodism: Theoretical and Methodological Considerations'." *Archive for the Psychology of Religion* 29, no. 1 (2007): 37-49.

Carter, Kelly D. "The High Church Roots of John Wesley's Appeal to Primitive Christianity." *Restoration Quarterly* 37 (1995): 65-79.

Cartwright, Michael G., and Gary R. Shiplett. "Closing Ranks on Open Communion: Two Views." *Quarterly Review* 8 (Spring 1988): 54-70.

Carver, Frank G. "Biblical Foundations for the 'Secondness' of Entire Sanctification [diag]." *Wesleyan Theological Journal* 22, no. 2 (Fall 1987): 7-23.

Case, L. D. "Origins of Methodist Publishing in America [reprint]." *Methodist History* 4 (April 1966): 29-41.

Castelo, Daniel. "Perfecting One Another: Friendship and the Moral Implications of Wesley's Small Groups." *Asbury Theological Journal* 64, no. 1 (2009): 4-21.

---. "Holiness Simpliciter: A Wesleyan Engagement and Proposal in Light of John Webster's Trinitarian Dogmatics of Holiness." *Wesleyan Theological Journal* 47, no. 2 (2012): 147-164.

Cecil, Robert. "Holy Dying: Evangelical Attitudes to Death [photos]." *History Today* 32 (August 1982): 30-34.

Chamberlain, Jeffrey S. "Moralism, Justification, and the Controversy over Methodism." *The Journal of Ecclesiastical History* 44 (1993): 652-78.

Chandler, D. R. "Towards The Americanizing of Methodism." *Methodist History* 8 (October 1974): 3-16.

Chapman, David M. "Holiness and Order: British Methodism's Search for the Holy Catholic Church." *Ecclesiology* 7, no. 1 (2011): 71-96.

Chapple, Richard Curtis. "Rediscovering Salvation as a Requirement for Full Membership." *The AME Zion Quarterly Review* 109 (July 1997): 26-35.

Cherry, Natalya. "Wesley's Doctrinal Distinctions in Developing the Faith That Marks the New Birth." Wesleyan Theological Journal 52, no. 2 (2017): 100-112.

Chilcote, Paul W. "John Wesley as Revealed by the Journal of Hester Ann Rogers." *Duke Divinity School Bulletin* 44 (Winter 1979): 33-43.

---. "John Wesley as Revealed by the Journal of Hester Ann Rogers, July 1775-October 1784." *Methodist History* 20, no. 3 (April 1982): 111-23.

---. "The Legacy of J. Ernest Rattenbury." *Methodist History* 21, no. 4 (July 1983): 207-24.

---. "John and Charles Wesley on 'God in Christ Reconciling'." *Methodist History* 47, no. 3 (2009): 132-145.

---. "Lessons from the Society Planting: Paradigm of Early Methodist Women: 2012 Aete Presidential Address." *Witness: Journal of the Academy for Evangelism in Theological Education* 27 (2013): 5-30.

Cho, J. C. "John Wesley's View on Baptism." *North East Asia Journal of Theology* 1, no. 9 (Spring 1972): 29-41.

---. "John Wesley's View on Baptism." *Wesleyan Theological Journal* 7, no. 1 (Spring 1972): 60-73.

---. "Adam's Fall and God's Grace: John Wesley's Theological Anthropology." *Evangelical Review of Theology* 10, no. 3 (July 1986): 202-13.

Christensen, Michael J. "Theosis and Sanctification: John Wesley's Reformation of a Patristic Doctrine." *Wesleyan Theological Journal* 31, no. 2 (Fall 1996): 71-94.

Church, Leslie F. "Pastor in the Eighteenth Century." *London Quarterly & Holborn Review* 181 (January 1956): 19-23.

Clapper, Gregory S. ""True Religion" and the Affections: A Study of John Wesley's Abridgement of Jonathan Edward's Treatises on Religious Affections." *Wesleyan Theological Journal* 19, no. 2 (Fall 1984): 77-89.

---. "Orthokardia: The Practical Theology of John Wesley's Heart Religion." *Quarterly Review* 10 (Spring 1990): 49-66.

---. "John Wesley's "Heart Religion" and the Righteousness of Christ." *Methodist History* 35, no. 3 (April 1997): 148-56.

---. "Wesley's 'Main Doctrines': Spiritual Formation and Teaching in the Wesleyan Tradition." *Wesleyan Theological Journal* 39, no. 2 (2004): 97-121.

---. "John Wesley's Abridgement of Isaac Watts' the Doctrine of the Passions Explained and Improved." *Wesleyan Theological Journal* 43 (2008): 28-32.

Clark, Brian Curtis. "Converting Mrs. Crouch: Women, Wonders, and the Formation of English Methodism, 1738-1741." *Journal of Ecclesiastical History* 65, no. 1 (2014): 66-83.

Clarke, Martin V. "John Wesley's Directions for Singing: Methodist Hymnody as an Expression of Methodist Beliefs in Thought and Practices." *Methodist History* 47, no. 1 (2009): 196-209.

Clarkson, G. E. "John Wesley and William Law's Mysticism." *Religion in Life* 42 (Winter 1973): 537-44.

Cleland, J. T. "A Presbyterian Look at John Wesley [Sermon]." *Duke Divinity School Bulletin* 28 (May 1963): 81-87.

Clements, Heather "The Church, Mental Disabilities, and Adult Faith Decisions: A Wesleyan Inquiry." *Wesleyan Theological Journal* 45, no. Fall (2010): 7-24.

---. "John Wesley, First Peoples of North America, and Christian Perfection." *Wesleyan Theological Journal* 46, no. 2 (2011): 150-167.

Clemons, James T. "John Wesley - Biblical Literalist?" *Religion in Life* 46 (Autumn 1977): 332-42.

---. "John Wesley's View of Suicide in Its Cultural Context." *Quarterly Review* 16 (Summer 1996): 135-49.

Clifford, Alan C. "The Gospel and Justification." *The Evangelical Quarterly* 57 (July 1985): 247-67.

Climenhaga, Daryl R. "Interpreting the Scriptures." *Brethren in Christ History and Life* 10 (December 1987): 198-209.

Clutterbuck, Richard. "Our Doctrines [Methodist; Fernley-Hartley Lecture]," *Epworth Review* 24 (July 1997): 21-33.

Coates, Greg. "Before American Methodists Became American: Methodist Countercultural Witness During the Revolutionary Era." *Wesleyan Theological Journal* 50, no. 2 (2015): 113-136.

Cockerill, Gareth L. "Jesus and the Greatest Commandment in Mark 10:17-22: A Test Case for John Wesley's " Theology of Love"." *Asbury Seminary Journal* 40, no. 1 (Spring 1985): 13-21.

Collins, Kenneth J. "A Hermeneutical Model for the Wesleyan Ordo Salutis." *Wesleyan Theological Journal* 19, no. 2 (Fall 1984): 23-37.

---. "John Wesley and the Means of Grace." *Asbury Seminary Journal* 40, no. 2 (Winter 1985): 23-31.

---. "John Wesley and the Means of Grace." *The Drew Gateway* 56, no. 3 (Spring 1986): 26-33.

---. "John Wesley's Platonic Conception of the Moral Law." *Wesleyan Theological Journal* 21, no. 1 and 2 (Spring-Fall 1986): 116-28.

---. "John Wesley and Liberation Theology: A Closer Look." *The Asbury Theological Journal* 42, no. 1 (1987): 85-90.

---. "John Wesley's Correspondence with His Father." *Methodist History* 26, no. 1 (October 1987): 15-26.

---. "The Continuing Significance of Aldersgate [response to "John Wesley against Aldersgate" by T W Jennings, 8:3-22 1988; rejoinder, 100-105]." *Quarterly Review* 8 (Winter 1988): 90-99.

---. "John Wesley's Concept of the Ministerial Office." *Wesleyan Theological Journal* 23, no. 1 and 2 (Spring-Fall 1988): 107-21.

---. "Twentieth-century Interpretations of John Wesley's Aldersgate Experience: Coherence and Confusion?" *Wesleyan Theological Journal* 24 (1989): 18-31.

---. "Children of Neglect: American Methodist Evangelicals," *Christian Scholar's Review* Vol. XX:1 (September 1990): 7-16.

---. "The Influence of Early German Pietism on John Wesley [Arndt and Francke]." *The Covenant Quarterly* 48 (November 1990): 23-42.

---. "Other Thoughts on Aldersgate: Has the Conversionist Paradigm Collapsed?" *Methodist History* 30, no. 1 (October 1991): 10-25.

---. "John Wesley's Critical Appropriation of Early German Pietism." *Wesleyan Theological Journal* 27, no. 1 and 2 (Spring-Fall 1992): 57-92.

---. "A Reply to Randy Maddox." *Methodist History* 31, no. 1 (October 1992): 51-54.

---. "John Wesley's Assessment of Christian Mysticism." *Lexington Theological Quarterly* 28, no. 4 (Winter 1993): 299-318.

---. "John Wesley's Relationship with His Wife as Revealed in His Correspondence." *Methodist History* 32, no. 1 (October 1993): 4-18.

---. "The Motif of Real Christianity in the Writings of John Wesley." *The Asbury Theological Journal* 49, no. 1 (Spring 1994): 49-62.

---. "The Soteriological Orientation of John Wesley's Ministry to the Poor." *The Asbury Theological Journal* 50, no. 1 (Spring 1995): 75-92.

---. "'Real Christianity' As Integrating Theme in Wesley's Soteriology: The Critique of a Modern Myth." The Asbury Theological Journal 51, No. 2 (Fall 1996): 15-45.

---. "The New Birth: John Wesley's Doctrine," *The Wesleyan Theological Journal* 32, no. 1 (Spring 1997): 53-68.

---. "A Reconfiguration of Power: The Basic Trajectory of John Wesley's Practical Theology," *The Wesleyan Theological Journal* 33, no. 1 (Spring 1998): 164-84.

---. "John Wesley's Topography of the Heart: Dispositions, Tempers and Affections," *Methodist History* 36, no. 3 (April 1998): 162-75.

---. "Why the Holiness Movement is Dead," *The Asbury Theological Journal* 54, No. 2, (Fall 1999) 27-36.

---. "Recent Trends in Wesley Studies and Wesleyan/ Holiness Scholarship," *The Wesleyan Theological Journal* 35, No. 1, (Spring 2000) 67-86.

---. "John Wesley's Critical Appropriation of Tradition in His Practical Theology," *The Wesleyan Theological Journal* 35, No. 2, (Fall 2000) 69-91.

---. "John Wesley," in *Historical Dictionary of the Holiness Movement*, pp. 266-68. Edited by William C. Kostlevy (Lanham, Maryland: Scarecrow Press, 2001).

---. "The Ongoing Decline of British and American Methodism: A Modernistic Saga." *The Asbury Theological Journal* 56 & 57, no. 2, 1 (2002): 67-82.

---. "The New Creation as a Multivalent Theme in John Wesley's Theology." *Wesleyan Theological Journal* 37, no. 2 (2002): 77-102.

---. "Rethinking the Systematic Nature of John Wesley's Theology." *Bulletin of the John Rylands University Library of Manchester* 86, no. 2 and 3 (2004): 309-330.

---. "The Promise of John Wesley's Theology for the 21st Century." *Asbury Theological Journal* 59, no. 1-2 (2004): 171-180.

---. "A Wesleyan Theology of Governance for Seminaries." *Asbury Journal* 64, no. 1 (2009): 83-91.

---. "The State of Wesley Studies in North America: A Theological Journey." *Wesleyan Theological Journal* 44, no. 2 (2009): 7-38.

---. "Is 'Canonical Theism' a Viable Option for Wesleyans?" *Wesleyan Theological Journal* 45, no. 2 (2010): 82-107.

---. "The Method of John Wesley's Practical Theology Reconsidered." Wesley and Methodist Studies 9, no. 2 (2017): 101-122.

Collins, Kenneth J., and Christine L. Johnson. "From the Garden to the Gallows: The Significance of Free Grace in the Theology of John Wesley." *The Wesleyan Theological Journal* 48, no. 2 (2013): 7-29.

Colson, Charles W. "Standing Tough Against All Odds: William Wilberforce [por]." *Christianity Today* 12 (6 September 1985): 26-33.

Conklin-Miller, Jeffrey A. "Peoplehood and the Methodist Revival." *Wesleyan Theological Journal* 46 (2011): 163-182.

Cooney, Jonathan. "The Shout Heard Round the World: Similarities and Differences between American and English Camp Meetings." *Methodist History* 50, no. 1 (2011): 40-51.

Coppedge, Allan. "John Wesley and the Issue of Authority in Theological Pluralism." *Wesleyan Theological Journal* 19, no. 2 (Fall 1984): 62-76.

Copplestone, J. Tremayne. "John Wesley and the American Revolution." *Religion in Life* 45 (Spring 1976): 89-105.

Cosby, Michael R. "Using the Wesleyan Quadrilateral to Teach Biblical Studies in Christian Liberal Arts Colleges." *Teach Theology & Religion* 4, no. 2 (2001): 71-80.

Coulter, Dale M. . "By Faith Alone: Pentecostals, Wesley, and the Reformation." Journal of the European Pentecostal Theological Association 37, no. 2 (2017): 123-134.

Couture, Pamela D. "Revelation in Pastoral Theology: A Wesleyan Perspective." *Journal of Pastoral Theology* 9 (1999): 21-34.

Cowley, T. "Les Debuts du Methodisme et les Courants Evangeliques dans la Societe Britannique." *Istina* 14 (October-December 1969): 387-412.

Crawford, Nathan. "Science and Theology in Conversation: Emergence Theories of Consciousness and Entire Sanctification." *Asbury Theological Journal* 64, no. 1 (2009): 40-53.

Creasman, Ron. "Why Do Missions? Probe of Wesley in Search of Motivational Resources for Missions." *Wesleyan Theological Journal* 38, no. 1 (2003): 210-225.

Crofford, James Gregory. "'Grace to All Did Freely Move:' Thoughts on Charles Wesley's 1741/1742 Hymns on God's Everlasting Love." *Wesley and Methodist Studies* 6 (2014): 37-62.

Crow, Earl P. "Wesley and Antinomianism." *Duke Divinity School Bulletin* 31 (Winter 1966): 10-19.

Cubie, David L. "Perfection in Wesley and Fletcher: Inaugural or Teleological?" *Wesleyan Theological Journal* 11 (Spring 1976): 22-37.

---. "Wesley's Theology of Love." *Wesleyan Theological Journal* 20, no. 1 (Spring 1985): 122-54.

---. "Placing Aldersgate in John Wesley's Order of Salvation." *Wesleyan Theological Journal* 24 (1989): 32-53.

---. "Early Methodism: A Paradigm for Non-Violence: An Exercise in "Vision Ethics"." *Wesleyan Theological Journal* 37, no. 1 (2002): 86-105.

---. ""Entire" Sanctification, the Platonic Doctrine of the Soul, and First Thessalonians 5:23"." *Wesleyan Theological Journal* 45, no. 2 (2010): 136-160.

Cule, John. "The Rev. John Wesley, M.A., 1703-1791: 'The Naked Empiricist' and Orthodox Medicine." *Journal of the History of Medicine and Allied Sciences* 45 (1990): 41-63.

Culp, John. "A Dialogue with the Process Theology of John B. Cobb, Jr." *Wesleyan Theological Journal* 15, no. 2 (Fall 1980): 33-44.

Cunningham, Floyd T. ""Justification by Faith": Richard Baxter's Influence Upon John Wesley." *Asbury Theological Journal* 64, no. 1 (2009): 55-66.

Cunningham, Joseph W. "Pneumatology through Correspondence: The Letters of John and 'John Smith' (1745-1748)." *Wesley and Methodist Studies* 1 (2009): 18-32.

---. "The Methodist Doctrine of Christian Perfection: Charles Wesley's Contribution Contextualized." *Wesley and Methodist Studies* 2 (2010): 25-44.

---. "A New Trajectory in Wesleyan Pneumatology: "Perceptible Inspiration" Reconsidered." *Wesleyan Theological Journal* 45, no. 2 (2010): 242-261.

---. "John Wesley's Moral Pneumatology: The Fruits of the Spirit as Theological Virtues." *Studies in Christian Ethics* 24, no. 3 (2011): 275-293.

Cushman, Robert E. "Theological Landmarks in the Revival Under Wesley." *Religion in Life* 28 (1957-58): 105-18.

---. "Orthodoxy and Wesley's Experimental Divinity [Wesley's idea of Doctrine]." *Quarterly Review* 8 (Summer 1988): 71-89.

Dabney, D. Lyle. "Jurgen Moltman and John Wesley's Third Article Theology." *Wesleyan Theological Journal* 29, no. 1 (Spring-Fall 1994): 140-48.

---. "What Has Aldersgate to Do with Wittenberg?" *Lutheran Forum* 42, no. 3 (2008): 47-50.

Dallimore, A. "Man Who Loves His Critics [George Whitefield]." *Christianity Today* 1 (19 August 1957): 14-16.

Daniel, W. Harrison. "The Young John Wesley as Cross-Cultural Witness: Investigations into Wesley's American Mission Experience and Implications for Today's Mission." *Missiology* 28, no. 4 (2000): 443-457.

Danker, Ryan N. "Fighting over the Dead: John Wesley, Ritualism, and the Politics of Church and State in 1870s England " *Wesley and Methodist Studies* 10, no. 1 (2018): 24-45.

Darsey, Steven. "John Wesley as Hymn and Tune Editor: The Evidence of Charles Wesley's 'Jesu, Lover of My Soul' and Martin Madan's HOTHAM." *The Hymn: A Journal of Congregational Song* 47 (January 1996): 17-24.

Davies, James A. "Small Groups: Are They Really So New [fig]." *Christian Education Journal* 5, no. 2 (1984): 43-52.

Davies, Rupert Eric. "The History and Theology of the Methodist Covenant Service." *Theology* 64 (1961): 62-68.

Dayton, Donald W. "Law and Gospel in the Wesleyan Tradition." *Grace Theological Journal* 12 (Fall 1991): 233-43.

---. "The Wesleyan Option for the Poor." *Wesleyan Theological Journal* 26, no. 1 (1991): 7-22.

---. "A Final Round with Larry Wood." *Pneuma* 28, no. 2 (2006): 265-270.

Dayton, Wilbur T. "The Bible in the Wesleyan Tradition." *Asbury Seminary Journal* 40, no. 1 (Spring 1985): 22-38.

Dean, William Walter. "The Methodist Class Meeting - The Significance of Its Decline." *The Proceedings of the Wesley Historical Society* 43 (December 1981): 41-48.

Deasley, Alex R. G., ed. "The Wesleyan Heritage in America [papers, Wesleyan Theological Society, Atlanta, Nov. 2-3 1984]." *Wesleyan Theological Journal* 20, no. 1 (Spring 1985): 7-154.

De Blasio, Marlon D. "Conversion, Justification, and the Experience of Grace in the Post-Aldersgate Wesley: Towards an Understanding of Who Is a Child of God." *Asbury Journal* 66, no. 2 (2011): 18-34.

DeGeorge, Rob. "Rehabilitating John Wesley's Christology in the Book of Hebrews: A Response to Hambrick and Lodahl." *Wesleyan Theological Journal* 53, no. 2 (2018): 165-193.

de Gruchy, Aubin. "Beyond Intention: John Wesley's Intentional and Unintentional Socio-Economic Influences on 18th Century England." *Journal of Theology for Southern Africa*, no. 68 (Spring 1989): 75-85.

Dell Colle, Ralph. "John Wesley's Doctrine of Grace in Light of the Christian Tradition." *International Journal of Systematic Theology* 4, no. 2 (2002): 172-189.

Dermer, Scott and Stephen Patrick Riley. "Interpreting Idolatry: Reading Scripture with the Fathers, Wesley, and Contemporary Exegesis." *Wesleyan Theological Journal* 48, no. 1 (2013): 149-161.

Derr, Colleen R. "The Role of Obedience in Child Faith Formation: Insights from the Teachings and Practices of John Wesley." *Christian Education Journal* 11, no. 2 (2014): 367-382.

Dey, Lala Kaylan K., ed. "Doctrinal Standards in United Methodism: The 1986 Frances Youngker Vosburgh Lectures." *The Drew Gateway* 57 (Fall 1987): 1-94.

Dicker, Gordon Stanley. "The Aldersgate Tradition and Its Critics." *Uniting Church Studies* 14, no. 1 (2008): 33-41.

Dieter, Melvin E. "The Development of 19th Century Holiness Theology." *Wesleyan Theological Journal* 20, no. 1 (Spring 1985): 61-77.

Dillman, Charles N. "Wesley's Approach to the Law in Discourse XXV on the Sermon on the Mount." *Wesleyan Theological Journal* 12, no. 12 (Spring 1977): 60-65.

Dinwiddie, Richard D. "Two Brothers who Changed the Course of Church Singing [John and Charles Wesley wrote an average of three hymns per week; pors; il]." *Christianity Today* 28, no. 13 (21 September 1984): 30-34.

Ditchfield, G.M. "John Wesley, Heterodoxy, and Dissent." *Wesley and Methodist Studies* 10, no. 2 (2018): 109-131.

Dodds, Adam. "Regeneration and Resistible Grace: A Synergistic Proposal." *Evangelical Quarterly* 83, no. 11 (2011): 29-48.

Donat, James G. "Empirical Medicine in the 18th Century: The Rev. John Wesley's Search for Remedies That Work." *Methodist History* 144, no. 4 (2006): 216-226.

Dorr, Donal J. "Total Corruption and the Wesleyan Tradition." *Irish Theological Quarterly* 31 (1964): 303-21.

---. "Wesley's Teaching on the Nature of Holiness." *London Quarterly & Holborn Review* 190 (July 1965): 234-39.

Dose, Kai. "A Note on John Wesley's Visit to Herrnhut in 1738." *Wesley and Methodist Studies* 7, no. 1 (2015): 117-120.

Doughty, William Lamplough. "Wesley and English Modernism." *Modern Churchman* 28 (1938): 70-80.

Douglas, David. "An American Investigates [Wesley's Aldersgate Experience]." *Epworth Review* 26 (January 1999): 60-65.

Dowdy, Roger. "A Service of Wesley Hymns [bibliog]." *Journal of Church Music* 30 (May 1988): 5-7.

Drakeford, John W. "How Growing Old Looks from Within: A Study of John Wesley's Perception of the Aging Process Revealed in His Journal's "Birthday Reflections"." *Journal of Religion and Aging* 1, no. 2 (Winter 1984): 39-51.

Dreyer, Frederick. "Faith and Experience in the Thought of John Wesley." *The American Historical Review* 88 (Fall 1983): 12-30.

---. "Evangelical Thought: John Wesley and Jonathan Edwards." *Albion* 19 (1987): 177-92.

---. "A "Religious Society under Heaven:" John Wesley and the Identity of Methodism." *Journal of British Studies* 25, no. 1 (2014): 62-83.

Drovdahl, Robert R. "Myth of Becoming; Myth of Being [developmentalism and Wesleyan perfection]." *Christian Education Journal* 13, no. Autumn (1992): 25-32.

Drovdahl, Robert R., and Les L. Steele. "Renewing the Self [Wesleyan Theological Perspective on Christian Education]." *Christian Education Journal* 15 (1995): 54-63.

Drury, John. "Luther and Wesley on Union and Impartation in Light of Recent Finnish Luther Research." *Wesleyan Theological Journal* 40 (2005): 58-68.

---. "Ten Dogmatic Theses on John Wesley's 'the Scripture Way of Salvation'." *Wesleyan Theological Journal* 51, no. 1 (2016): 214-223.

Dunlap, E. Dale. "Baptism and the Christian Life: A United Methodist View [reply, K Penzel]." *Perkins Journal* 34, no. 2 (Winter 1981): 7-15.

Dunlap, Pamela Couture. "On the Danger of Reading the Works of John Wesley [editorial]." *Quarterly Review* 7 (Spring 1987): 3-8.

Dunning, H. Ray. "Systematic Theology in a Wesleyan Mode [reply, W J Abraham]." *Wesleyan Theological Journal* 17, no. 1 (Spring 1982): 15-22.

---. "Toward a Wesleyan Ecclesiology." *Wesleyan Theological Journal* 22, no. 1 (Spring 1987): 112-17.

Durbin, L. M. "Nature of Ordination in Wesley's View of the Ministry." *Methodist History* 9 (April 1971): 3-20.

Dryer, Frederick. "John Wesley: Ein Englisher Pietist." *Methodist History 40 no 2 Ja 2002* (2002): 71-84.

Eby, Patrick A. "John and Charles Wesley's Use of John Milton: Trinity and Heresy." *Methodist History* 44, no. 2 (2006): 115-124.

Eckhart, R. A. "Wesley and the Philosophers." *Methodist Review* 112 (1929): 357-70.

Eddy, Geoffrey Thackray. "Formica Contra Leonem: An Eighteenth Century Conflict Reassessed." *Methodist History* 38, no. 2 (January 2000): 71-81.

Edwards, M. "Reluctant Lover; John Wesley as Suitor." *Methodist History* 12 (January 1974): 46-62.

Edwards, Rem B. "John Wesley's Non-Literal Literalism and Hermeneutics of Love." *Wesleyan Theological Journal* 51, no. 2 (2016): 26-40.

Endicott, Lucas. "Settling the Printing Business: John Dickins and the Methodist Episcopal Book Concern from 1789 to 1798." *Methodist History* 48, no. 2 (2010): 81-91.

English, Charles Middleton. "John Wesley and the French Catholic Tradition." *Studies on Voltaire and the Eighteenth Century* 303 (1992): 441-44.

English, Donald. "Revisitazione di Aldersgate: Storia e Teologia Della Missione Metodista." *Protestantesimo* 47, no. 2 (1992): 82-95.

English, John C. "John Wesley and the Principal of Ministerial Succession." *Methodist History* 2, no. 2 (January 1964): 31-36.

---. "The Heart Renewed: John Wesley's Doctrine of Christian Initiation." *Wesleyan Quarterly Review* 4 (1967): 115-92.

---. "Sacrament of Baptism According to the Sunday Service of 1784." *Methodist History* 5 (January 1967): 10-16.

---. "John Wesley and Francis Rous." *Methodist History* 6 (July 1968): 28-35.

---. "John Wesley and the Anglican Moderates of the Seventeenth Century." *Anglican Theological Review* 51 (July 1969): 203-20.

---. "John Norris and John Wesley on the 'Conduct of the Understanding'." *The Proceedings of the Wesley Historical Society* 37 (February 1970): 101-4.

---. "Freedom Under Grace: Papers Presented to the Methodist History Symposium." Baker University; Baldwin, Kansas (1984).

---. "John Wesley and the English Enlightenment: An `Appeal to Men of Reason and Religion'." *Studies on Voltaire and the Eighteenth Century* 263 (1989): 400-403.

---. "John Wesley's Studies as an Undergraduate." *The Proceedings of the Wesley Historical Society* 47 (May 1989): 29-37.

---. "John Wesley and Isaac Newton's "System of the World"." *The Proceedings of the Wesley Historical Society* 48 (October 1991): 69-86.

---. "John Wesley's Indebtedness to John Norris [epistemology and education]." *Church History* 60 (March 1991): 55-69.

---. "John Wesley's Scientific Education." *Methodist History* 30, no. 1 (1991): 42-51.

---. "John Wesley and the French Catholic Tradition." *Studies on Voltaire and the Eighteenth Century* 303 (1992): 1-4.

---. "'Dear Sister': John Wesley and the Women of Early Methodism." *Methodist History* 33, no. 1 (October 1994): 26-33.

---. "John Wesley and the Rights of Conscience." *Journal of Church and State* 37 (1995): 349-63.

---. "John Wesley and the Liturgical Ideals of Thomas Cranmer." *Methodist History* 35 (July 1997): 222-32.

---. "The Path to Perfection in Pseudo-Macarius and John Wesley." *Pacifica: Journal of the Melbourne College of Divinity* 11, no. 1 (February 1998): 54-62.

---. "John Wesley and His 'Jewish Parishioners': Jewish-Christian Relationships in Savannah, Georgia, 1736-1737," *Methodist History* 36, no. 4 (July 1998): 220-27.

---. "John Wesley, the Establishment of Religion and the Separation of Church and State." *Journal of Church and State* 46, no. 1 (2004): 83-97.

---. "John Wesley Meets Laetitia Pilkington." *Methodist History* 42, no. 2 (2004): 88-97.

---. "References to St. Augustine in the Works of John Wesley." *Asbury Theological Journal* 60, no. 2 (2005): 5-24.

Estep, James Riley Jr. "John Wesley's Philosophy of Formal Childhood Education," *Christian Education Journal* 1, no. 2 (1997): 43-52.

Estrada-Carrasquillo, Wilmer. "The Relational Character of Wesley's Theology and Its Implications for an Ecclesiology for the Other: A Latino Pentecostal Testimony." *The Asbury Journal* 73, no. 1 (2018): 105-120.

Evans, Robert. "Another Look at John Wesley's Early Revivals." *Church Heritage* 20, no. 3 (2018): 139-155.

Fassett, Thomas White Wolf. "A Return to the Genius of Wesley: May we joyously demonstrate the power of love through personal and social holiness [review of report to General Board of Church and Society, 2 October 1998]," *Christian Social Action* 11 (November 1998): 9-12.

Faulkner, John Alfred. "Wesley the Mystic." *London Quarterly Review* 153 (1930): 145-60.

Felton, Gayle Carlton. "John Wesley and the Teaching Ministry: Ramifications for Teaching Education in the Church Today." *Religious Education* 92 (Winter 1997): 92-106.

Felleman, Laura. "John Wesley's Natural Philosophy: A Survey of Several Misconceptions." *Methodist History* 44, no. 3 (2006): 170-176.

---. "John Wesley's Survey of the Wisdom of God in Creation: A Methodological Inquiry." *Perspectives on Science and Christian Faith: Journal of the American Scientific Affiliation* 58, no. 1 (2006): 68-73.

---. "The Evidence of Things Not Seen: John Wesley's Faithful Convictions: Charles Bonnet's Inferential Conjectures." *Wesleyan Theological Journal* 42 (2007): 52-64.

Ferguson, Duncan S. "John Wesley on Scripture: The Hermeneutics of Pietism." *Methodist History* 22, no. 4 (July 1984): 234-45.

Ferrel, Lowell O. "John Wesley and the Enthusiasts [roots of Holiness-Pentecostal tensions]." *Wesleyan Theological Journal* 23, no. 1 and 2 (Spring-Fall 1988): 180-87.

Fiddick, Harold G. "The Care of Souls: John Wesley on the Preacher's Work and Ways." *Methodist Recorder* 73, no. 3 (1932): 9.

Field, David N. "John Wesley as a Public Theologian: The Case of Thoughts Upon Slavery." *Scriptura* 114 (2015).

Fletcher, John 1729-1785. "Letters from John Fletcher to John Wesley [July 4 1774, August 14 1774, August 1 1775]," *The Asbury Theological Journal* 53, no. 1 (Spring 1998): 91-96.

Flores, Daniel F., edt., and Thelma Herrera-Flores, edt. "Two Remarkable Stories: Lost Entries of John Wesley's Journal." *Methodist History* 38, no. 4 (2000): 251-257.

Flowers, Margaret G., and Douglas R. Cullum. "A Sometime Diversion: The Hymn Translations and Original Hymns of John Wesley." *Methodist History 41 no 1 O 2002* (2002): 295-308.

Flowers, Margaret G., Wayne McCown, and Douglas R. Cullum. "18th-Century Earthquakes and Apocalyptic Expections." *Methodist History* 42, no. 4 (2004): 222-235.

Forbes, Bruce D. ""And Obey God, etc": Methodism and American Indians [bibliog]." *Methodist History* 23, no. 1 (October 1984): 3-24.

Ford, Coleman M. "'A Pure Dwelling Place for the Holy Spirit': John Wesley's Reception of the Homilies of Macarius." Expository Times 130, no. 4 (2018): 157-166.

Ford, David C. "Saint Makarios of Egypt and John Wesley: Variations on the Theme of Sanctification." *Greek Orthodox Theological Review* 33 (1988): 285-312.

Forsaith, Peter. "The Romney Portrait of John Wesley." *Methodist History* 42, no. 4 (2004): 249-255.

Foss, H. "Thought Development of John Wesley." *Methodist Review* 63 (1903): 895ff.

Fox, Harold G. "John Wesley and Natural Philosophy." *University of Dayton Review* 7, no. 1 (1970): 1-9.

Frank, Thomas E. "The Dynamics of Methodism's Heritage." *Ecumenical Trends* 16 (May 1987): 81-85.

Franklin, Patrick S. "John Wesley in Conversation with the Emerging Church." *Asbury Journal* 63 (2008): 75-93.

Frazier, J. Russell. "John Wesley's Covenantal and Dispensational View of Salvation History." *Wesley and Methodist Studies* 1 (2009): 33-54.

Freeman, George H. "Wesley and the Poor: Theory and Practice from Then until Now." *Word and Deed* 8 (2005): 55-68.

Friedman, Matt. "Active Faith: Lessons from Wesley," *Regeneration Quarterly* 4 (Fall 1998): 32-34.

Friedman, Matt. "A Macarian-Wesleyan Theology of Mission." *Asbury Journal* 67 (2012): 93-111.

Frost, Brian. "Orthodoxy and Methodism." *London Quarterly & Holborn Review* 189 (1964): 13-22.

---. "The Idea of Fullness in the Hymns of Charles Wesley." *Sobornost (incorporating Eastern Churches Review), 4,* no. 7 (1965): 373-82.

Frost, Francis. "The Three Loves: A Theology of the Wesley Brothers [W. F. Flemington Lectures, Wesley House, Cambridge, 1995]," *Epworth Review* 24 (July 1997): 86-116.

Fuhrman, Eldon R. "Speaking the Truth in Love: Dual Emphases in Wesleyan Thought [bibliog]." *Wesleyan Theological Journal* 11 (Spring 1976): 5-21.

Gadsby, Gordon and Francis Dewhurst. "John Wesley's Contribution to the Evolution of Alternative and Holistic Healing." *Epworth Review* 26 (January 1999): 143-61.

Gaines, Timothy R. "Can Ethics Be Wesleyan?: Moral Theology and Holiness Identity." *Wesleyan Theological Journal* 51, no. 1 (2016): 155-167.

Gale, M. Andrew. "'Justice, Mercy, Truth:' A Theological Concept in the Sermons of John Wesley." *Wesleyan Theological Journal* 51, no. 2 (2016): 109-124.

Gallaway, Craig B. "Patterns of Worship in Early Methodist Hymnody and the Task of Hymnal Revision [bibliog]." *Quarterly Review* 7 (Fall 1987): 14-29.

Galliers, Brian J. N. "Baptism in the Writings of John Wesley." *The Proceedings of the Wesley Historical Society* 32 (1960): 121-24,153-57.

Garrison, R. B. "Vital Interaction: Scripture and Experience: John Wesley's Doctrine of Authority." *Religion in Life* 25 (1925): 563-73.

George, A. Raymond "Ordination in Methodism." *London Quarterly & Holborn Review* 176 (April 1951): 159-69.

---. "Private Devotion in the Methodist Tradition." *Studia Liturgica* 2 (1963): 223-36.

---. "The Real Presence and the Lord's Supper." *The Proceedings of the Wesley Historical Society* 34 (1964): 181-87.

---. "Foundation Document of the Faith, Pt 9: Methodist Statements." *Expository Times* 91 (June 1980): 260-63.

---. "The Sunday Service 1784." *Doxology* 1 (1984): 5-13.

Georgian, Elizabeth A. "Medicine and Politics: The Primitive Physic and Early American Methodism." *Wesley and Methodist Studies* 8, no. 1 (2016): 36-51.

Gerlach, Sandra. "John Wesley, Inquirer Seeking Grace: The Moravian View." *Methodist History* 45, no. 4 (2007): 223-231.

Gibson, William. "Samuel Wesley's Conformity Reconsidered." 47, no. 2 (2009): 68-83.

Giffin, John. "Scriptural Standards in Religion: John Wesley's Letters to William Law and James Hervey." *Studia Biblica et Theologica* 16 (1988): 143-68.

Giffin, Ryan K. "The Good Work of Justification, Sanctification, and Glorification: John Wesley's Soteriological Explanation of Philippians 1:6." The Asbury Journal 73, no. 1 (2018): 121-137.

Godbold, A. "Francis Asbury and his Difficulties with John Wesley and Thomas Rankin." *Methodist History* 3 (April 1965): 3-19.

Godsey, John D. "The Interpretation of Romans in the History of the Christian Faith." *Interpretation* 34 (January 1980): 3-16.

Gonzalez, Justo L. "Wesley's Heritage and the Global Church." *Methodist History* 43, no. 2 (2005): 115-130.

Goodwin, Charles H. "John Wesley: Revival and Revivalism, 1736-1768." *Wesleyan Theological Journal* 31, no. 1 (Spring 1996): 171-89.

---. "Setting Perfection too High: John Wesley's Changing Attitudes Toward the 'London Blessing'," *Methodist History* 36, no. 2 (January 1998): 86-96.

---. "John Wesley's Indebtedness to Jonathan Edwards." *Epworth Review* 25 (April 1998): 89-96.

Gorman, Joe. "Grace Abounds: The Missiological Implications of John Wesley's Inclusive Theology of Other Religions." *Wesleyan Theological Journal* 48, no. 1 (2013): 38-53.

---. "The Vital Relationship between Holiness and Health: Rekindling John Wesley's Holistic View of Salvation." *Wesleyan Theological Journal* 51, no. 2 (2016): 89-108.

Graham, David A. "The Chalcedonian Logic of John Wesley's Christology." International Journal of Systematic Theology 20, no. 1 (2018): 84-103.

Graham, Fred Kimball. "John Wesley's Choice of Hymn Tunes [12 examples]." *The Hymn: A Journal of Congregational Song* 39 (October 1988): 29-37.

Graves, A. S. "John Wesley's Variation in Belief." *Methodist Review* 47 (1887): 192.

Greathouse, William M. "Sanctification and the Christus Victor Motif in Wesleyan Theology." *Wesleyan Theological Journal* 7, no. 1 (Spring 1972): 47-59.

Greathouse, William M. "Sanctification and the Christus Victor Motif in Wesleyan Theology." *Wesleyan Theological Journal* 38, no. 2 (2003): 217-229. [Reprint of the earlier 1972 article.]

Green, Joel B. "Contribute or Capitulate? Wesleyans, Pentecostals, and Reading the Bible in a Post-Colonial Mode." *Wesleyan Theological Journal* 39, no. 1 (2004): 74-90.

Greeves, Frederic. "John Wesley and Divine Guidance." *London Quarterly & Holborn Review* 162 (1937): 379-85.

Grider, J. Kenneth. "Evaluation of Timothy Smith's Interpretation of Wesley [pp 68-87 Spr 80]." *Wesleyan Theological Journal* 15, no. 2 (Fall 1980): 64-69.

---. "The Nature of Wesleyan Theology." *Wesleyan Theological Journal* 17, no. 2 (Fall 1982): 43-57.

---. "Wesleyanism and the Inerrancy Issue." *Wesleyan Theological Journal* 19, no. 2 (Fall 1984): 52-61.

Griffin, Eric Richard. "Practical Catholicism: John Wesley's theology of Bishops Reconsidered." *Churchman: Journal of Anglican Theology* 112, no. 4 (1998): 324-38.

Grislis, E. "Wesleyan Doctrine of the Lord's Supper [bibliog]." *Duke Divinity School Bulletin* 28 (May 1963): 99-110.

Gschwandtner, Christina M. "A Wesleyan Model for Reconciliation and Evangelism? Conversation with Hegel and Levinas." *Wesleyan Theological Journal* 37, no. 1 (2002): 70-85.

Gunter, W. Stephen. "Thinking Theologically About Evangelism." *Quarterly Review* 19 (Spring 1999): 35-52.

---. "John Wesley, a Representative of Jacobus Arminius." *Wesleyan Theological Journal* 42, no. 2 (2007): 65-82.

Guyette, Fred. "Jesus as Prophet, Priest, and King: John Wesley and the Renewal of an Ancient Tradition." *Wesleyan Theological Journal* 40 (2005): 88-101.

Haartman, Keith. "Religious Ecstasy and Personality Transformation in John Wesley's Methodism: Theoretical and Methodological Considerations." *Archive for the Psychology of Religion* 29, no. 1 (2007): 3-35.

Haas, John W., Jr. "Eighteenth Century Evangelical Responses to Science: John Wesley's Enduring Legacy." *Science and Christian Belief* 6 (October 1994): 83-100.

---. "John Wesley's Views on Science and Christianity: An Examination of the Charge of Anti-science." *Church History* 63 (September 1994): 378-92.

---. "John Wesley's Vision of Science in the Service of Christ." *Perspectives on Science and Christian Faith: Journal of the American Scientific Affiliation* 47 (December 1995): 234-43.

Hall, Kevin. "Wesley's Disabling Fall." *Journal of Religion, Disability & Health* 15, no. 2 (2011): 197-209.

Hall, T. "Christian's Life; Wesley's Alternative to Luther and Calvin." *Duke Divinity School Bulletin* 28 (May 1963): 111-26.

Hall, Thor. "Wesley Og Hans Kvinner." *Teologisk Forum* 2, no. 2 (1988): 43-66.

Hambrick, C. H. "Lessons From an "Unsuccessful" Missionary." *Practical Anthropology* 8 (July-August 1961): 186-88. Editorial.

Hambrick, Matthew, and Michael Lodahl. "Responsible Grace in Christology? John Wesley's Rendering of Jesus in the Epistle to the Hebrews." *Wesleyan Theological Journal* 43 (2008): 86-103.

Hamilton, Barry W. "The Establishmentarian Turn in Middle Methodism." *Wesleyan Theological Journal* 50, no. 2 (2015): 137-155.

Hammond, Geordan. "John Wesley and Georgia: Success or Failure?" *Proceedings of the Wesley Historical Society* 56, no. 6 (2008): 297-305.

---. "John Wesley's Mindset at the Commencement of His Georgia Sojourn: Suffering and the Introduction of Primitive Christianity to the Indians." *Methodist History* 41, no. 1 (2008): 16-25.

---. "High Church Anglican Influences on John Wesley's Conception of Primitive Christianity, 1732-1735." *Anglican and Episcopal History* 78, no. 2 (2009): 174-207.

---. "Versions of Primitive Christianity: John Wesley's Relations with the Moravians in Georgia, 1735-1737 " *Journal of Moravian History* 6 (2009).

----. "The Wesleys' Sacramental Theology and Practice in Georgia." *Proceedings of the Charles Wesley Society* 13 (2009): 53-73.

---. "John Wesley and "Imitating" Christ." *Wesleyan Theological Journal* 45 (2010): 197-212.

Hancock, Brannon. "Dangerous Liaisons: Wesleyan-Holiness Encounters with Popular Culture." *Wesleyan Theological Journal* 51, no. 1 (2016): 188-201.

Hannah, Vern A. "Original Sin and Sanctification: A Problem for Wesleyans." *Wesleyan Theological Journal* 18, no. 2 (1983): 47-53.

Hansen, Douglas, and Robert Drovdahl. "The Holding Power of Love: John Wesley and D.W. Winnicott in Conversation." *Journal of Psychology and Christianity* 25, no. 1 (2006): 54-62.

Hanshaw, Mark E. "A Hindu Vision of Grace for a Western Christian Community." *Religion East & West*, no. 10 (2010): 15-34.

Harland, H. Gordon. "John Wesley [life and work; por]." *Touchstone: Heritage and Theology in a New Age* 2, no. 3 (October 1984): 5-17.

Harman, Allan. "The Impact of Matthew Henry's Exposition on Eighteenth-Century Christianity." *Evangelical Quarterly* 82, no. 1 (2010): 3-14.

Harmon, Nolan B., and John W. Bardsley. "John Wesley and the Articles of Religion." *Religion in Life* 22 (1952-53): 280-91.

Harper, K. "[William] Law and [John] Wesley." *Church Quarterly Review* 163 (January-March 1982): 61-71.

Harper, Steve. "John Wesley: Spiritual Guide." *Wesleyan Theological Journal* 20, no. 2 (Fall 1985): 91-96.

---. "Wesley's Sermons as Spiritual Formation Documents." *Methodist History* 26, no. 3 (April 1988): 131-38.

Harrington, Susan F. "Friendship Under Fire: George Whitefield and John Wesley, 1739-1741." *Andover Newton Quarterly* 15 (January 1975): 167-81.

Harris, Elizabeth J. "Methodist Inter Faith Practitioners and the Wesleys." *Epworth Review* 35, no. 3 (2008): 72-83.

Hart, David. "Baptism and Conversion Narratives in Eighteenth-Century Methodism: A Norfolk Case Study." *Wesley and Methodist Studies* 8, no. 1 (2016): 16-34.

Hasker, William. "Holiness and Systemic Evil: A Response to Albert Truesdale." *Wesleyan Theological Journal* 19, no. 1 (Spring 1984): 60-62.

Hatton, Peter. "John Wesley, Jeremy Taylor, Seneca and Control [self-management]." *Epworth Review* 17 (Spring 1990): 69-82.

Haverly, Thomas P. "Conversion Narratives: Wesley's Aldersgate Narrative and the Portrait of Peter in the Gospel of Mark." *Wesleyan Theological Journal* 24 (1989): 54-73.

Hawn, C. Michael. "Hymnody for Children, pt 1 [il]." *The Hymn: A Journal of Congregational Song* 36, no. 1 (January 1985): 19-26.

Haywood, Clarence Robert. “Was John Wesley a Political Economist?” *Church History* 33 (September 1964): 314-21.

Headley, Anthony J. “Marriage and Ministry: Conjugal and Occupational Conflicts in Wesley’s Life and Ministry.” *Asbury Theological Journal* 65, no. 1 (2010): 83-96.

Hearden, Maura. “Our Lady of Sacramental Communion: Marian Possibilities Emerging from Catholic-Methodist Dialogue.” *Pro Ecclesia* 19, no. 1 (2010): 69-92.

Heitzenrater, Richard P. “Oxford Diaries and the First Rise of Methodism.” *Methodist History* 12 (July 1974): 110-35.

---. “The Present State of Wesley Studies.” *Methodist History* 22, no. 4 (July 1984): 221-31.

---. “Wesley Studies in the Church and the Academy.” *Perkins Journal* 37 (Spring 1984): 1-6.

---. “John Wesley’s Principles and Practice of Preaching” *Methodist History* 37 (January 1999): 89-106.

---. “Plain Truth: Sermons as Standards of Doctrine.” *The Drew Gateway* 57 (Fall 1987): 16-30.

---. "An Unpublished Wesley Letter on Health and Ireland [Je 15 1789, Peard Dickinson]." *Methodist History* 27, no. 2 (January 1989): 119-23.

---. "The Second Rise of Methodism: Georgia [J Wesley's journals]." *Methodist History* 28, no. 2 (January 1990): 117-32.

---. "A Wesley Letter on Deeds, Sashes, and Schedules," *Methodist History* 36, no. 2 (January 1998): 125-31.

---. "John Wesley's *A Christian Library*, Then and Now." *American Theological Library Association: Proceedings* 55 (2001): 133-146.

---. "John Wesley and America." *Proceedings of the Wesley Historical Society* 54, no. 3 (2003): 85-114.

---. "John Wesley's Early Sermons." *The Proceedings of the Wesley Historical Society* 37 (1969-70): 110-128.

Hempton, David. "Methodism and the Law." *Bulletin of the John Rylands University Library of Manchester* 70 (Autumn 1988): 93-107.

Hendricks, George E., and M. Elton Hendricks. "Mr. Wesley, since You Wanted to Help the Poor, Why Did You Ignore the English Poor Law of Your Day?" *The Asbury Journal 70*, no. 2 (2015): 55-77.

Hendricks, M. Elton. "John Wesley and Natural Theology [prevenient grace]." *Wesleyan Theological Journal* 18, no. 2 (Fall 1983): 7-17.

Henning, Robert. "Reform and Holiness for Prisoners: A Wesleyan Mission for the Twenty-First Century." *Wesleyan Theological Journal* 38, no. 1 (2003): 187-209.

Henry, G. C. "John Wesley's Doctrine of Free Will." *London Quarterly & Holborn Review* 185 (July 1960): 200-204.

Henzel, Jan. "When Conversion Is Joy and Death Victory: Historical Foundations of the Doctrine of Perseverance." *Tyndale Bulletin* 54, no. 2 (2003): 123-148.

Hiatt, R. Jeffrey. "John Wesley's Approach to Mission." *Asbury Journal* 68, no. 1 (2013): 108-124.

Hildebrandt, Franz. "John Wesley, 1703-1791." *Scottish Journal of Theology* 4, no. 1 (1951): 39-54.

---. "Wesley's Churchmanship." *The Drew Gateway* 31 (Spring 1961): 147-62.

---. "Wesley's Christology." *The Proceedings of the Wesley Historical Society* 33 (June 1962): 122-24.

Hindmarsh, D. Bruce. "The Inner Life of Doctrine: An Interdisciplinary Perspective on the Calvinist-Arminian Debate among Methodists." *Church History* 83, no. 2 (2014): 367-397.

---. "Spiritual Experience and Early Evangelical Correspondence: The Letters of John Wesley and Ann Bolton, 1768-91." *Huntington Library Quarterly* 79, no. 3 (2016): 24.

Hindley, J. C. "Philosophy of Enthusiasm; A Study in the Origins of 'Experimental Theology'." *London Quarterly & Holborn Review* 182 (April 1957): 99-109.

---. "Philosophy of Enthusiasm; A Study in the Origins of 'Experimental Theology'." *London Quarterly & Holborn Review* 182 (July 1957): 199-210.

Hobbs, R. Gerald. "With a Thousand Tongues: The Wesleys and Christian Song." *Touchstone: Heritage and Theology in a New Age* 2, no. 3 (October 1984): 18-29.

Hofler, D. "Methodist Doctrine of the Church." *Methodist History* 6 (October 1967): 25-35.

Hogden, Margaret T. "The Negro in the Anthropology of John Wesley." *Journal of Negro History* 19 (1934): 308-23.

Hohenstein, Charles R. "'Lex Orandi, Lex Credendi': Cautionary Notes." *Wesleyan Theological Journal* 32, no. 2 (Fall 1997): 140-57.

Holden, Harrington William. *John Wesley in Company with High Churchmen.* London: Church Press, 1869.

Holeman, Virginia T. "Theology for Better Counseling: Help from within the Wesleyan-Holiness Theological Tradition." *Journal of Psychology & Theology* 42, no. 4 (2014): 369-378.

Holeman, Virginia T., and Anthony J. Headley. "Integration Based Upon Wesleyan Theology." *Journal of Psychology & Christianity* 33, no. 4 (2014): 335-343.

Holland, Bernard G. "The Background to the 1967 Methodist Service for Infant Baptism." *Church Quarterly Review* 2 (1969): 43-54.

---. "The Conversions of John and Charles Wesley and Their Place in Methodist Tradition." *The Proceedings of the Wesley Historical Society* 38 (1971): 45-53, 65-71.

---. "`A Special Madness': The Effect of John Wesley's Early Preaching." *The Proceedings of the Wesley Historical Society* 39 (1973): 77-85.

Holland, L. M. "John Wesley and the American Revolution." *Journal of Church and State* 5 (November 1963): 199-213.

Holland, L.M. and R. F. Howell. "John Wesley's Concept of Religious and Political Authority." Journal of Church and State 6 (Autumn 1964): 296-313.

Hooker, Morna D. "Scriptural Holiness: The Wesley's Use of Scripture." *Wesleyan Theological Journal* 50, no. 2 (2015): 7-24.

Hood, Jared C. ""I Never Read Calvin": George Whitefield, a Calvinist Untimely Born." *Churchman* 125, no. Spring (2011): 7-20.

---. "Whitefield: The Heart of an Evangelist." *Reformed Theological Review* 69, no. 3 (2010): 164-179.

Hope, N. V. "Aldersgate; An Epoch in British History." *Christianity Today* 7 (26 April 1963): 3-4.

Horst, Mark L. "Experimenting with Christian Wholeness: Method in Wesley's Theology." *Quarterly Review* 7 (Summer 1987): 11-23.

Hoskins, Steven T. "Eucharist and Eschatology in the Writings of the Wesleys." *Wesleyan Theological Journal* 29, no. 1 (Spring-Fall 1994): 64-80.

---. "The Wesleyan/Holiness Movement in Search of Liturgical Identity." *Wesleyan Theological Journal* 32, no. 2 (Fall 1997): 121-39.

Hosman, G. B. "Problem of Church and State in the Thought of John Wesley as Reflecting his Understanding of Providence and his View of History [dissertation abstract]." *The Drew Gateway* 41 (Fall 1970): 40.

Houston, Joel. "A Change of Heart in Bristol? John Wesley's Doctrine of Election in Perspective, 1739-1768." *Wesleyan Theological Journal* 51, no. 2 (2016): 68-78.

Howard, Harry L. "John Wesley: Tory or Democrat?" *Methodist History* 31, no. 1 (October 1992): 38-46.

Howard, I. "Wesley versus Phoebe Palmer; An Extended Controversy." *Wesleyan Theological Journal* 6, no. 1 (Spring 1971): 31-40.

Howcroft, Kenneth G. "Reason, Interpretation and Postmodernism: Is there a Methodist Way of reading the Bible?" *Epworth Review* 25 (July 1998): 28-41.

Hughes, Melanie Dobson. "The Holistic Way: John Wesley's Practical Piety as a Resource for Integrated Health Care." *Journal of Religion and Health* 47, no. 2 (2008): 237-252.

Hughes, Richard A. ""Make Us One with Christ:" Essay on the Anglican-Methodist Dialogue." *Journal of Ecumenical Studies* 49, no. 3 (2014): 443-457.

Hughes, Robert D. "Wesley Roots of Christian Socialism." *The Ecumenist* 13 (1975): 49-53.

Hughes, Trevor H. "Jeremy Taylor and John Wesley." *London Quarterly & Holborn Review* (October 1949): 296-304.

Hulley, Leonard D. "An Interpretation of John Wesley's Doctrine of Perfect Love." *Theologia Evangelica* 23 (March 1990): 21-29.

Hunsicker, David S. "John Wesley: Father of Today's Small Group Concept?" *Wesleyan Theological Journal* 31, no. 1 (Spring 1996): 192-211.

Hunter, Fredrick. "The Origins of Wesley's Covenant Service." *London Quarterly & Holborn Review* 164 (1939): 78-87.

---. "Manchester Non-Jurors and Wesley's High Churchism." *London Quarterly & Holborn Review* 172 (1947): 56-61.

Hunter, George. "John Wesley as Church Growth Strategist." *Wesleyan Theological Journal* 21, no. 1 and 2 (Spring-Fall 1986): 24-33.

Huntley, Dana. "At Home with the Wesleys." *British Heritage* 32, no. 5 (2011): 36-39.

Hynson, Leon O. "John Wesley's Concept of Liberty of Conscience." *Wesleyan Theological Journal* 7, no. 1 (Spring 1972): 36-46.

---. "John Wesley and Political Reality." *Methodist History* 12 (October 1973): 37-42.

---. "Social Concerns of Wesley; Theological Foundations." *Christian Scholar's Review* 4, no. 1 (1974): 36-42.

---. "Christian Love: The Key To Wesley's Ethics." *Methodist History* 14 (October 1975): 44-55.

---. "Creation and Grace in Wesley's Ethics." *The Drew Gateway* 46, no. 1-3 (1975-1976): 41-55.

---. "War, the State, and the Christian Citizen in Wesley's Thought." *Religion in Life* 45 (Summer 1976): 204-19.

---. "John Wesley and the "Unitas Fratrum": A Theological Analysis." *Methodist History* 18 (October 1979): 26-60.

---. "Evangelism and Social Ethics in Wesley's Theology." *The AME Zion Quarterly Review* 93, no. 2 (July 1981): 2-18.

---. "A Wesleyan Theology of Evangelism." *Wesleyan Theological Journal* 17, no. 2 (Fall 1982): 26-42.

---. "Human Liberty as Divine Right: A Study in the Political Maturation of John Wesley." *Journal of Church and State* 25 (Winter 1983): 57-85.

---. "Original Sin as Privation: An Inquiry into a Theology of Sin and Sanctification." *Wesleyan Theological Journal* 22, no. 2 (Fall 1987): 65-83.

---. "John Wesley's Theology of the Kingdom of God." *Wesleyan Theological Journal* 23, no. 1 and 2 (Spring-Fall 1988): 46-57.

---. "Wesley's 'Thoughts Upon Slavery': A Declaration of Human Rights." *Methodist History* 33, no. 1 (October 1994): 46-57.

---. "Wesley, Jennings, and the Poor." *Evangelical Journal* 13 (1995): 39-44.

---. "Religion and Politics, Truth and Toleration: Toward a Wesleyan Political Philosophy." *Evangelical Journal* 15 (Spring 1997): 18-32.

Inbody, Tyron. "Where United Methodists and Presbyterians Differ on Sanctification." *Journal of Theology (UTS)* 105, Summer (2001): 75-98.

Jackson, Jack. "Collecting and Preserving Disciples: Verbal Proclamation in Early Methodist Evangelism." *Wesley and Methodist Studies* 2 (2010): 45-66.

Jackson, Marion A. "An Analysis of the Source of John Wesley's "Directions for Renewing our Covenant with God"." *Methodist History* 30, no. 3 (April 1992): 176-84.

Jafta, L. "Some Aspects of Methodist Spirituality." *Studia Historiae Ecclesisasticae* 18 (1992): 61-76.

Jallais, Therese-Marie. "Le Cheminement Theologique De John Wesley (1703-1791) Avec Le Catholisme." *Revue d'Histoire et de Philosophie Religieuse* 88, no. 3 (2008): 295-314.

Jarvis, Clive. "Gilbert Boyce: General Baptist Messenger and Opponent of John Wesley." *Baptist Quarterly* 39, no. 5 (2002): 244-259.

Jennings, Theodore W., Jr. "John Wesley Against Aldersgate." *Quarterly Review* 8 (Fall 1988): 3-22.

---. "Wesley's Preferential Option for the Poor." *Quarterly Review* 9 (Fall 1989): 10-29.

---. "John Wesley on the Origin of Methodism." *Methodist History* 29, no. 2 (January 1991): 76-86.

---. "The Meaning of Discipleship on Wesley and the New Testament." *Quarterly Review* 13 (Spring 1993): 3-20.

Johnson, Richard O. "The Development of the Love Feast in Early American Methodism." *Methodist History* 19, no. 2 (January 1981): 67-83.

Johnson, W. Stanley. "Christian Perfection as Love for God [reply, W M Arnett]." *Wesleyan Theological Journal* 18, no. 1 (Spring 1983): 50-60.

---. "John Wesley's Concept of Enthusiasm." *Kardia* 3 (1988): 27-38.

Joling-van der Sar, Gerda. "The Controversy between William Law and John Wesley." *English Studies* 87, no. 4 (2006): 442-465.

Jones, B. E. "Reason and Religion Joined; The Place of Reason in Wesley's Thought." *London Quarterly & Holborn Review* 189 (April 1964): 110-13.

Jones, Beth Felker. "The Future of Wesleyan Theology Is Revival." *Wesleyan Theological Journal* 51, no. 1 (2016): 37-50.

Jones, Robert. "Characteristics of Chaplaincy: A Methodist Understanding." *Epworth Review* 37, no. 4 (2010): 5-9.

Joseph, P. V. "An Appraisal of Prevenient Grace in John Wesley's Soteriology." 7, no. 2 (2010): 135-153.

Josselyn, Lynne. "The Comparative Eucharist Views of John Wesley and John Nevin with an Emphasis on Christian Nurture and the Admission of Children to the Lord's Table." *New Mercersburg Review* 4 (1988): 18-35.

Joy, James R. "Wesley, Man of a Thousand Books and a Book." *Religion in Life* 8 (Winter 1939): 71-84.

Kallstad, Thorvald. "The Application of the Religio-Psychological Role Theory." *Journal for the Scientific Study of Religion* 26 (Spring 1987): 367-74.

---. "John Wesley Och Mystiken." *Teologisk Forum* 2, no. 2 (1988): 7-42.

Kantzer, Kenneth S. "If Only Wesley Were Here [Wesley's Contributions Praised; Editorial]." *Christianity Today* 35 (11 March 1991): 25.

Keefer, Luke L. "John Wesley: Disciple of Early Christianity [reply, H A Snyder, C. L. Bence]." *Wesleyan Theological Journal* 19, no. 1 (Spring 1984): 23-32.

---. "John Wesley and English Arminianism." *Evangelical Journal* 4, no. 1 (Spring 1986): 15-28.

---. "Characteristics of Wesley's Arminianism." *Wesleyan Theological Journal* 22, no. 1 (Spring 1987): 88-100.

---. "John Wesley, The Methodists, and Social Reform in England." *Wesleyan Theological Journal* 25, no. 1 (1990): 7-20.

---. "Holiness Affecting Our Witness." *Brethren in Christ History and Life* 31, no. 1 (2008): 53-72.

---. "How Useful Is the Wesleyan Quadrilateral for the Brethren in Christ?" *Brethren in Christ History and Life* 33 (2010): 117-133.

Kellerman, Bill Wylie. "Free in Obedience [Wesley and Methodism; il]." *Witness* 77 (October 1994): 6.

---. "To Stir up God's Good Trouble: John Wesley and the Methodist Revival Movement." *Sojourners* 13, no. 3 (March 1984): 20-23.

---. "Free in Obedience [Wesley and Methodism]." *Witness* 77, no. 6 (October 1994).

Kent, John H. S. "John Wesley's Churchmanship." *The Proceedings of the Wesley Historical Society* 35 (1965): 10-14.

Kerr, Nathan R. "Speaking Gracefully: The Dynamic of Language in the Economy of Reconciliation." *Wesleyan Theological Journal* 37, no. 1 (2002): 106-130.

Keysor, Charles W. "Methodism's Silent Minority: A Voice for Orthodoxy." *Christian Advocate* 10 (14 July 1966): 9-10.

---. "The Story of Good News." *Good News* 14 (March-April 1981): 8-25;50-53.

Killian, Charles. "Bishop Daniel A. Payne: An Apostle of Wesley." *Methodist History* 24, no. 2 (January 1986): 107-19.

Kimbrough, S. T. "John Wesley: Editor-Poet-Priest." *Methodist History* 43, no. 2 (2005): 131-159.

King, Rob. "Eastern Patristic Spirit-Christology for Contemporary Wesleyan Faith Practice." *Wesleyan Theological Journal* 38, no. 2 (2003): 103-123.

Kingdon, Harold. "John Wesley: Bible Scholar Extraordinaire." *Asbury Seminary Journal* 40, no. 1 (Spring 1985): 39-54.

Kingdon, Robert Maccune. "Laissez-Faire or Government Control: A Problem for John Welsey." *Church History* 26 (December 1957): 342-54.

Kinkel, Gary Steven. "The Big Chill: The Theological Disagreement which Separated John Wesley and Count Zinzendorf." *Unitas fratrum* 27-28 (1990): 89-112.

Kirkham, Donald H. "John Wesley's "Calm Address": The Response of the Critics." *Methodist History* 14 (October 1975): 13-23.

Kishida, Yuki. "John Wesley's Ethics and Max Weber." *Wesleyan Quarterly Review* 4 (1967): 43-58.

Kisker, Scott. "Justified but Unregenerate? The Relationship of Assurance to Justification and Regeneration in the Thought of John Wesley." *Wesleyan Theological Journal* 28, no. 1-2 (Spring-Fall 1993): 44-58.

---. "The Evangelistic Mission of Pointing to the Cross: A Response to Dr. Beth Felker Jones." In *Exploring Christian Mission Beyond Christendom.* Indianapolis: University of Indianapolis, 2010.

Kissack, R. "Wesley's Concept on His Own Ecclesiastical Position." *London Quarterly & Holborn Review* 186 (January 1961): 57-60.

Kitshoff, M. C., and J. W. Claasen. "John Wesley as Aldersgate-ervaring: 'n Herwaardering [Eng abst, bibliog]." *Hervormde Teologiese Studies* 45 (November 1989): 948-67.

Klaiber, Walter Z. „Aus Glauben, damit aus Gnaden: der Grundsatz paulinischer Soteriologie und die Gnadenlehre John Wesleys," *Zeitschrift fur Theologie und Kirche* 88, no. 3 (1991): 313-38.

Knapp, Jeffrey H. "Throwing the Baby out with the Font Water: The Development of Baptismal Practice in the Church of the Nazarene." *Worship 76 no 3 My 2002* (2002): 225-244.

Knickerbocker, Waldo E., Jr. "Arminian Anglicanism and John and Charles Wesley." *Memphis Theological Seminary Journal* 29 (Fall 1991): 79-97.

Knight, Henry H., III. "The Relation of Love to Gratitude in the Theologies of Edwards and Wesley." *Evangelical Journal* 6 (Spring 1988): 3-12.

---. "The Significance of Baptism for the Christian Life: Wesley's Pattern of Christian Initiation." *Worship* 63 (March 1989): 133-42.

---. "The Baptismal Shaping of Christian Lives: Wesley's Class Meetings and Service of Covenant Renewal." *Doxology* 7 (1990): 17-22.

---. "Worship and Sanctification." *Wesleyan Theological Journal* 32, no. 2 (Fall 1997): 5-14.

---. "John Wesley: Mentor for an Evangelical Revival." *Wesleyan Theological Journal* 32 (Spring 1997): 179-86.

---. "Love and Freedom "by Grace Alone" in Wesley's Soteriology: A Proposal for Evangelicals." *Pneuma 24 no 1 Spr 2002* (2002): 57-67.

---. "John Wesley and the Quest for Holiness." In *From Aldersgate to Azusa Street* 17-26. Eugene: Pickwick, 2010.

Knight, John. A. "Aspects of Wesley's Theology After 1770." *Methodist History* 6 (April 1968): 33-42.

---. "John Fletcher's Influence on the Development of Wesleyan Theology in America." *Wesleyan Theological Journal* 13 (Spring 1978): 13-33.

Kolodziej, Benjamin A. "Issac Watts, the Wesleys, and the Evolution of 18th-Century English Congregational Song." *Methodist History* 42, no. 4 (2004): 236-248.

Koskie, Steven Joe. "Reading the Way to Heaven: A Wesleyan Theological Hermeneutic of Scripture." *Journal of Theological Interpretation Supplements* 8 (2014).

Kurowski, Mark T. "The First Step toward Grace: John Wesley's Use of the Spiritual Homilies of Macarius the Great," *Methodist History* 36, no. 2 (January 1998): 113-24.

Kwok, Wai-luen. "John Wesley's Evangelical Movement and the 18th Century English Society." *Jian Dao* 37 (2012): 55-81.

Lacy, H. E. "Authority in John Wesley." *London Quarterly & Holborn Review* 189 (April 1964): 114-19.

Lamp, Jeffrey S. "Creational Christology: A Rationale for Wesleyans to Care for the Created Order." *Wesleyan Theological Journal* 44, no. 1 (2009): 91-103.

Lancaster, Sarah Heaner. "Baptism and Justification: A Methodist Understanding." *Ecclesiology* 4, no. 3 (2008): 289-307.

Langford, Thomas Anderson. "John Wesley's Doctrine of Justification by Faith." *Bulletin of the United Church of Canada Committee on Archives and History* 29 (1980-1982): 47-62.

---. "John Wesley's Doctrine of Sanctification." *Bulletin of the United Church of Canada Committee on Archives and History* 29 (1980-1982): 63-73.

---. "Is There Such a Thing as Wesleyan Theology?" *Epworth Review* 15, no. 2 (1988): 67-72.

Lansdown, Richard. "Method in the Madness." History Today 68, no. 9 (2018): 52-61.

Larkins, J. S. "John Wesley among the Colonies: Wesleyan Theology in the Face of the American Revolution." *Methodist History* 45, no. 4 (2007): 232-243.

Law, Samuel K. "Waltzing with Wesley: Wesleyan Theology as a Renewing Framework for Chinese Christian Spirituality and Global Identity." Asbury Journal 72, no. 1 (2017): 20-43.

Lawson, John. "Wesley Rides Again." *Christianity Today* 4 (25 April 1960): 12-13.

---. "Saving Faith as Wesley Saw It." *Christianity Today* 8 (24 April 1964): 3-4.

---. "The Conversion of the Wesleys: 1738 Reconsidered." *The Asbury Theological Journal* 43, no. 2 (Fall 1988): 7-44.

Leclerc, Diane. "Holiness and the Paradox of Power: Toward a Wesleyan Theology of Dis-Ability." *Wesleyan Theological Journal* 44, no. 1 (2009): 55-69.

Lee, J. W. "John Wesley: A Methodist Evolutionist." *Southern Magazine* 4 (1894): 348.

Lee, Peter K. H. "A Wesleyan Perspective [Christianity and Buddhism; Reply to D W Mitchell, pp 5-13]." *Ching Feng: A Journal on the Encounter of Religion and Culture in Asia* 29, no. 1 (March 1986): 16-19.

Leffel, G. Michael. "Prevenient Grace and the Re-Enchantment of Nature: Toward a Wesleyan Theology of Psychotherapy and Spiritual Formation." *Journal of Psychology and Christianity* 23, no. 2 (2004): 130-139.

Leger, J. Augustin. "Wesley's Place in Catholic Thought." *Constructive Quarterly* 2 (1914): 329-60.

Leland, Scott. "Methodist Theology in America in the 19th Century." *Religion in Life* 25 (Winter 1955-1956): 87-98.

Lidgett, John Scott. "The Theological Issues." *London Quarterly & Holborn Review* 163 (1938): 171-74.

Lim, Isaac. "Wesleyan Preaching and the Small Group Ministry: Principles and Practices." *Asia Journal of Theology* 3 (October 1989): 509-23.

Lindstrom, Harald G. "The Message of John Wesley and the Modern Man." *The Drew Gateway* 4 (1955): 186-95.

Littell, F. H. "Discipline of Discipleship in the Free Church Tradition." *The Mennonite Quarterly Review* 35 (April 1961): 111-19.

Littell, Franklin H. "The Methodist Class Meeting as an Instrument of Christian Discipline." *World Parish* 9, no. 1 (February 1961): 14-24.

Lloyd, Gareth. "'a Cloud of Perfect Witnesses': John Wesley and the London Disturbances, 1760-1763." *Asbury Theological Journal 56-57 no 2-1 Fall-Spr 2001-2002* (2002): 117-136.

Lockyer, Thomas F. "Luther and Wesley." *The Proceedings of the Wesley Historical Society* 8 (1911-1912): 61-66.

Lodahl, Michael E. ""The Witness of the Spirit": Questions of Clarification for Wesley's Doctrine of Assurance." *Wesleyan Theological Journal* 23, no. 1 and 2 (Spring-Fall 1988): 188-97.

---. "The Cosmological Basis for John Wesley's "Gradualism"." *Wesleyan Theological Journal* 32, no. 1 (Spring 1997): 17-32.

Lofthouse, W. F. "Wesley's Doctrine of Christian Perfection." *London Quarterly & Holborn Review* 159 (1934): 178-88.

---. "John Wesley's Letters to His Brother." *London Quarterly & Holborn Review* 185 (January 1960): 60-65.

---. "John Wesley's Letters to His Brother." *London Quarterly & Holborn Review* 185 (April 1960): 133-39.

Lowery, Kevin Twain. "Empiricism and Wesleyan Ethics." *Wesleyan Theological Journal* 46, no. 1 (2011): 150-162.

Loyer, Kenneth. "A Review Essay: "Coming to Terms with Perfection"." *Asbury Journal* 65, no. 2 (2010): 99-104.

Luchetti, Lenny. "A Homiletic New Birth: How Empathy Drove John Wesley to the Fields." Wesleyan Theological Journal 52, no. 2 (2017): 200-209.

---. "Theological Empathy and John Wesley's Missional Field Preaching." Great Commission Research 8, no. 2 (2017): 177-186.

Luik, John C. "Marxist and Wesleyan Anthropology and the Prospects for a Marxist-Wesleyan Dialogue." *Wesleyan Theological Journal* 18, no. 2 (Fall 1983): 54-66.

Luker, David. "Revivalism in Theory and Practice: The Case of Cornish Methodism [1791-1871]." *The Journal of Ecclesiastical History* 37, no. 4 (October 1986): 603-19.

Lunn, Arnold. "The Mind of John Wesley." *Review of Churches* 5 (1928): 497-507.

Lyerly, Cynthia Lynn. "Francis Asbury and the Opposition to Early Methodism." *Methodist History* 54, no. 4 (2016): 248-258.

Lyles, Jean Caffey. "The Bicentennial of American Methodism: 1784-1984." *Ecumenical Trends* 13, no. 4 (April 1984): 49-55.

Lyon, Robert W. "Baptism and Spirit-Baptism in the New Testament." *Wesleyan Theological Journal* 14, no. 1 (1979): 14-26.

Lyons, George. "Hermeneutical Bases for Theology: Higher Criticism and the Wesley Interpreter [reply, M A Weigelt]." *Wesleyan Theological Journal* 18, no. 1 (Spring 1983): 63-78.

MacMillan, Ken. "John Wesley and the Enlightened Historians." *Methodist History* 38, no. 2 (January 2000): 121-32.

Madden, Deborah. "Medicine and Moral Reform: The Place of Practical Piety in John Wesley's Art of Physic." *Church History* 73, no. 4 (2004): 741-758.

---. "The Limitation of Human Knowledge: Faith and the Empirical Method in John Wesley's Medical Holism." *History of European Ideas* 32, no. 2 (2006): 162-172.

Maddix, Mark. "John Wesley's Educational Philosophy." *Evangelical Journal* 27, no. 1 (2009): 16-21.

---. "Scripture as Formation: The Role of Scripture in Christian Formation." *Wesleyan Theological Journal* 46, no. 1 (2011): 134-149.

---. "Christian Nurture and Conversion: A Conversation between Horace Bushnell and John Wesley." *Christian Education Journal* 9, no. 2 (2012): 309-325.

---. "Moral Exemplarity and Relational Atonement: Toward a Wesleyan Approach to Discipleship." *Wesleyan Theological Journal* 50, no. 1 (2015): 67-82.

Maddock, Ian J. "Solving a Trans-Atlantic Puzzle?: John Wesley, George Whitefield, and 'Free Grace' Indeed!" *Wesley and Methodist Studies* 8, no. 1 (2016): 1-15.

Maddox, Randy L. "Responsible Grace: The Systematic Perspective of Wesleyan Theology." *Wesleyan Theological Journal* 19, no. 2 (Fall 1984): 7-22.

---. "Responsible Grace: The Systematic Nature of Wesley's Theology Reconsidered." *Quarterly Review* 6, no. 1 (Spring 1986): 24-34.

---. "Karl Rahner's Supernatural Existential: A Wesleyan Parallel?" *Evangelical Journal* 5 (Spring 1987): 3-14.

---. "Wesleyan Theology and the Christian Feminist Critique." *Wesleyan Theological Journal* 22 (1987): 101-11.

---. "Respected Founder/Neglected Guide: The Role of Wesley in American Methodist Theology." *Methodist History* 37 (January 1999): 71-88.

---. "John Wesley: Practical Theologian? [practical theology as Glaubenslehre]." *Wesleyan Theological Journal* 23, no. 1 and 2 (Spring-Fall 1988): 122-47.

---. "John Wesley and Eastern Orthodoxy: Influences, Convergences and Differences." *The Asbury Theological Journal* 45, no. 2 (Fall 1990): 29-53.

---. "Celebrating Wesley - When?" *Methodist History* 29, no. 2 (January 1991): 63-75.

---. "Wesley and Inclusive Grammar: A Note for Reflection." *Sacramental Life* 4, no. 4 (1991): 40-43.

---. "Continuing the Conversation." *Methodist History* 30, no. 4 (July 1992): 235-41.

---. "Opinion, Religion and "Catholic Spirit": John Wesley on Theological Integrity [Theological Convictions]." *The Asbury Theological Journal* 47, no. 1 (Spring 1992): 63-87.

---. "Wesley and the Question of Truth or Salvation Through other Religions." *Wesleyan Theological Journal* 27 (Spring-Fall 1992): 7-29.

---. "Wesley as Theological Mentor: The Question of Truth or Salvation Through Other Religions." *Wesleyan Theological Journal* 27, no. 1-2 (Spring-Fall 1992): 7-29.

---. "Wesleyan Resources for a Contemporary Theology of the Poor?" *The Asbury Theological Journal* 49 (Spring 1994): 35-47.

---. "Reading Wesley as a Theologian." *Wesleyan Theological Journal* 30, no. 1 (Spring 1995): 7-54.

---. "Holiness of Heart and Life: Lessons from North American Methodism," *The Asbury Theological Journal* 50, no. 2 (Fall 1995): 151-72.

---. "Kingswood School Library Holdings (Ca.1775)." *Methodist History 41 no 1 O 2002* (2002): 342-370.

---. "The Collection of Books Owned by the Charles Wesley Family." *Wesleyan Theological Journal* 38, no. 2 (2003): 175-216.

---. "'Vital Orthodoxy': A Wesleyan Dynamic for 21st Century Christianity." *Methodist History* XLII, no. 1 (2003): 3-19.

---. "Remnants of John Wesley's Personal Library." *Methodist History* 42, no. 2 (2004): 122-128.

---. "Psychology and Wesleyan Theology: Precedents and Prospects for a Renewed Engagement." *Journal of Psychology and Christianity* 23, no. 2 (2004): 101-109.

---. "Josiah Tucker on Justification: Source for a Wesley Letter." *Methodist History* 44, no. 3 (2006): 166-169.

---. "Celebrating the Whole Wesley: A Legacy for Contemporary Wesleyans." *Methodist History* 43, no. 2 (2005): 74-89.

---. "Anticipating the New Creation: Wesleyan Foundations for Holistic Mission." *Asbury Theological Journal* 62, no. 1 (2007): 49-66.

---. "John Wesley on Holistic Health and Healing." *Methodist History* 46, no. 1 (2007): 4-33.

---. "John Wesley's Precedent for Theological Engagement with the Natural Sciences." *Wesleyan Theological Journal* 44, no. 1 (2009): 23-54.

---. "The Rule of Christian Faith, Practice and Hope: John Wesley and the Bible." *Epworth Review* 38, no. 2 (2011): 6-37.

---. "New John Wesley Letter to Charles Wesley." *Methodist History* 50, no. 3 (2012): 187-188.

---. "A Zealous (but Respected) Adversary: John Lewis's Correspondence with John Wesley." *Wesley and Methodist Studies 7*, no. 1 (2015): 121-148.

---. "John Wesley on 'Patriotism'." Wesley and Methodist Studies 9, no. 2 (2017): 184-188.

Maddox, Randy L., and Timothy Underhill. "Untwisting the Tangled Web: Charles Wesley and Elizabeth Story." *Wesley and Methodist Studies* 8, no. 2 (2016): 175-183.

Madron, Thomas W. "John Wesley on Race: A Christian View of Equality." *Methodist History* 2, no. 4 (1964): 24-34.

---. "Some Economic Aspects of John Wesley's Thought Revisited." *Methodist History* 4 (October 1965): 33-45.

---. "No Justice Without Love [Wesley, Institutions of Political Order, and the Fight Against Injustice; Photos]." *Christian Social Action* 4 (June 1991): 13-16.

Malony, H. Newton. "John Wesley and the Eighteenth Century Therapeutic Uses of Electricity." *Perspectives on Science and Christian Faith: Journal of the American Scientific Affiliation* 47 (December 1995): 244-54.

Manchester, Eric. "Why Is Evangelism Important If One Can Be Saved without the Gospel?" *Wesleyan Theological Journal* 37, no. 1 (2002): 158-170.

Mann, Mark H. "Wesley, Word, and Table: The Rise and Fall of Eucharistic Practice in Early Methodism." *Wesleyan Theological Journal* 51, no. 2 (2016): 54-67.

Manor, James. "Coming of Britain's Age of Empire and Protestant Theology, 1750-1839." *Zeitschrift fur Missionswissenschaft und Religionswissenschaft* 61, no. 1 (1977): 38-54.

Marriot, Thomas. "The Rev. John Wesley M.A. and William Wilberforce, Esq on Perfection and Practical Christianity." *Wesleyan Methodist Magazine* 68 (1845): 364-65.

Marshall, I. H. "Sanctification in the Teaching of John Wesley and John Calvin." *The Evangelical Quarterly* 34 (April-June 1962): 75-82.

Martin, A. W., Jr. ""Then and Now": Wesley's Notes as a Model for United Methodists Today." *Quarterly Review* 10 (Summer 1990): 25-47.

Martin, Robert K. "Toward a Wesleyan Sacramental Ecclesiology." *Ecclesiology* 9, no. 1 (2013): 19-38.

Martin, Roger B. "English Evangelicals and the Golden Age of Private Philanthropy 1730-1850." *The Princeton Seminary Bulletin* 4, no. 3 (1983): 187-95.

Martin, Troy W. "John Wesley's Exegetical Orientation: East or West." *Wesleyan Theological Journal* 26, no. 1 (1991): 104-38.

Martyn, Stephen. "The Journey to God: Union, Purgation and Transformation within the Ascent of Mount Carmel and a Plain Account of Christian Perfection." *Asbury Journal* 67 (2012): 138-157.

Maser, Frederick E. "John Wesley's Only Marriage [With reply by Frank Baker, pp 42-45]." *Methodist History* 16 (October 1977): 33-41.

---. "Second Thoughts on John Wesley." *The Drew Gateway* 49 (Winter 1978): 1-56.

---. "The Unknown John Wesley." *The Drew Gateway* 49, no. 2 (1978): 1-28.

---. "Discovery [J Wesley's Authorship of the Poem "Georgia"]." *Methodist History* 21, no. 3 (April 1983): 169-71.

---. "Wesley, Whitefield, and Olivers." [editor] *Methodist History* 37 (January 1999): 131-33.

---. "Discovery [Text of John Wesley's Letter to James Barry, 1778; Methodist Work on the Isle of Man]." *Methodist History* 22, no. 1 (October 1983): 67-70.

---. "Wesley on Important Issues." *Methodist History* 37 (October 1998): 59-65.

---. "New Paths for Research." *Methodist History* 25, no. 4 (July 1987): 256-57.

---. "Researchers Rescue Wesley [Response to Excerpt From Hanby Letter, 25:256-257 Jl 1987]." *Methodist History* 26, no. 2 (January 1988): 127-28.

---. "A Lost Letter Leads to a Research Project [Robert Southey's Life of Wesley]." *Methodist History* 27, no. 4 (July 1989): 254-56.

---. "Something New and Something Old in a Wesley Letter [to E Bennis, F 12 1773]." *Methodist History* 29, no. 1 (October 1990): 44-46.

---. "Rediscovery of an Old Story [J Wesley's account of his family's haunted home]." *Methodist History* 31, no. 1 (October 1992): 47-50.

---. "New Notes On An Important Wesley Letter [to Rev Samuel Walker, S 3 1756]." *Methodist History* 31, no. 2 (January 1993): 118-22.

---. "Facts About Preaching and Methodism Not Generally Known." *Methodist History* 32 (April 1994): 195-99.

---. "More About John Wesley." *Methodist History* 32 (January 1994): 133-36.

---. "[Sayings Attributed to J Wesley; C Wesley in Bristol]." *Methodist History* 33, no. 1 (October 1994): 58-60.

---. "Another View of Wesley and the Methodists." *Methodist History* 34 (October 1995): 59-60.

---. "John Wesley and Queen Elizabeth [Wesley's opinion of monarch]." *Methodist History* 33, no. 3 (April 1995): 192-94.

---. "A Bible and the Man Who Saved Wesley's Life [Dr Fothergill]." *Methodist History* 34, no. 3 (April 1996): 190-91.

---. "Wesley Trivia [his sisters]." *Methodist History* 26, no. 4 (July 1988): 252-54.

---. "New Light on the Methodists and the Revolutionary War [letters to Lord Dartmouth from Webb and J Wesley]." *Methodist History* 28, no. 1 (October 1989): 57-65.

---. "Things You've Really Wanted to Know About the Wesleys." *Methodist History* 29, no. 2 (January 1991): 119-21.

---. "An Unpublished Letter of John Wesley to Hannah Ball, Mr 29, 1769 [commentary by C A Green]." *Methodist History* 29, no. 3 (April 1991): 184-86.

---. "Rare Wesley Items are Where You Find Them [Lessons for children]." *Methodist History* 30, no. 3 (April 1992): 185-86.

---. "A Discovery That is Not A Discovery and yet is A Discovery [letter of J Wesley to Penelope Newman, Ap 22 1775, with text]." *Methodist History* 31, no. 3 (April 1993): 177-79.

---. "What is Missing from Wesley?," *Methodist History* 36, no. 3 (April 1998): 191-93.

---. "A Letter from a Female Friend to John Wesley." *Methodist History* 39, no. 1 (2000): 60-63.

Massa, Mark S. "The Catholic Wesley: A Revisionist Prolegomenon." *Methodist History* 22, no. 1 (October 1983): 38-53.

Master, F. E. "Problem in Preaching: An Analysis of the Preaching Power of John Wesley." *London Quarterly & Holborn Review* 182 (April 1957): 110-17.

Matsumoto, Hiroaki. "John Wesley's Understanding of Man." *Wesleyan Quarterly Review* 4 (1967): 83-102.

Matthaei, Sondra Higgins. "Practical Divinity: Ministry in the Wesleyan Tradition." *Quarterly Review* 12 (Winter 1992): 57-68.

Matthews, Rex D. "John Wesley's Idea of Christian Perfection Reconsidered." *Wesleyan Theological Journal* 50, no. 2 (2015): 25-67.

Mattke, R. A. "Integration of Truth in John Wesley [II Tim 2:15]." *Wesleyan Theological Journal* 8 (Spring 1973): 3-13.

Mbennah, Emmanuel D. and J. M. Vorster. "The Influence of Arminian Conception of Predestination on the 18th-century Wesleyan Revival." *Studia Historiae Ecclesisasticae* 24, no. 1 (1998): 161-87.

McAdoo, Henry R. "A Theology of the Eucharist: Brevient and the Wesleys." *Theology* 97 (July-August 1994): 245-56.

McCarthy, Daryl. "Early Wesleyan Views of Scripture." *Wesleyan Theological Journal* 16, no. 2 (Fall 1981): 95-105.

McCormack, James T. "The Forgotten Notes of John Wesley." *Irish Biblical Studies* 8 (1986): 22-42.

McCormick, Kelly S. "Theosis in Chrysostom and Wesley: An Eastern Paradigm on Faith and Love." *Wesleyan Theological Journal* 26, no. 1 (1991): 38-103.

McCutcheon, William J., and William Neill. "United Methodist Evangelicals in Two Generations: The 1920s and 1930s." *Explor* 2, no. 2 (Fall 1976): 59-72.

McDonald, Fredrick W. "John Wesley the Theologian." *Methodist Recorder* 31 (1891): 257.

McDonald, William. ""What Shall We Do for the Rising Generation?" Methodist Catechisms, 1745-1934." *Wesleyan Theological Journal* 43, no. 2 (2008): 177-192.

---. "A Luther Wesley Could Appreciate: Toward Convergence on Sanctification." Pro Ecclesia 20, no. 1 (2011): 43-63.

McEllhenney, John G. "John Wesley and Samuel Johnson: A Tale of Three Coincidences." *Methodist History* 21, no. 3 (April 1983): 143-55.

---. "Two Critiques of Wealth: John Wesley and Samuel Johnson Assess the Machinations of Mammon." *Methodist History* 32 (April 1994): 147-59.

McElwain, Randall D. "Biblical Language in the Hymns of Charles Wesley." *Wesley and Methodist Studies* 1 (2009): 55-70.

McEwan, David B. "The Living and Written Voice of God: John Wesley's Reading, Understanding, and Application of Scripture." *Wesleyan Theological Journal* 46, no. 1 (2011): 106-119.

---. "Wesleyan Connectionalism and Nazarene Ecclesiology: Insights and Implications for Future Directions." *Didache: Faithful Teaching* 13, no. 2 (2014): 1-11.

---. "Loving God, Loving Neighbour: A Wesleyan Perspective on the Implications for Mission." *Crucible: Theology and Ministry* 6, no. 2 (2015): 1-9.

---. "'A Continual Enjoyment of the Three-One God': John Wesley and the Life of God in the Soul." *Phronema* 33, no. 1 (2018): 49-72.

McGonigle, Herbert. "Pneumatological Nomenclature in Early Methodism." *Wesleyan Theological Journal* 8 (1973): 61-72.

McInelly, Brett C. "Writing the Revival: The Intersections of Methodism and Literature in the Long 18th Century." *Literature Compass* 12, no. 1 (2016): 12-21.

McKenna, David L. "John Wesley and the Megatrends [social change; guest editorial; por]." *Christianity Today* 28, no. 17 (23 November 1984): 18-19.

---. "That Amazing Grace [250th Anniversary of John Wesley's Aldersgate experience]." *Christianity Today* 32 (13 May 1988): 22-23.

McKinney, Maxine. "Social Action Roots in United Methodism." *Engage/Social Action* 13, no. 2 (Fall 1985): 53-56.

Meadows, Philip R. "Methodist Society as the New Creation." *Wesleyan Theological Journal* 39, no. 2 (2004): 74-96.

Meeuwsen, James. "Original Arminianism and Methodistic Arminianism Compared." *Reformed Review* 14 (1960): 21-36.

Meistad, Tore. "Systematic Theology and Ethics in the Wesleyan Tradition: Some Methodological Reflections." *Quarterly Review* 19 (Spring 1999): 53-71.

Melton, J. G. "Annotated Bibliography of Publications About the Life and Work of John Wesley." *Methodist History* 7 (July 1969): 29-46.

Mercer, Jerry L. "The Destiny of Man in John Wesley's Eschatology." *Wesleyan Theological Journal* 2 (1967): 56-65.

Meredith, W. H. "John Wesley, Christian Socialist." *Methodist Review* 61 (1901): 426ff.

Merritt, John G. ""Dialogue" Within a Tradition: John Wesley and Gregory of Nyssa Discuss Christian Perfection." *Wesleyan Theological Journal* 22, no. 2 (Fall 1987): 92-116.

Miguez Bonino, Jose. "Conversion, New Creature and Commitment." *International Review of Mission* 72 (July 1983): 324-32.

Miller, Donald G. "Some Observations on the New Testament Concept of "Witness"." *The Asbury Theological Journal* 43, no. 1 (Spring 1988): 55-71.

Miller, Kenneth H. "Experiential Christianity and John Wesley's Alternative to System-Building." *Evangelical Journal* 11 (Fall 1993): 76-90.

---. "The Church and Its Discipline in the Thought of John Wesley." *Evangelical Journal* 13 (Fall 1995): 63-73.

Mills, W. Douglas. "The Wesleyan Essentials of Faith." *Word and Deed* 8 (2005): 15-31.

Mills, William H. "John Wesley and Evolution." *Popular Science Monthly* 46 (1894-1895): 284-85.

Miskov, Jennifer. "Missing Links: Phoebe Palmer, Carrie Judd Montgomery, and Holiness Roots within Pentecostalism." *PentecoStudies* 10, no. 1 (2011): 8-28.

Mitton, Charles Leslie. "Two Stages of the Christian Life." *London Quarterly & Holborn Review* 177 (July 1952): 192-200.

Momany, Christopher P. "Wesley's General Rules: Paradigm for Postmodern Ethics." *Wesleyan Theological Journal* 28, no. 1-2 (Spring-Fall 1993): 7-22.

---. "The True Nature of Virtue: A Holiness Ethic for the Twenty-First Century." *Wesleyan Theological Journal* 51, no. 1 (2016): 145-154.

Monk, Robert C. "Educating Oneself for Ministry: Francis Asbury's Reading Patterns [rev fr The Divine Drama in History and Liturgy, ed by J E Booty, 1984]." *Methodist History* 29, no. 3 (April 1991): 140-54.

Moore, Allen J. "Some Distinctive Characteristics of Methodist Theological Education." *Quarterly Review* 18 (Fall 1998): 211-26.

Moore, D. Marselle. "Development in Wesley's Thought on Sanctification and Perfection." *Wesleyan Theological Journal* 20, no. 2 (Fall 1985): 29-53.

Moore, Mary Elizabeth. "Poverty, Human Depravity, and Prevenient Grace." *Quarterly Review* 16 (Winter 1996): 343-60.

Morgan, David T. "Dupes of Designing Men: John Wesley and the American Revolution." *Historical Magazine of the Protestant Episcopal Church* 44 (June 1975): 121-31.

Morris, Nicola. "Predicting a 'Bright and Prosperous Future': Irish Methodist Membership (1855-1914)." *Wesley and Methodist Studies* 2 (2010): 91-114.

Morton, Russell. "John 14:12-21 as Paradigm for the Wesleyan Understanding of Mission." *Wesleyan Theological Journal* 39, no. 1 (2004): 91-103.

Mosala, Itumeleng J. "Wesley Read From the Experience of Social and Political Deprivation in South Africa." *Journal of Theology for Southern Africa*, no. 68 (Spring 1989): 86-91.

Moulton, Wilfred J. "John Wesley's Doctrine of Christian Perfection: A Lecture." *Methodist Recorder* 65 (1924): 19.

---. "John Wesley's Doctrine of Perfect Love." *London Quarterly Review* 144 (1925): 14-27.

Mtshiselwa, Ndikho. "'Surely, Goodness and Mercy Shall Follow Me...': Reading Psalm 23:6 in Conversation with John Wesley." *Studia historiae ecclesiasticae* 41, no. 2 (2015): 116-130.

Mullen, Wilbur H. "John Wesley's Method of Biblical Interpretation." *Religion in Life* 47 (Spring 1978): 99-108.

Mumford, Norman W. "The Organization of the Methodist Church During the Time of John Wesley." *Quarterly Review* 171 (1946): 35-40; 128-35.

Murphree, Mark. "'Pure Religion and Undefiled': A Wesleyan Analysis of Ibn Turayl's Hai Ebn Yokda." *Wesleyan Theological Journal* 48, no. 1 (2013): 106-116.

Murphy-Geiss, Gail E. "The First Family Values of Methodism: The Wesleys." *Methodist History* 42, no. 3 (2004): 148-166.

Napier, Nathaniel J. "A Wesleyan Critque of the Leviathan of Capitalism." *Review & Expositor* 110, no. 2 (2013): 191-209.

Nausner, Helmut. "Some Notes on Christian Perfection [reply, W K Pyles]." *Quarterly Review* 3 (Spring 1983): 71-82.

---. "The Meaning of Wesley's General Rules; An Interpretation: tr by J S O'Malley." *The Asbury Theological Journal* 44, no. 2 (Fall 1989): 43-60.

---. "Mission in Methodist Perspective: Some Personal Deliberations." *Methodist History* 49, no. 1 (2010): 51-57.

Neal, John C. "The Methodist Episcopal Church and Early Wesleyan Missions in the Caribbean." *Methodist History* 50, no. 1 (2011): 16-27.

Nelson, James D. "The Strangeness of Wesley's Warming." *Journal of Theology (United Theological Seminary)* 92 (1988): 12-24.

Newport, Kenneth G. C. "Premillennialism in the Early Writings of Charles Wesley." *Wesleyan Theological Journal* 32, no. 1 (Spring 1997): 85-106.

Newton, J. A. "Perfection and Spirituality in the Methodist Tradition." *Church Quarterly Review* 3 (October 1970): 95-103.

---. "The Ecumenical Wesley." The Ecumenical Review 24 (April 1972): 160-75.

---. "The Heart Strangely Warmed: Eastern Orthodox and the Free Church Tradition in the West [Methodism; por]." Sobornost (incorporating Eastern Churches Review) 6, no. 2 (1984): 43-54.

---. "John Wesley's Theology in Historical Perspective." Journal of the Lincolnshire Methodist History Society 4, no. 1 (1988): 28-38.

---. "Spirituality and Sanctification." One In Christ: A Catholic Ecumenical Review 24, no. 3 (1988): 218-22.

Nichols, Kathryn. "Charles Wesley's Eucharistic Hymns: Their Relationship to the Book of Common Prayer." *The Hymn: A Journal of Congregational Song* 39 (April 1988): 13-21.

---. "The Theology of Christ's Sacrifice and Presence in Charles Wesley's Hymns on the Lord's Supper." *The Hymn: A Journal of Congregational Song* 29 (October 1988): 19-29.

Nicholson, Roy Stephen. "John Wesley's Personal Experience of Christian Perfection." *The Asbury Seminarian* 6, no. 1 (1952): 65-89.

---. "John Wesley and Ecumenicity." *Wesleyan Theological Journal* 2, no. 1 (Spring 1967): 66-81.

---. "The Holiness Emphasis in Wesleys' Hymns." *Wesleyan Theological Journal* 5, no. 1 (Spring 1970): 13-22.

Niles, Lori Haynes. "Toward a Wesleyan Theology of Failure." *Wesleyan Theological Journal* 43 (2008): 120-132.

Nilsen, E. Anker. "En Pyskodynamisk Analyse Av John Wesleys Religiose Opplevelser." *Norsk Teologisk Tidsskrift* 76, no. 1 (1975): 35-42.

Noble, Thomas A. "John Wesley as a Theologian: An Introduction." *Didache: Faithful Teaching* 7, no. 2 (2007).

---. "John Wesley as a Theologian: An Introduction." *Evangelical Review of Theology* 34, no. 3 (2010): 238-257.

---. "To Serve the Present Age: Authentic Wesleyan Theology Today." *Wesleyan Theological Journal* 46, no. 1 (2011): 73-89.

Nockles, Peter. "'Emissaries of Babylon' or 'Brothers in Christ'? Charles Wesley and Anti-Catholicism." *Wesley and Methodist Studies* 2 (2010): 3-24.

---. "Reactions to Robert Southey's Life of Wesley (1820) Reconsidered." *Journal of Ecclesiastical History* 63, no. 1 (2012): 61-80.

Noll, Mark A. "Romanticism and the Hymns of Charles Wesley." *The Evangelical Quarterly* 46 (October-December 1974): 195-223.

---. "John Wesley and the Doctrine of Assurance." *Bibliotheca Sacra* 132 (April-June 1975): 161-77.

Noppen, J. P. van. "Hymns as Literature, Language and Discourse: Wesleyan Hymns as a Case Example." *Hymn* 56, no. 3 (2005): 22-30.

Noro, Yoshio. "The Character of John Wesley's Faith." *Wesleyan Quarterly Review* 4 (1967): 10-26.

---. "Wesley's Understanding of Christian Perfection." *Wesleyan Quarterly Review* 4 (1967): 27-42.

---. "Wesley's Theological Epistemology." *The Iliff Review* 28 (1971): 59-67.

Norwood, Frederick A. "Wesleyan and Methodist Historical Studies, 1960-1970; A Bibliographic Article." *Church History* 40 (June 1971): 182-99.

---. "Wesleyan and Methodist Historical Studies, 1960-1970 [reprint, bibliog essay]." *Methodist History* 10 (January 1972): 23-44.

Nuttall, G. F. "John Wesley Presides [review article]." *London Quarterly & Holborn Review* 191 (July 1966): 200-204.

Nygren, Ellis H. "John Wesley's Changing Concept of the Ministry." *Religion in Life* 31 (1962): 264-74.

---. "Implications in Wesleyan Thought for a Critique of Existentialism." *Wesleyan Theological Journal* 6, no. 1 (Spring 1971): 23-30.

Oakes, Kenneth. "Temporality as Rupture and Remainder: Wesley, Pinnock, and St. Thomas." *Wesleyan Theological Journal* 39, no. 2 (2004): 39-53.

O'Brien, Glen. "A Trinitarian Revisioning of the Wesleyan Doctrine of Christian Perfection." *Aldersgate Papers* 2 (2001): 17-68.

---. "A Beautiful Virgin Country Ready for a Revival of Bible Holiness: Early Holiness Evangelists in Australia." *Wesleyan Theological Journal* 42, no. 2 (2007): 155-181.

---. "Joining the Evangelical Club: The Movement of the Wesleyan-Holiness Churches in Australia Along the Church-Sect Continuum." *The Journal of Religious History* 32, no. 3 (2008): 320-344.

---. "They Made a Pentecostal out of Her: The Church of God (Cleveland) in Australia." *Lucas Evangelical History Journal* 1 (2009): 67-99.

---. "Anti-Americanism and Wesleyan-Holiness Churches in Australia." *Journal of Ecclesiastical History* 61, no. 2 (2010): 314-43.

---. "Why Brengle? Why Coutts? Why Not?" *Word and Deed: A Journal of Salvation Army Theology and Ministry* November (2010): 5-24.

---. "John Wesley and Athanasius on Salvation in the Context of the Debate over Wesley's Debt to Eastern Orthodoxy." *Phronema* 28, no. 2 (2013): 35-53.

---. "John Wesley, the Uniting Church, and the Authority of Scripture." *Pacifica: Australasian Theological Studies* 27, no. 2 (2014): 170-183.

Oden, Amy G. "John Wesley's Notion of Watchfulness: 'A Mighty Exertion'." Wesleyan Theological Journal 52, no. 2 (2017): 151-170.

Oden, Thomas C. "What are 'Established Standards of Doctrine': A Response to Richard Heitzenrater [5:6-27 Fall 1985]." *Quarterly Review* 7 (Spring 1987): 41-62.

Ogden, Schubert M. "Process Theology and the Wesleyan Witness [bibliog]." *Perkins Journal* 37 (Spring 1984): 18-33.

Oglevie, Heather. "Entire Sanctification and the Atonement: A Wesleyan Demonstration" *Wesleyan Theological Journal* 50, no. 1 (2015): 38-52.

Olivers, Thomas. "A Descriptive and Plaintive Elegy on the Death of the Late Reverend John Wesley, 1791 [ed by H D Rack; poem]." *Epworth Review* 18 (May 1991): 35-40.

Olson, Mark K. "Aldersgate II and the Birth of the Servant State." Wesleyan Theological Journal 43 (2008): 154-176.

---. "Strange Bedfellows: Reappraisal of Mildred Wynkoop's a Theology of Love." Wesleyan Theological Journal 45, no. 2 (2010): 196-217.

---. "The Stillness Controversy of 1740: Tradition Shaping Scripture Reading." Wesleyan Theological Journal 46, no. 1 (2011): 120-133.

---. "John Wesley's Doctrine of Sin Revisited." Wesleyan Theological Journal 47, no. 2 (2012): 53-71.

---. "The New Birth in the Early Wesley." Wesleyan Theological Journal 52, no. 2 (2017): 79-99.

Olson, Roger. "Arminianism Is Evangelical Theology." *Wesleyan Theological Journal* 46, no. 2 (2011): 7-24.

Olsson, Karl A. "Influence of Pietism on Social Action." *Moravian Theological School Bulletin* No 1 (1965): 45-56.

O'Malley, J. Steven. "Recovering the Vision of Holiness: Wesley's Epistemic Basis." *The Asbury Theological Journal* 41, no. 1 (Spring 1986): 3-17.

---. "Pietist Influences in the Eschatological Thought of John Wesley and Jurgen Moltmann." *Wesleyan Theological Journal* 29, no. 1 (Spring-Fall 1994): 127-39.

---. "Pietistic Influence on John Wesley: Wesley and Gerhard Tersteegen." *Wesleyan Theological Journal* 31, no. 2 (Fall 1996): 48-70.

---. "Co-Laborers in the Harvest: John Wesley and the Evangelicals." *Evangelical Journal* 24, no. 1 (2006): 9-18.

---. "The Pietist Link to Wesley's Deathbed Confession." *Wesleyan Theological Journal* 51, no. 2 (2016): 79-88.

---. "Pietism and Wesleyanism: Setting the Stage for a Theological Discussion." Wesleyan Theological Journal 53, no. 1 (2018): 56-78.

Ong, Walter J. "Peter Ramus and the Naming of Methodism." *Journal of the History of Ideas* 14 (1953): 235-48.

Oord, Thomas Jay. "Types of Wesleyan Philosophy: General Landscape and Personal Research Agenda." *Wesleyan Theological Journal* 39, no. 1 (2004): 154-162.

---. "Love as a Methodological and Metaphysical Source for Science and Theology." *Wesleyan Theological Journal* 45, no. 1 (2010): 81-107.

---. "Love, Wesleyan Theology and Psychological Dimension of Both." *Journal of Psychology and Christianity* 31, no. 2 (2012): 144-156.

Orcibal, Jean. "Les Spirituels francais et espagnols chez John Wesley et ses Contemporains." *Revue de l'Histoire des Religions* 139 (1951): 50-109.

---. "L'Originalite Theologique de John Wesley et les Spiritualites du Continent." *Revue Historique* 222 (1959): 51-80.

Osborn, G. R. "Methodism and Education; John Wesley's Contribution." *London Quarterly & Holborn Review* 181 (October 1956): 259-64.

Oswalt, John N. "Wesley's use of the Old Testament in His Doctrinal Teachings [with index to OT passages in Sugden's edition of J. Wesley's Standard Sermons]." *Wesleyan Theological Journal* 12 (Spring 1977): 39-53.

---. "John Wesley and the Old Testament Concept of the Holy Spirit." *Religion in Life* 48 (Autumn 1979): 283-92.

Ott, Philip W. "John Wesley and the Non-Naturals." *Preventive Medicine* 9 (1980): 578-84.

---. "John Wesley on Health: A Word for Sensible Regimen." *Methodist History* 18, no. 3 (April 1980): 193-204.

---. "John Wesley on Mind and Body: Toward an Understanding of Health as Wholeness." *Methodist History* 27, no. 2 (January 1989): 61-72.

---. "John Wesley on Health and Wholeness." *Journal of Religion and Health* 30 (Spring 1991): 43-57.

---. "Medicine as Metaphor: John Wesley on Therapy of the Soul." *Methodist History* 33, no. 3 (April 1995): 179-91.

---. "John Wesley on Health as Wholeness." *Journal of Religion and Health* 30 (Spring 1991): 43-57.

Otto, Marc. ""We Cannot Know Much, but We May Love Much": Mystery and Humility in John Wesley's Narrative Ecology." *Wesleyan Theological Journal* 44, no. 1 (2009): 118-140.

Outler, Albert C. "Evangelism in the Wesleyan Spirit." *Andover Newton Quarterly* 14 (January 1974): 212-24.

---. "John Wesley as a Theologian: Then as Now." *Methodist History* 12 (July 1974): 63-82.

---. "John Wesley: Folk Theologian." *Theology Today* 34 (1977): 150-60.

---. "John Wesley's Interest in the Early Fathers of the Church." *The Bulletin Committee on Archives and History of the United Church of Canada* 29 (1983): 5-17.

---. "The Rediscovery of John Wesley Through His Faith and Doctrine." *Historical Bulletin* 12 (1983): 4-10.

---. "Spirit and Spirituality." *Quarterly Review* 8, no. 2 (Summer 1988): 3-18.

Oxford Institute of Methodist Theological Studies. "First,1959: Biblical Theology." *London Quarterly & Holborn Review* 184 (July 1959): 162-274.

Parkes, William. "John Wesley: Field Preacher." *Methodist History* 30, no. 4 (July 1992): 217-34.

---. "Watchnight, Covenant Service, and the Love-Feast in Early British Methodism." *Wesleyan Theological Journal* 32, no. 2 (Fall 1997): 35-58.

Pask, A. H. "Influence of Arminius on John Wesley." *London Quarterly & Holborn Review* 185 (October 1960): 258-63.

Pasquarello, M. "On the Trinity" John Wesley: Homiletical Theologian." *Asbury Theological Journal* 61, no. 1 (2006): 97-108.

Pearson, Sharon Clark. "Sacred Songs/Sacred Service." *Wesleyan Theological Journal* 32, no. 2 (Fall 1997): 15-34.

Pellowe, William Charles Smithson. "John Wesley's Use of the Bible." *Methodist Review* 106 (1923): 353-74.

---. "John Wesley's Use of Doctrine." *Methodist Review* 107 (1924): 101-7.

Pembroke, Neil F. "From Self-Doubt to Assurance: The Psychological Roots of John Wesley's Early Spiritual Development." *Journal of Psychology and Christianity* 13 (Fall 1994): 242-53.

Peterson, Brent. "Eucharist: The Church's Political Response to Suffering and Vocational Empowerment to Suffering Love." *Wesleyan Theological Journal* 43 (2008): 146-164.

---. "A Post-Wesleyan Eucharistic Ecclesiology: The Presence of Christ in the Eucharist as the Memory of the Facing Event between Christ and the Church." *Proceedings of the North American Academy of Liturgy* (2011): 181-202.

Peterson, Claire Brown. "Pride in Perfection: A Thomistic Defense of John Wesley's Doctrine of Entire Sanctification." Wesleyan Theological Journal 53, no. 2 (2018): 102-124.

Peterson, Michael L. "Orthodox Christianity, Wesleyanism, and Process Theology." *Wesleyan Theological Journal* 15, no. 2 (Fall 1980): 45-58.

Phillips, Thomas E. "The Mission of the Church in Acts: Inclusive or Exclusive?" *Wesleyan Theological Journal* 38, no. 1 (2003): 125-137.

Phipps, William E. "John Wesley on Slavery." *Quarterly Review* 1 (Summer 1981): 23-31.

Pilkington, Frederick. "Methodism and Episcopacy." *Contemporary Review* 193 (1958): 303-7.

Pillow, Thomas Wright. "John Wesley's Doctrine of the Trinity." *The Cumberland Seminarian* 24, no. 1 (Spring 1986): 1-10.

Pinnock, Clark H. "The Beauty of God: John Wesley's Reform and Its Aftermath." *Wesleyan Theological Journal* 38, no. 2 (2003): 57-68.

Pinomaa, L. "Tro, Lag, Helgelse hos Luther, Calvin och John Wesley." *Norsk Teologisk Tidsskrift* 69, no. 1-2 (1968): 107-18.

Plant, Stephen and Plested, Marcus. "Macarius, St. Gregory of Nyssa, and the Wesleys." *Epworth Review* 33, no. 1 (2006): 22-30.

Platt, Fredric. "The Work of the Holy Spirit (The Conversion of John Wesley)." *London Quarterly & Holborn Review* 163 (1938): 175-78.

Pletzer, Randy. "Roots - a Return to Wesleyan Methodism." *Evangelical Journal* 27, no. 1 (2009): 35-40.

Porter, L. E. "James Hervey, 1714-1758; A Bicentenary Appreciation." *The Evangelical Quarterly* 31 (January- March 1959): 4-20.

Potter, Claire. "The Influence of Danish Missionaries to India on Susanna Wesley's Methods of Education and Its Subsequent Influence on John Wesley." *Methodist History* 52, no. 3 (2014): 148-167.

Proctor, W. C. G. "Toplady on Predestination." *Churchman: Journal of Anglican Theology* 77 (March 1963): 30-37.

Pugh, Ben. "The Wesleyan Way Entire Sanctification and Its Spin-Offs--a Recurring Theme in Evangelical Devotion." *Evangelical Review of Theology* 38, no. 1 (2014): 4-21.

Rack, Henry D. "The Decline of the Class-Meeting and the Problem of Church Membership in Nineteenth-Century Methodism." *The Proceedings of the Wesley Historical Society* 39 (February 1973): 12-21.

---. "Religious Societies and the Origin of Methodism [Societies for the Reformation of Manners]." *The Journal of Ecclesiastical History* 38 (October 1987): 582-95.

---. "John Wesley: Journals and Diaries [Starting with oneself: spiritual confessions, pt 6]." *Expository Times* 101 (May 1990): 228-31.

---. "John Wesley as Theologian." *Epworth Review* 27 (January 2000): 43-47.

---. "Wesley Portrayed: Character and Criticism in Some Early Biographies." *Methodist History* 43, no. 2 (2005): 90-114.

---. "A Man of Reason and Religion? John Wesley and the Enlightenment " *Wesley and Methodist Studies* 1 (2009): 2-17.

Radford, J. Grange. "John Wesley's Witness to Christ: Yesterday and Today." *Methodist Magazine* 161 (161): 261-64.

Rainey, David. "The Established Church and Evangelical Theology: John Wesley's Ecclesiology." *International Journal of Systematic Theology* 12, no. 4 (2010): 420-434.

---. "Beauty in Creation: John Wesley's Natural Philosophy." Wesley and Methodist Studies 9, no. 1 (2017): 18-35.

Rainy, Principal. "Characteristics of Wesley and His Teaching: The Sermon." *Methodist Recorder* 31, no. 1 (1891): 215.

Rakestraw, Robert V. "John Wesley as a Theologian of Grace." *Journal of the Evangelical Theological Society* 27 (June 1984): 193-203.

---. "Human Rights and Liberties in the Political Ethics of John Wesley." *Evangelical Journal* 3 (1985): 63-78.

---. "The Contributions of John Wesley Toward an Ethic of Nature." *The Drew Gateway* 56, no. 3 (Spring 1986): 14-25.

Ramsey, Paul. "A Letter to James Gustafson." *The Journal of Religious Ethics* 137 (Spring 1985): 71-100.

Randolph, J. R. "John Wesley and the American Indian; a Study in Disillusionment [preprint]." *Methodist History* 10 (April 1972): 3-11.

Rankin, Stephen W. "A Perfect Church: Toward a Wesleyan Missional Ecclesiology." *Wesleyan Theological Journal* 38, no. 1 (2003): 83-104.

Rattenbury, John Ernest. "The Doctrine of Assurance." *London Quarterly & Holborn Review* 178 (January 1953): 65-66.

Raymond, Allan. "I Fear God And Honour The King: John Wesley and the American Revolution." *Church History* 45 (September 1976): 316-28.

Reed, Rodney L. "Calvin, Calvinism, and Wesley: The Doctrine of Assurance in Historical Perspective." *Methodist History* 32, no. 1 (October 1993): 31-43.

---. "Worship, Relevance, and the Preferential Option for the Poor in the Holiness Movement." *Wesleyan Theological Journal* 32, no. 2 (Fall 1997): 80-104.

Reeve, R. "John Wesley, Charles Simeon, and the Evangelical Revival." *Canadian Journal of Theology* 2 (October 1956): 203-14.

Reichard, Joshua D. "From Causality to Relationality: Toward a Wesleyan Theology of Concursus." *Wesleyan Theological Journal* 49 (2014): 122-138.

Reist, I. W. "John Wesley's View of the Sacraments; A Study in the Historical Development of a Doctrine." *Wesleyan Theological Journal* 6, no. 1 (Spring 1971): 41-54.

---. "John Wesley's View of Man; A Study in Free Grace versus Free Will." *Wesleyan Theological Journal* 7, no. 1 (Spring 1972): 25-35.

---. "John Wesley and George Whitefield: A Study in the Integrity of Two Theologies of Grace." *The Evangelical Quarterly* 47 (January-March 1975): 26-40.

Richardson, N. S. "John Wesley on Separation from the Church." *American Quarterly Church Review* 14 (1861): 63-74.

Richey, Russell E. "Shady Grove, Garden, and Wilderness: Methodism and the American Woodland." *Methodist History* 54, no. 4 (2016): 231-247.

Rieger, Joerg. "The Means of Grace, John Wesley, and the Theological Dilemma of the Church Today," *Quarterly Review: A Journal of Theological Resources for Ministry* 17 (Winter 1997): 377-93.

Rigg, James Harrison. "The Sacrament of the Lord's Supper." *Methodist Recorder* 31 (1891): 190-91.

Rightmire, R. David. "Subordination of Ecclessiology and Sacramental Theology to Pneumatology in the Nineteenth-Century Holiness Movement." *Wesleyan Theological Journal* 47, no. 2 (2012): 27-35.

Riss, Richard M. "John Wesley's Christology in Recent Literature." *Wesleyan Theological Journal* 45, no. 1 (2010): 108-129.

Rivers, Isabel. "John Wesley and the Language of Scripture, Reason, and Experience." *Prose Studies* 4 (1981): 252-84.

Robbins, Keith. "John Wesley, Methodism and Globalization." *Epworth Review* 34, no. 4 (2007): 23-37.

Rogal, Samuel J. "John Wesley's Daily Routine." *Methodist History* 8 (October 1974): 41-51.

---. """The Elder unto the Well-beloved": The Letters of John Wesley." *Journal of Religious Studies* 7 (Fall 1979): 73-87.

---. "Scripture Quotation in Wesley's Earnest Appeal." *Research Studies* 47 (1979): 181-88.

---. "The Contribution of John and Charles Wesley to the Spread of Popular Religion." *Grace Theological Journal* 4, no. 2 (Fall 1983): 233-44.

---. "John Wesley at Edinburgh: 1751-1790." *Trinity Journal* 4 (Spring 1983): 18-34.

---. "John Wesley's Arminian Magazine." *Andrew University Seminary Studies* 22 (Summer 1984): 231-47.

---. "Methodism on the Hustings: Woodrow Wilson and "John Wesley's Place in History" [bicentennial address, 1903]." *Perkins Journal* 38 (Spring 1985): 9-18.

---. "John Wesley and Mary Queen of Scots: A Love Affair with History." *Methodist History* 24, no. 4 (July 1986): 216-26.

---. "John Wesley's 87th Year: Good is the Work of the Lord." *Journal of Religion and Aging* 4, no. 1 (1987): 67-77.

---. "John Wesley Takes a Wife." *Methodist History* 27, no. 1 (October 1988): 48-55.

---. "John Wesley's Journal: Prescriptions for the Social, Spiritual and Intellectual Ills of Britain's Middle Class." *Andrew University Seminary Studies* 26 (Spring 1988): 33-42.

---. "Electricity: John Wesley's Curious and Important Subject"." *Eighteenth Century Life* 13 (November 1989): 79-90.

---. "John Wesley Takes Tea [Significance of His Tea Drinking]." *Methodist History* 32, no. 4 (July 1994): 222-28.

---. "Ladies Huntington, Glenorchy, and Maxwell: Militant Methodist Women." *Methodist History* 32, no. 2 (January 1994): 126-32.

---. "John Wesley Takes Tea [significance of his tea drinking]." *Methodist History* 32, no. 4 (July 1994): 222-28.

---. "John Wesley as Editor and Encyclopedist," *The Asbury Theological Journal* 52, no. 2 (Fall 1997): 81-89.

---. "On Keyboard and Breadboard: The Wesley Family Courts the London Scene." *Methodist History* 38, no. 4 (2000): 242-250.

---. "Scripture References, Allusions, and Echoes in Works by Charles and John Wesley." *Trinity Journal* 25, no. 1 (2004): 75-91.

---. "Legalizing Methodism: John Wesley's Deed of Declaration and the Language of the Law." *Methodist History* 144, no. 2 (2006): 105-114.

---. "'The Bible Told Them So: A Look at the Wesleys' Reliance Upon the Scriptures.'" Methodist History 56, no. 3 (2018): 133-148.

Rogers, C. A. "John Wesley and Jonathan Edwards." *Duke Divinity School Bulletin* 31 (Winter 1966): 20-38.

Rogers, Charles Allen. "John Wesley and William Tilly." *The Proceedings of the Wesley Historical Society* 35 (1966): 137-41.

Rousseau, George Sebastian. "John Wesley's Primitive Physics (1747)." *Harvard Library Bulletin* 16 (1968): 242-56.

Rowe, Kenneth E. Ed. "Rare Scrapbook of Wesley Prints [gathered by Abel Stevens; Discovery; Facsimile]." *Methodist History* 22, no. 4 (July 1984): 261-63.

---. "Charles Wesley Letter Sheds Light on John Wesley's Political Activism During the Revolutionary War." *Methodist History* 45, no. 3 (2007): 190-193.

Rowe, Stringer G. "Wesley's Dilemmas." *Wesleyan Methodist Magazine* 126 (1903): 428-30.

Ruffle, Douglas W. "Holiness and Happiness Shall Cover the Earth." *Quarterly Review* 19 (Spring 1999): 73-82.

Runyon, Theodore H. "Carl Michalson as a Wesleyan Theologian." *The Drew Gateway* 51, no. 2 (Winter 1980): 1-13.

---. "Wesley and `Right Experience'." *Papers of the Canadian Methodist Historical Society* 7 (1989): 55-65.

---. "The Role of Experience in Religion [for J Wesley; rev fr Drew G 57:44-55 Fall 1987; indexed in RIO 19]." *International Journal for Philosophy of Religion* 31 (June 1992): 187-94.

---. "The New Creation: The Wesleyan Distinctive." *Wesleyan Theological Journal* 31, no. 2 (Fall 1996): 5-19.

Rupp, Gordon E. "Confessio Augustana: A Methodist Appraisal [discussion, pp 95-97]." *LWF Report*, no. 6/7 (1979): 83-94.

Russell, Andrew C.. "Polemical Solidarity: John Wesley and Jonathan Edwards Confront John Taylor on Original Sin." *Wesleyan Theological Journal* 47, no. 2 (2012): 72-88.

Ruth, Lester. "A Little Heaven Below: The Love Feast and Lord's Supper in Early American Methodism." *Wesleyan Theological Journal* 32, no. 2 (Fall 1997): 59-79.

Ryan, Linda Ann. "Wesleyan Perspectives on the Education of Girls in Eighteenth-Century England." *Wesley and Methodist Studies* 8, no. 2 (2016): 135-154.

Ryder, Mary R. "Avoiding the "Many-Headed Monster": Wesley and Johnson on Enthusiasm." *Methodist History* 23, no. 4 (July 1985): 214-22.

Sakakibara, Gan. "A Study of John Wesley's Economic Ethics." *Wesleyan Quarterly Review* 4 (1967): 59-72.

Sanchez, Jonathan D. "John Wesley, on the Etiology of Evil: A Pastoral Reconstruction of Wesley's Theodicy Based on Genesis 1:31." *Apuntes* 34, no. 4 (Win 2014): 137-149.

Sanders, Cheryl J. "African-American Worship in the Pentecostal and Holiness Movements." *Wesleyan Theological Journal* 32, no. 2 (Fall 1997): 105-20.

Sanders, John. ""Open Theism": A Radical Revision or Miniscule Modification of Arminianism." *Wesleyan Theological Journal* 38, no. 2 (2003): 69-102.

Sanders, Paul S. "John Wesley and Baptismal Regeneration." *Religion in Life* 23 (1954): 591-603.

---. "What God Hath Joined Together?" *Religion in Life* 29 (1960): 491-500.

---. "Wesley's Eucharistic Faith and Practice." *Anglican Theological Review* 48 (April 1966): 157-74.

---. "The Puritans and John Wesley." *Work and Worship* 17, no. 2 (1967): 13-19.

Sangster, William Edwin. "Wesley and Sanctification." *London Quarterly & Holborn Review* 171 (1946): 214-21.

Satterwhite, John H. "A New Direction for Wesley Theological Seminary." *The AME Zion Quarterly Review* 94, no. 3 (October 1982): 48-50.

Schlimm, Matthew R. "The Puzzle of Perfection: Growth in John Wesley's Doctrine of Perfection." *Wesleyan Theological Journal* 38, no. 2 (2003): 124-142.

---. "Defending the Old Testament's Worth: John Wesley's Reaction to the Rebirth of Marcionism." *Wesleyan Theological Journal* 42, no. 2 (2007): 28-51.

Schneeberger, Vilem D. „Schlichte Wahrheit; Eine Aufgabe der Theologie?" *Communio Viatorum: A Theological Journal* 17, no. 1-2 (1974): 47-61.

---. „Der Begriff der Christlichen Freiheit bei John Wesley." *Communio Viatorum: A Theological Journal* 20, no. 1-2 (1977): 47-61.

---. „Haushalter Gottes (Beitrag zum Thema Verzicht im Blick auf Christliche Lebenshaltung)." *Communio Viatorum: A Theological Journal* 23, no. 1-2 (1980): 65-70.

Schofield, Robert E. "John Wesley and Science in 18th Century England." *Isis* 44 (1953): 331-40.

Schofield, Robert A. "Methodist Spiritual Condition in Georgian Northern England." *Journal of Ecclesiastical History* 65, no. 4 (2014): 780-802.

Schwartz, William Andrew. "How 'Truth' Limits Inter-Religious Dialogue: What Wesleyans Might Learn from Buddhism " *Wesleyan Theological Journal* 48, no. 1 (2013): 99-105.

Scott, David. "Racial Images in John Wesley's Thoughts Upon Slavery." *Wesleyan Theological Journal* 43 (2008): 87-100.

Scroggs, R. "John Wesley as Biblical Scholar." *Journal of Biblical Religion* 28 (October 1960): 415-22.

Seaborn, Joseph William, Jr. "Wesley's Views on the Uses of History." *Wesleyan Theological Journal* 21, no. 1 and 2 (Spring-Fall 1986): 129-36.

Seaman, Matthew. "Dark Green Religion and the Wesleyan Tradition: Harmony and Dissonance." *Wesleyan Theological Journal* 48, no. 1 (2013): 135-148.

Sell, Alan P. F. "John Chater: From Independent Minister to Sandemanian Author." *Baptist Quarterly* 31 (July 1985): 100-117.

Selleck, J. Brian. "An Historical Consideration of Worship and the Cure of Souls." *The Drew Gateway* 54, no. 2-3 (1984): 25-51.

---. "John Wesley and Spiritual Formation." *Doxology* 7 (1990): 6-16.

Severson, Eric R. "Ethical Dialogue: Trinitarian Externality as a Pattern for Evangelism and Missions." *Wesleyan Theological Journal* 38, no. 1 (2003): 105-124.

Shelton, R. Larry. "John Wesley's Approach to Scripture in Historical Perspective." *Wesleyan Theological Journal* 16, no. 1 (Spring 1981): 23-50.

---. "The Trajectory of Wesleyan Theology." *Wesleyan Theological Journal* 21, no. 1 and 2 (Spr-Fall 1986): 159-75.

Shetler, Brian. "Prophet and Profit: John Wesley, Publishing, and the Arminian Magazine." *Wesleyan Theological Journal* 49 (Fall 2014): 187-204.

Shier-Jones, Angela. "The Church and the World: Christianity and Culture from a Wesleyan Perspective." *Word and Deed* 8 (2006): 61-82.

Shipley, David C. "Wesley and Some Calvinistic Controversies." *The Drew Gateway* 25 (Summer 1955): 195-210.

---. "The Development of Theology in American Methodism in the 19th Century." *London Quarterly & Holborn Review* 28 (1959): 249-64.

Shockley, Grant S. "Methodism, Society and Black Evangelism in America; Retrospect and Prospect." *Methodist History* 12 (July 1974): 145-82.

Shontz, William H. "Anglican Influence on John Wesley's Soteriology." *Wesleyan Theological Journal* 32, no. 1 (Spring 1997): 33-52.

Short, Chad. "Wesleyan Theology and the Postmodern Quest for Meaning and Identity." *Wesleyan Theological Journal* 39, no. 2 (2004): 216-246.

Shopshire, James M. "A Retrospective View of the Seventh Oxford Institute of Methodist Theological Studies [Jl 26-Ag 5 1983; conf rpt]." *The AME Zion Quarterly Review* 95, no. 2 (July 1983): 6-21.

Shrier, Paul, and Cahleen Shrier. "Acts of Mercy as Mimesis: A Neuroscientific Critique of John Wesley's Means of Grace in Sanctification." *Journal of Pastoral Theology* 15, no. 1 (2005): 1-17.

---. "Wesley's Sanctification Narrative: A Tool for Understanding the Holy Spirit's Work in a More Physical Soul." *Pneuma: The Journal of the Society for Pentecostal Studies* 31, no. 2 (2009): 225-241.

Shriver, Donald W., jr., and E. Richard Knox. "Taxation in the History of Protestant Ethics [bibliog]." *The Journal of Religious Ethics* 13 (Spring 1985): 134-60.

Simon, John Smith. "Mr. Wesley's Notes upon the New Testament." *The Proceedings of the Wesley Historical Society* 9 (March 1914): 97-104.

---. "Wesley's Ordinations." *The Proceedings of the Wesley Historical Society* 9 (1914): 145-54.

Simpson, William C. Jr. "Pastors, Preachers, and the Healing Arts: The Wesleyan Tradition," *Living Pulpit* 6, no. 2 (April-June 1997): 22-23.

---. "John Wesley and Pentecostal Power." *Living Pulpit* 13, no. 2 (2004): 34-35.

Singleton, John. "At the Roots of Methodism: Wesley Intensely Interested In Social Issues." *Christian Social Action* 12 (Fall 1999): 30.

---. "At the Roots of Methodism: Wesley's Words Strike a Chord Today: Social Justice Ministry and Methodism Go Back to Its Founder." *Christian Social Action* 13, no. 2 (2000): 26-27.

Skuce, Stephen. "A Firm and Generous Faith: Towards an Authentic Wesleyan Inter-Faith Understanding." *Studies in Interreligious Dialogue* 19, no. 1 (2009): 66-80.

Sledge, Robert W. "What Bohler Got from Wesley." *Methodist History* 45, no. 4 (2007): 214-222.

Smith, H. "How Wesley Dealt With Erring Preachers." *Methodist Quarterly Review* 76 (1927): 401-11.

Smith, H. L. "Wesley's Doctrine of Justification; Beginning and Process [preprint]." *Duke Divinity School Bulletin* 28 (May 1963): 88-98. Same. Lond QHR 189:120-8 Ap'64.

Smith, James W. "Some Notes on Wesley's Doctrine of Prevenient Grace." *Religion in Life* 34 (1964): 68-80.

Smith, John Q. "Occupational Groups among the Early Methodists of the Keighley Circuit." *Church History* 57, no. 2 (June 1988): 187-96.

Smith, Robert D. "John Wesley and Jonathan Edwards on Religious Experience: A Comparative Analysis." *Wesleyan Theological Journal* 25, no. 1 (1990): 130-46.

Smith, Thomas W. "Authority and Liberty: John Wesley's View of Medieval England." *Wesley and Methodist Studies* 7, no. 1 (2015): 1-26.

Smith, Timothy L. "The Holy Spirit in the Hymns of the Wesleys [reply, T C Mitchell, pp 48-57]." *Wesleyan Theological Journal* 16, no. 2 (Fall 1981): 20-47.

---. "Notes on the Exegesis of John Wesley's "Explanatory Notes Upon the New Testament"." *Wesleyan Theological Journal* 16, no. 1 (Spring 1981): 107-13.

---. "Chronological List of John Wesley's Sermons and Doctrinal Essays." *Wesleyan Theological Journal* 17, no. 2 (Fall 1982): 88-110.

---. "George Whitefield and Wesleyan Perfectionism [reply, L. O. Hynson]." *Wesleyan Theological Journal* 19, no. 1 (Spring 1984): 63-85.

---. "John Wesley and the Wholeness of Scripture." *Interpretation* 39 (July 1985): 246-62.

---. "John Wesley and the Second Blessing." *Wesleyan Theological Journal* 21, no. 1 and 2 (Spring-Fall 1986): 137-58.

---. "Whitefield and Wesley on Righteousness by Grace." *TSF Bulletin* 9, no. 4 (March-April 1986): 5-8.

---. "The Spirit's Gifts: Then and Now." *Christianity Today* 34 (19 March 1990): 25-26.

Smith, Warren Thomas. "The Wesleys in Georgia: An Evaluation." *The Journal of the Interdenominational Theological Center* 6 (Spring 1979): 157-67.

---. "Sketches of Early Black Methodists." *The Journal of the Interdenominational Theological Center* 9 (Fall 1981): 1-18.

---. "Eighteenth Century Encounters: Methodist-Moravian." *Methodist History* 24, no. 3 (April 1986): 141-56.

Snyder, Howard A. "John Wesley, a Man for our Times." *Christianity Today* 16 (23 June 1972): 8-11.

---. "The Church as Holy and Charismatic." *Wesleyan Theological Journal* 15, no. 2 (Fall 1980): 7-32.

---. "The Holy Reign of God [in Wesleyan-Holiness theology fr J Wesley to E S Jones]." *Wesleyan Theological Journal* 24 (1989): 74-90.

---. "John Wesley and Macarius the Egyptian." *The Asbury Theological Journal* 45, no. 2 (Fall 1990): 55-60.

---. "The Babylonian Captivity of Wesleyan Theology." *Wesleyan Theological Journal* 39, no. 1 (2004): 7-34.

---. "John Wesley, Irenaeus, and Christian Mission: Rethinking Western Christian Theology." The Asbury Journal 73, no. 1 (2018): 138-159.

---. "Works of Grace and Providence: The Structure of John Wesley's Theology." Wesley and Methodist Studies 10, no. 2 (2018): 151-176.

Spaulding, H. W. "Practicing Holiness: Consideration of Action in the Thought of John Wesley." *Wesleyan Theological Journal* 40, no. 1 (2005): 110-137.

Speaks, Ruben L. "Christian Perfection and Human Liberation: The Wesleyan Synthesis [lecture, bicentennial celebration of Methodism, London, Eng, Ag 1984]." *The AME Zion Quarterly Review* 96, no. 4 (January 1985): 29-44.

---. "Christian Perfection and Human Liberation: The Wesleyan Synthesis." The AME Zion Quarterly Review 104 (April 1992): 5-17.

Spivey, Ronald V. "Methodism and the Means of Grace." *London Quarterly & Holborn Review* 182 (July 1957): 188-92.

Stanger, Frank B. "Reopening of John Wesley's City Road Chapel: A Call for Methodist Renewal." *Methodist History* 17 (April 1979): 178-95.

Stanley, F. L., ed. "John Wesley, An Unpublished Letter." *Methodist History* 4 (October 1965): 59-60.

Staples, Rob L. "Sanctification and Selfhood; A Phenomenological Analysis of the Wesleyan Message." *Wesleyan Theological Journal* 7, no. 1 (Spring 1972): 3-16.

---. "John Wesley's Doctrine of the Holy Spirit." *Wesleyan Theological Journal* 21, no. 1 and 2 (Spring-Fall 1986): 91-115.

Stark, David M. "'Lo! For Us the Wilds Are Glad!': Charles Wesley's Proclamation of Isaiah." *Wesleyan Theological Journal* 51, no. 2 (2016): 41-53.

Starkey, Lycurgus M. "The Holy Spirit and the Wesleyan Witness." *Religion in Life* 49 (Spring 1980): 72-80.

Starr, Roger. "Religion in the Unheavenly City [contrasting purposes and objects]." *First Things: A Monthly Journal of Religion and Public Life*, no. 13 (May 1991): 14-21.

Steele, Richard B. "John Wesley's Synthesis of the Revival Practices of Jonathan Edwards, George Whitefield, Nicholas von Zinzendorf." *Wesleyan Theological Journal* 30, no. 1 (Spring 1995): 154-72.

Stein, K. James. "Philipp Jakob Spener's Hope for Better Times for the Church: Contribution in Controversy." *The Covenant Quarterly* 37 (August 1979): 3-20.

---. "Baltimore 1784: Historical - Theological - Ecclesiastical [Methodist Christmas Conf; bibliog]." *Methodist History* 23, no. 1 (October 1984): 25-43.

---. "Martin Luther and the Beginnings of United Methodism." *Explor: A Journal of Theology* 8 (Spring 1986): 31-39.

Stephens, W. P. "Understanding Islam - in Light of Bullinger and Wesley." *Evangelical Quarterly* 81, no. 1 (2009): 23-37.

Stephenson, John. "The Doctrine of Christian Holiness as Taught by John Wesley." *Primitive Methodist Quarterly Review* 4,5 (1882-1883).

Stepp, Todd A. "Authentic Christian Worship." *Wesleyan Theological Journal* 45, no. 2 (2010): 218-241.

Stiles, Kenton M. "In the Beauty of Holiness: Wesleyan Theology, Worship, and the Aesthetic." *Wesleyan Theological Journal* 32, no. 2 (Fall 1997): 194-217.

Stoeffler, F. Ernest. "Infant Baptism: Entry into Covenant." *Christian Advocate* 4 (24 May 1962): 10-11.

---. "Wesleyan Concept of Religious Certainty; Its Pre-history and Significance." *London Quarterly & Holborn Review* 189 (April 1964): 128-39.

---. "Religious Roots of the Early Moravian and Methodist Movements." *Methodist History* 24, no. 3 (April 1986): 132-40.

Stoolz, K. "John Wesley and Evolution: A Reply to W.W. Sweet." *The Christian Century* 40 (1923): 663.

Strawson, W. "Wesley's Doctrine of the Last Things." *London Quarterly & Holborn Review* 184 (July 1959): 240-49.

---. "John Wesley's Two-Fold Belief About the Church: The Gospel and the Unity of the Church." *Methodist Recorder* 5 (1961): 389-90.

Stevenson, George John. "John Wesley and Luther." *Methodist Recorder* 23 (1883): 826.

Stevenson, R. T. "An Eighteenth Century Club." *Bibliotheca Sacra* 54 (1897): 66-85.

Stiles, Kenton M. "Theological Aesthetics: A Wesleyan Sampling of Cuisine." *Wesleyan Theological Journal* 42, no. 1 (2007): 160-182.

Straker, Ian. "Comments on Selected Themes [a Symposium on John H. Wigger's American Saint: Francis Asbury and the Methodists]." *Methodist History* 48, no. 4 (2010): 216-222.

Streiff, Patrick. "John William Fletcher's Shaping of Wesleyan Theology in Its Approach Beyond Christianity." *Methodist History* 52, no. 2 (2014): 78-93.

Stringer, J. H. "Promise of Sanctification; A Study in a Famous Wesley Passage." *London Quarterly & Holborn Review* 180 (January 1955): 26-30.

Stromberg, Peter G. "Wesleyan Sanctification and the Ethic of Self-Realization." *Ethos* 43, no. 4 (2015): 423-443.

Suchocki, Marjorie Hewitt. "Coming Home: Wesley, Whitehead, and Women." *The Drew Gateway* 57, no. 3 (Fall 1987): 31-43.

Suter, Keith D. "Christians and Personal Wealth." *Asia Journal of Theology* 3 (October 1989): 643-50.

Sweet, W. W. "John Wesley and Scientific Discovery." *The Christian Century* 40 (1923): 663.

Swift, W. F. "Brothers Charles and John." *London Quarterly & Holborn Review* 182 (October 1957): 275-80.

---. "John Wesley's Lectionary; with Notes on Some Later Methodist Lectionaries." *London Quarterly & Holborn Review* 183 (October 1958): 298-304.

Sylvest, Edwin E. "Wesley desde el Margen Hispano." *Apuntes: Reflexiones Teologicas desde el Margen Hispano* 1, no. 2 (Summer 1981): 14-19.

Tan, Seng-Kong. "The Doctrine of the Trinity in John Wesley's Prose and Poetic Works." *Journal for Christian Theological Research 7 2002* (2002).

Taran, Peter. "John Wesley's Giftedness." *Ecumenical Trends* 16 (May 1987): 86-88.

Tau, Kyle. "A Wesleyan Analysis of the Nazarene Doctrinal Stance on the Lord's Supper." *Wesleyan Theological Journal* 43, no. 2 (2008): 101-122.

Thiessen, Carol R. "John Wesley Alive [Refiner's fire; The Man from Aldersgate]." *Christianity Today* 25 (2 October 1981): 84.

Thomas, Howe Octavius Jr. "John Wesley's Awareness and Application of the Method of Distinguishing Between Theological Essentials and Theological Opinions." *Methodist History* 26, no. 2 (January 1988): 84-97.

---. "John Wesley's Understanding of the Theological Distinction Between 'Essentials' and 'Opinions'." *Methodist History* 33, no. 3 (April 1995): 139-48.

---. "Whenceforth Wesley: John Wesley's Theology from Then to Now." *Methodist History* 43, no. 4 (2005): 258-272.

Thompson, Andrew C. ""To Stir Them up to Believe, Love, Obey"--Soteriological Dimensions of the Class Meeting in Early Methodism." *Methodist History* 48, no. 3 (2010): 160-178.

---. "Outler's Quadrilateral, Moral Psychology and Theological Reflection in the Wesleyan Tradition." *Wesleyan Theological Journal* 46 (2011): 49-72.

Thompson, Andrew C. "The Practical Theology of the General Rules." *The Asbury Journal* 68, no. 2 (2013): 6-27.

Thompson, Claude. "Wesley's Doctrines of Christian Perfection." *Together* (May 1962): 45.

Thompson, E. W. "Episcopacy; John Wesley's View." *London Quarterly & Holborn Review* 181 (April 1956): 113-17.

---. "John Wesley, Superintendent." *London Quarterly & Holborn Review* 184 (October 1959): 325-30.

Thompson, Henry O. "Biography as Theology: A Review Article." *The Drew Gateway* 51, no. 1 (Fall 1980): 43-50.

Thompson, Richard. "Holy Word, Holy People: (Re) Placing Scripture in Wesleyan-Holiness Thought and Practice." *Wesleyan Theological Journal* 51, no. 1 (2016): 51-64.

Thornley, John. "John Wesley's View on Temperance." *United Free Churches Magazine* 29 (1886): 423-25.

Thornton, Wallace, Jr. "The Revivalist Movement and the Development of a Holiness/Pentecostal Philosophy of Missions." *Wesleyan Theological Journal* 38, no. 1 (2003): 160-186.

Thorsen, Donald A. "Experimental Method in the Practical Theology of John Wesley [Anglican and British empirical roots]." *Wesleyan Theological Journal* 24 (1989): 117-41.

---. "Ecumenism, Spirituality, and Holiness: Exploring Wesley and the Variety of Christian Spiritualities." *Wesleyan Theological Journal* 41, no. 1 (2006): 189-204.

---. "Sola Scriptura and the Wesleyan Quadrilateral." *Wesleyan Theological Journal* 41, no. 2 (2006): 7-27.

---. "Holiness in Postmodern Culture." *Wesleyan Theological Journal* 43, no. 2 (2008): 123-135.

---. "The Wesleyan Impulse in Teaching." *Asbury Theological Journal* 63, no. 2 (2008): 49-58.

---. "Jesus, Ecumenism, and Interfaith Relations: A Wesleyan Perspective." *Wesleyan Theological Journal* 47, no. 1 (2012): 59-71.

---. "A Wesleyan-Holiness Perspective on the Church: Towards a Common Vision." *Journal of Ecumenical Studies* 50, no. 2 (2015): 295-298.

---. "Tulip Vs. Acura: Reframing Differences between Calvin and Wesley." *Wesleyan Theological Journal* 50, no. 2 (2015): 96-112.

Timpe, Randie L. "John Wesley and B F Skinner: Casualty, Freedom, and Responsibility [bibliog]." *Journal of Psychology and Christianity* 4, no. 3 (Fall 1985): 28-34.

Tippett, A. R. "Church Which is His Body; A Model from Physical Anthropology." *Missiology* 2 (April 1974): 147-59.

Topolewski, John Leo. "Mr. Wesley's Trust Clause: Methodism in the Vernacular." *Methodist History* 37 (April 1999): 143-61.

Towns, Elmer L. "John Wesley and Religious Education." *Religious Education* 65 (1970): 318-28.

Tracy, Wesley D. "Christian Education in the Wesleyan Mode [discussion of Kingswood School; reply, JD Beals]." *Wesleyan Theological Journal* 17, no. 1 (Spring 1982): 30-53.

---. "John Wesley, Spiritual Director: Spiritual Guidance in Wesley's Letters [letters to Anne Bolton]." *Wesleyan Theological Journal* 23, no. 1 and 2 (Spring-Fall 1988): 148-62.

---. "Economic Policies and Judicial Oppression as Formative Influences on the Theology of John Wesley." *Wesleyan Theological Journal* 27 (Spring-Fall 1992): 30-56.

Tripp, David H. ""Observe the Gradation!" John Wesley's Notes on the New Testament." *Quarterly Review* 10 (Summer 1990): 49-64.

---. "John and Charles Wesleys' Hymns of the Lord's Supper." *The Harp: A Review of Syriac and Oriental Studies* 5 (1992): 131-55.

---. "Clement of Alexandria and the Wesley Brothers." *The Proceedings of the Wesley Historical Society* 49 (1994): 113-16.

---. ""Standard Sermons": History for History's Sake, Denominational Manifesto, Doctrinal "Standard"." *Asbury Theological Journal 56-57 no 2-1 Fall-Spr 2001-2002* (2002): 97-116.

Truesdale, Albert L. "Christian Holiness and the Problem of Systematic Evil [reply, W Hasker]." *Wesleyan Theological Journal* 19, no. 1 (Spring 1984): 39-59.

Tsoumas, T. "Methodism and Bishop Erasmus." *Greek Orthodox Theological Review* 2, no. 2 (1956): 63-73.

Turley, Brian K. "John Wesley and War." *Methodist History* 29, no. 2 (January 1991): 96-111.

Turner, E. E. "John Wesley and Mysticism." *Methodist Review* 113 (1930): 16-31.

Turner, John M. "John Wesley: Theologian for the People." *Journal of United Reform Church History Society* 3 (1986): 320-28.

---. "Victorian Values - Or Whatever Happened to John Wesley's Scriptural Holiness?" *The Proceedings of the Wesley Historical Society* 46 (1988): 165-84.

Tuttle, Robert G., Jr. "Can United Methodists Be Charismatics?" *Circuit Rider* 2, no. 6 (April 1978): 3-6.

Tyson, John R. "John Wesley and William Law: A Reappraisal [Appendices]." *Wesleyan Theological Journal* 17, no. 2 (Fall 1982): 58-78.

---. "Charles Wesley and the German Hymns [identity of translator]." *The Hymn: A Journal of Congregational Song* 35 (July 1984): 153-57.

---. "Charles Wesley's Sentimental Language [reply to E Sharpe, 53,149-164 1981]." *The Evangelical Quarterly* 57 (July 1985): 269-75.

---. "Charles Wesley's Theology of Redemption." *Wesleyan Theological Journal* 20, no. 2 (Fall 1985): 7-28.

---. "God's Everlasting Love: Charles Wesley and the Predestinarian Controversy." *Evangelical Journal* 3, no. 2 (Fall 1985): 47-62.

---. "Essential Doctrines and Real Religion: Theological Method in Wesley's Sermons on Several Occasions." *Wesleyan Theological Journal* 23, no. 1 and 2 (Spring-Fall 1988): 163-79.

---. "Sin, Self and Society: John Wesley's Hamartiology Reconsidered [his Sermons on several occasions]." *The Asbury Theological Journal* 44, no. 2 (Fall 1989): 77-89.

---. "Transfiguration of Scripture." *The Asbury Theological Journal* 47, no. 2 (Fall 1992): 17-41.

---. "Why Did John Wesley 'Fail'?: A Reappraisal of Wesley's Evangelical Economics." *Methodist History* 35, no. 3 (April 1997): 176-87.

---. "Christian Liberty as Full Redemption: Charles Wesley's Approach." *Wesleyan Theological Journal* 38, no. 2 (2003): 143-174.

---. "We the People": John Wesley's Critique of Liberal Democracy." *Wesleyan Theological Journal* 40 (2005): 102-122.

---. "Charles Wesley and the Language of Evangelical Experience: The Poetical Hermeneutic Revisited." *Asbury Theological Journal* 61, no. 1 (2006): 25-46.

Urwin, Evelyn Clifford. "The 'Warmed Heart' and Its Social Consequences: The Conversion of John Wesley." *London Quarterly & Holborn Review* 163 (1938): 211-14.

Ury, M. William. "A Wesleyan Concept of "Person"." *Wesleyan Theological Journal* 38, no. 2 (2003): 30-56.

Van Der Walle, Bernie A. "Crafted and Co-Opted: The Early Christian and Missionary Alliance's Selective and Self-Serving Use of the Life and Writings of John Wesley." Wesley Theological Journal 53, no. 2 (2018): 125-143.

Van Doornik, Merwin. "Your Master Proclaim: A Tribute to John and Charles Wesley." *Reformed Worship*, no. 8 (Summer 1988): 14-16.

van Noppen, J.-P. "Le Cantique Methodiste: Une Approach Historique et Stylistique," *Bulletin de la Societe Royale d'Histoire du Protestantisme Belge*, vol. 123 (December 1999): 27-42.

---. "Methodist Discourse and Industrial Work Ethic: A Critical Theolinguistic Approach," *Revue Belge de Philologie et d'Histoire* 73, no. 3 (1995): 693-714.

---. "Le Discours Methodiste: Une Analyse Critique du Contenu," *Revue Belge de Reflexion Protestante*, vol. 3 (1999): 13-38.

---. "The English Hymn: A discourse Perspective." *Belgian Association of Anglicists in Higher Education* (2001).

van Noppen J. –P. and J. Gillespie. "L'Image de la Servante Domestique Dans la Fiction Edifiante Methodiste." *Bulletin de la Societe Royale d'Histoire du Protestantisme Belge* 125 (2001).

Vick, E. W. H. "John Wesley's Teaching Concerning Perfection." *Andrew University Seminary Studies* 4 (July 1966): 201-17.

Vickers, J. A. "Gibbes Family of Hilton Park; An Unpublished Correspondence of John Wesley." *Methodist History* 6 (April 1968): 43-61.

---. "Lambeth Palace Library; Some Items of Methodist Interest from the Fullman Papers." *Methodist History* 9 (July 1971): 22-29.

---. "On Indexing John Wesley." *The Indexer* 11, no. 4 (October 1979): 189-97.

---. "A New Whitefield Letter [to J Wesley; text]." *The Proceedings of the Wesley Historical Society* 48 (February 1992): 119-22.

---. "Son to Sophia: a Byway of Methodist History." *Methodist History* 35 (July 1997): 214-21.

Vickers, Jason E. "On Friendship: John Wesley's Advice to the People Called Methodists." *Wesleyan Theological Journal* 42 (2007): 32-49.

---. "Albert Outler and the Future of Wesleyan Theology: Retrospect and Prospect." *Wesleyan Theological Journal* 43 (2008): 56-67.

---. "The Wesleys of Blessed Memory: Hagiography, Missions and the Study of World Methodism." *International Bulletin of Missionary Research* 36, no. 3 (2012): 143-147.

---. "The Holy Spirit and Holy Communion: Towards a Wesley Liturgy of the Atonement." *Wesleyan Theological Journal* 50, no. 1 (2015): 23-37.

Villa-Vicencio, Charles. "Towards a Liberating Wesleyan Social Ethic for South Africa Today." *Journal of Theology for Southern Africa*, no. 68 (Spring 1989): 92-102.

Vondey, Wolfgang. "Wesleyan Theology and the Disjointing of the Protestant Scripture." *Wesleyan Theological Journal* 46, Fall (2011): 70-85.

Wagley, Laurence, A. "The Wesleyan Revival and Forgiveness of Sin." *Liturgy* 4 (1991): 87-93.

Wagner, Paul S. "John Wesley's Use of German Hymn Tunes." *Hymn* 57 (2006): 27-38.

Wainwright, Geoffrey. "Methodism's Ecclesial Location and Ecumenical Vocation." *One In Christ: A Catholic Ecumenical Review* 19, no. 2 (1983): 104-34.

---. "The Assurance of Faith: A Methodist Approach to the Question Raised by the Roman Catholic Doctrine of Infallibility." *One In Christ: A Catholic Ecumenical Review* 22, no. 1 (1986): 44-61.

---. "Perfect Salvation in the Teaching of Wesley and Calvin." *Reformed World* 40, no. 2 (1988): 898-909.

---. "The Sacraments in Wesleyan Perspective." *Doxology* 5 (1988): 5-20.

---. "Why Wesley was a Trinitarian." *The Drew Gateway* 59 (Spring 1990): 26-43.

---. "Wesley and the Communion of Saints." *One In Christ: A Catholic Ecumenical Review* 27, no. 4 (1991): 332-45.

---. "Worship According to Wesley." *Australian Journal of Liturgy* 3 (1991): 5-20.

Wakefield, Gordon. "Literature du Desert Chez John Wesley." *Irenikon: Revue des Moines de Chevetonge* 51, no. 2 (1978): 155-70.

Wakefield, Gordon Stevens. "Traditions of Spiritual Guidance: John Wesley and the Methodist System." *The Way* 31 (1991): 69-91.

Walker, Maxine. "John Wesley and T.S. Eliot Dialogue on Christianity and Culture." *Wesleyan Theological Journal* 40 (2005): 239-253.

Wall, James M. "Give All You Can: Newt Gingrich Meets John Wesley [editorial]." *The Christian Century* 112 (Fall 1995): 99-100.

Wall, Robert E. "John's John: A Wesleyan Theological Reading of 1 John " *Wesleyan Theological Journal* 46 (2011): 105-141.

Wall, Robert W. "Toward a Wesleyan Hermeneutics of Scripture." *Wesleyan Theological Journal* 30, no. 2 (Fall 1995): 50-67.

Wallace, Charles. "Simple and Recollected: John Wesley's Life-style." *Religion in Life* 46 (Summer 1977): 198-212.

Walls, Jerry L. "John Wesley's Critique of Martin Luther." *Methodist History* 20, no. 1 (October 1981): 29-41.

---. "The Free Will Defense, Calvinism, Wesley, and the Goodness of God." *Christian Scholar's Review* 13, no. 1 (1984): 19-33.

---. "What is Theological Pluralism [United Methodist Book of Discipline; doctrinal statements]." *Quarterly Review* 5 (Fall 1985): 44-62.

---. "As the Waters Cover the Sea: John Wesley on the Problem of Evil." *Faith and Philosophy* 13 (October 1996): 534-62.

Walters, O. S. "Concept of Attainment in John Wesley's Christian Perfection." *Methodist History* 10 (April 1972): 12-29.

---. "John Wesley's Footnotes to Christian Perfection." *Methodist History* 12 (October 1973): 19-36.

Walters, Stanley D. "Strange Fires: A Biblical Allusion in John Wesley's Hymns." *Methodist History* 17 (October 1978): 44-58.

Warner, Laceye. "Towards a Wesleyan Evangelism." *Methodist History 40 no 4* (2002): 230-245.

---. "Spreading Scriptural Holiness: Theology and Practices of Early Methodism for the Contemporary Church." *Asbury Theological Journal* 63, no. 1 (2008): 115-138.

Watson, David Lowes. "Christ our Righteousness: The Center of Wesley's Evangelistic Message." *Perkins Journal* 37 (Spring 1984): 34-47.

Watson, David L. "Spiritual Formation in Ministerial Training: The Wesleyan Paradigm: Mutual Accountability [Perkins School of Theology, Dallas]." *The Christian Century* 102 (6-13 February 1985): 122-24.

Watson, David Lowes. "Justification by Faith and Wesley's Evangelistic Message." *Wesleyan Theological Journal* 21, no. 1 and 2 (Spring-Fall 1986): 7-23.

---. "The Much-Controverted Point of Justification by Faith and the Shaping of Wesley's Evangelical Message." *Wesleyan Theological Journal* 21, no. 1 and 2 (Spring-Fall 1986): 7-23.

Watson, Kevin M. "The Form and Power of Godliness: Wesleyan Communal Discipline as Voluntary Suffering." *Wesleyan Theological Journal* 43 (2008): 165-183.

Watson, Philip Saville. "Wesley and Luther on Christian Perfection." *The Ecumenical Review* 15 (April 1963): 291-302.

Watts, A. McKibbin, ed. "John and Charles Wesley: 250th Anniversary of Their Conversion." *Touchstone: Heritage and Theology in a New Age* 6 (May 1988): 4-37.

Watty, William W. "Man and Healing: A Biblical and Theological View [WCC consultation on health and wholeness; Port of Spain, Trinidad, 1979]." *Point Series* 10, no. 2 (1981): 147-60.

Webb, J. R. "Young John Wesley; A New Monument [Savannah, plate]." *Methodist History* 8 (January 1970): 33-35.

Weber, Theodore R. "Political Order in Ordo Salutis: A Wesleyan Theory of Political Institutions." *Journal of Church and State* 37 (Summer 1995): 537-54.

Webster, Robert. "Sensing the Supernatural: John Wesley's Empirical Epistemology and the Pursuit of Divine Knowledge." *Sewanee Theological Review* 54, no. 3 (2011): 254-281.

Weissenbacher, A.C. "John Wesley and the Natural Law of Jean Porter and Pamela Hall." *Wesleyan Theological Journal* 49 (Fall 2014): 187-204.

---. "The Neuroscience of Wesleyan Soteriology: The Dynamic of Both Instanteousness and Gradual Change." *Zygon* 51, no. 2 (2016): 347-360.

Wellings, Martin. "John Wesley's Preachers: A Social and Statistical Analysis of the British and Irish Preachers Who Entered the Methodist Itinerancy before 1791." *Epworth Review* 37, no. 2 (2010): 74-75.

Wells, Harold. "Wesley on Stewardship and Economics [Good News to the Poor: John Wesley's Evangelical Economics, by T W Jennings, Jr.]." *Quarterly Review* 13 (Summer 1993): 85-91.

Werner, David. "John Wesley's Question: "How Is Your Doing?"." *Asbury Theological Journal* 65, no. 2 (2010): 68-93.

Wesley, John. "John Wesley and Robert Hall Junior [letter of July 7,1789]." *Methodist History* 8 (October 1969): 87.

---. "John Wesley Letter of 1789." *Methodist History* 7 (July 1969): 47.

---. "Unpublished Wesley Letter." *Methodist History* 7 (April 1969): 52.

---. "Primitive Physic: or, An Easy and Natural Method of Curing Most Diseases." *Weavings* 2 (November-December 1987): 37-40.

---. "Devotions and Prayers of John Wesley. Sel. (Quiet Heart)." *Decision* 50, no. 37 (2009).

---. "Turning Points #4: John Wesley." *Outreach* 10, Nov/Dec (2011): 28.

Wesley, John, and Randy Maddox. "John Wesley's Earliest Defense of the Emerging Revival in Bristol." *Wesley and Methodist Studies* 6, no. 2014 (2014): 124-153.

West, Nathaniel. "John Wesley a Premillenarian." *Christian Workers Magazine* 17 (1916): 96-101.

Westerfield-Tucker, Karen B.. "On the Occasion; Charles Wesley's Hymns on the London Earthquakes of 1750." *Methodist History* 42, no. 4 (2004): 197-221.

---. "`Plain and Decent': Octagonal Space and Methodist Worship." *Studia Liturgica* 24, no. 2 (1994): 129-44.

---. "Liturgical Expression of Care for the Poor in the Wesleyan Tradition: A Case Study for the Ecumenical Church." *Worship* 69 (January 1995): 51-64.

---. "John Wesley's Prayer Book Revision." *Methodist History* 34, no. 4 (July 1996): 230-47.

---. "On the Occasion; Charles Wesley's Hymns on the London Earthquakes of 1750." *Methodist History* 42, no. 4 (2004): 197-221.

---. "On the Occasion: Charles Wesley's Hymns on the London Earthquakes of 1750." *Hymn* 56 (2005): 38.

---. "North American Methodism's Engagement with Liturgical Renewal." *Liturgy* 26, no. 4 (2011): 57-66.

---. "'Wesleyan'? 'Wesleyan Tradition'? Worship and Liturgical Practices among the Spiritual Descendants of John and Charles Wesley." *Wesleyan Theological Journal* 53, no. 2 (2018): 30-53.

Weyer, Michael. „Die Aldersgate-Erfahrung John Wesleys." *Okumenische Rundschau* 37 (July 1988): 311-20.

Whedon, Daniel A. "John Wesley's View of Entire Sanctification." *Wesleyan Methodist Magazine* 85 (1862): 1015-20; 1090-93.

Wheeler, Sondra Ely. "Transforming Mercy: John Wesley's Legacy in Moral Theology." *Wesleyan Theological Journal* 53, no. 1 (2018): 43-55.

Whidden, Woodrow W. "Sola Scriptura, Inerrantist Fundamentalism, and the Wesleyan Quadrilateral:; is 'No Creed but the Bible' a Workable Solution?" *Andrew University Seminary Studies* 35 (Autumn 1997): 211-26.

---. "Wesley on Imputation: A Truly Reckoned Reality or Antinomian Polemical Wreckage?," *The Asbury Theological Journal* 52, no. 2 (Fall 1997): 63-70.

---. "Wesley's Theology of Preaching and Its Implications for Worship." *Toronto Journal of Theology* 15, no. 2 (1999): 183-192.

White, Charles Edward. "What Wesley Practiced and Preached about Money." *Leadership: A Practical Journal for Church Leaders* 8 (Winter 1987): 27-29.

---. "The Decline of the Class Meeting." *Methodist History* 38, no. 4 (2000): 258-267.

White, Charles E. "John Wesley's Use of Church Discipline." *Methodist History* 29 (1991): 112-18.

White, H. W. "Wesley's Death Through the Eyes of the Press." *London Quarterly & Holborn Review* 184 (January 1959): 45-46.

Whitesel, Bob. "A Holistic Good News: Missional, Effective Evangelism and Lessons Learned While Traveling in the Hoof Prints of Wesley." *Great Commission Research Journal* 5, no. 1 (2013): 52-65.

Whitesel, Bob. "Church Growth before McGavran: The Methodological Parallels of John Wesley." *Great Commission Research Journal 6* (Win 2015): 187-202.

Whitney, G. W. "The Opinions of John Wesley." *Universalist Quarterly View* 30-32 (1873-1875): 317-0, 434-54, 185-98, 90-8, 323-43.

Wiersma, Noelle S. Griffin. "The Wesleyan Tradition and Qualitative Inquiry in Contemporary Counseling Psychology: Heart and Mind as Art and Science." *Christian Scholar's Review* 36, no. 2 (2007): 167-183.

Wigger, John H. "John Wesley and Francis Asbury." *Methodist History* 54, no. 4 (2016): 271-284.

Williams, A. H. "John Wesley's Preferment to St Daniel's Church, near Pembroke." *The Proceedings of the Wesley Historical Society* 48 (May 1992): 155.

Williams, Garry J. "Was Evangelicalism Created by the Enlightenment?" *Tyndale Bulletin* 53 no 2 2002 (2002): 283-312.

Williams, Kevin F. "'To be capable of God. . .' --John Wesley's understanding of 'Christian Perfection' as the link between his theology and his spirituality," *Studia Historiae Ecclesisasticae* 23 (1997): 15-38.

Wilson, Charles R. "Relevance of John Wesley's Distinctive Correlation of Love and Law." *Wesleyan Theological Journal* 12 (Spring 1977): 54-59.

Wilson, David D. "The Importance of Hell for John Wesley." *The Proceedings of the Wesley Historical Society* 34 (1963): 12-16.

Wilson, D. D. "John Wesley and Mystical Prayer." *London Quarterly & Holborn Review* 193 (January 1968): 61-69.

Wilson, D.R. "'Thou Shal[T] Walk with Me in White': Afterlife and Vocation in the Ministry of Mary Bosanquet Fletcher." *Wesley and Methodist Studies* 1 (2009): 71-85.

---. "A Sermon by Mary Fletcher (Nee Bosanquet), on Exodus 20, Preach at Madeley in the Parish Vincarage on the Evening of Whitsunday, 8 June 1794 Transcribed, Introduced, and Annotated by D.R. Wilson." *Wesley and Methodist Studies* 2 (2010).

Wilson, Paul Scott. "Wesley's Homiletic: Law and Gospel for Preaching." *Toronto Journal of Theology* 10 (1994): 215-25.

Wilson, Philip S. "Wesley and Luther on Christian Perfection." *The Ecumenical Review* 15 (1963): 291-302.

Wimberly, Edward P. "The Black Christian Experience and the Holy Spirit." *Quarterly Review* 8, no. 2 (Summer 1988): 19-35.

Winckles, Andrew O. "'Excuse What Difficiencies You Will Find': Methodist Women and Public Space in John Wesley's Arminian Magazine." *Eighteenth-Century Studies* 46, no. 3 (2013): 415-429.

Wingeier-Rayo, Philip. "The Early Methodist Revival, Base Christian Communities and Pentecostalism in Latin America: A Comparison of Ecclesiology." *Apuntes* 21, no. 4 (2001): 132-147.

---. "A Wesleyan Theology of Religions: A Re-Reading of John Wesley through His Encounters with Peoples of Non-Christian Faiths." Methodist Review, no. 10 (2018): 1-22.

Wingeier-Rayo, and Paul Chilcote. "The Wesleyan Revival and Methodism in Cuba." *Quarterly Review* 17 (Fall 1997): 207-21.

Witherington, Ben. "'Elementary my dear Watson': The Effect of Richard Watson on American Methodism [bibliog]." *Ashland Theological Journal* 20 (1988): 29-46.

Withrow, Lisa R. "A Wesleyan View on "Making Disciples"." *Journal of Theology (UTS)* 105, Summer (2001): 3-17.

Wood, A. Skevington. "Lessons From Wesley's Experience." *Christianity Today* 7 (April 1963): 4-6.

---. "John Wesley, Theologian of the Spirit." *Evangelical Review of Theology* 4 (1980): 176-88.

---. "The Eighteenth Century Methodist Revival Reconsidered." *The Evangelical Quarterly* 53 (July-September 1981): 130-48.

Wood, Charles M. "Methodist Doctrine: An Understanding [paper presented at 10th Oxford Institute of Methodist Theological Studies]," *Quarterly Review: A Journal of Theological Resources for Ministry* 18 (Summer 1998): 167-82.

Wood, Darren Cushman. "John Wesley's Use of the Atonement." *Asbury Journal* 62, no. 2 (2007): 55-70.

---. "Suffering with the Crucified Christ: The Function of the Cross in the Works of John Wesley and Dorothee Soelle." *Wesleyan Theological Journal* 43 (2008): 184-202.

Wood, Laurence W. "Wesley's Epistemology." *Wesleyan Theological Journal* 10 (Spring 1975): 48-59.

---. "Exegetical-Theological Reflections on the Baptism with the Holy Spirit." *Wesleyan Theological Journal* 14, no. 2 (Fall 1979): 51-63.

---. "Thoughts Upon the Wesleyan Doctrine of Entire Sanctification with Special Reference to Some Similarities with the Roman Catholic Doctrine of Confirmation." *Wesleyan Theological Journal* 15, no. 1 (Spring 1980): 88-99.

---. "The Rediscovery of Pentecost in Methodism [conversion and apologetics of J. Fletcher]," *The Asbury Theological Journal*, 53, no. 4 (Spring 1998): 7-34.

---. "Pentecostal Sanctification in Wesley and Early Methodism." *Pneuma* 21, no. 2 (1999): 251-287.

---. "Can Pentecostals Be Wesleyans? My Reply to Don Dayton's Rejoinder." *Pneuma* 128, no. 1 (2006): 120-130.

---. "The Origin, Development, and Consistency of John Wesley's Theology of Holiness." *Wesleyan Theological Journal* 43 (2008): 33-55.

---. "The Need for a Contextual Interpretation of John Wesley's Sermons." *Wesleyan Theological Journal* 45, no. 1 (2010): 259-267.

---. "An Interpretation of the United Methodist Liturgy of Christian Baptism: 'By Water and the Spirit,' in the Matrix of John Wesley, John Fletcher, and Joseph Benson." *Wesleyan Theological Journal* 50, no. 2 (2015): 156-185.

---. "Conflicting Views of the New Birth between John and Charles Wesley with a Timeline Narrative Explaining How and Why the Distinction between Justifying Faith and Entire Sanctifying Grace Was Developed." Wesleyan Theological Journal 52, no. 2 (2017): 40-78.

---. "John Wesley's Mission of Spreading Scriptural Holiness: A Case Study in World Mission and Evangelism." The Asbury Journal 73, no. 1 (2018): 8-49.

Wood, Timothy L. ""That They May Be Free Indeed": Liberty in the Early Methodist Thought of John Wesley and Francis Asbury." *Methodist History* 38, no. 4 (2000): 231-241.

Woodruff, Jennifer Lynn. "John Calvin, the Wesleys, and John Williamson Nevin on the Lord's Supper." *Methodist History* XLI, no. 4 (2003): 159-178.

Woolley, Tim. "A Community of Selective Memory? Hugh Bourne, William Clowes and Primitive Methodist Historiography." *Wesley and Methodist Studies* 2 (2010): 67-90.

Worden, Barbara S. "The Emotional Evangelical: Blake and Wesley." *Wesleyan Theological Journal* 18, no. 2 (Fall 1983): 67-79.

Wright, C. J. "Methodism and the Church of England." *Modern Churchman* 45 (December 1955): 345-52.

---. "Methodism and the Church of England." *Modern Churchman* 46 (March 1956): 52-54.

Wright, John W. "'Use' and 'Enjoy' in John Wesley: John Wesley's Participation within the Augustinian Tradition." *Wesley and Methodist Studies* 6 (2014): 3-36.

Wright, Ronald W., Greg Diamond, and Philip Budd. "An Experienced Presence: An Intersubjective Perspective on John Wesley's Early Theology." *Journal of Psychology and Christianity* 23, no. 2 (2004): 155-164.

Wynkoop, Mildred Bangs. "Hermeneutical Approach to John Wesley." *Wesleyan Theological Journal* 6, no. 1 (Spring 1971): 13-22.

---. "John Wesley: Mentor or Guru?" *Wesleyan Theological Journal* 10 (Spring 1975): 5-14.

---. "Theological Roots of the Wesleyan Understanding of the Holy Spirit." *Wesleyan Theological Journal* 14, no. 1 (1979): 77-98.

Yates, Arthur S. "Wesley and His Bible." *Methodist Recorder* 5 (1960): 8.

Yates, Kelly Diehl. "The Wesleyan Trilateral: Prevenient Grace, Catholic Spirit, and Religious Tolerance." *Wesleyan Theological Journal* 48, no. 1 (2013): 54-61.

Yeager, Jonathan. "John Wesley's Conflict with James Hervey and Its Effects in Scotland'." *Journal of Religious History* 34, no. 4 (2010): 398-413.

Yeich, Brian. "Poetry as the Handmaid of Piety: Hymns as a Catalyst for Human Development in Early Methodism." *Asbury Journal* 67, no. 1 (2012): 77-92.

Yoon, Young Hwi. "The Spread of Antislavery Sentiment through Proslavery Tracts in the Transatlantic Evangelical Community, 1740's-1770's." *Church History* 81, no. 2 (2012): 348-377.

Yong, Amos. "A Heart Strangely Warmed on the Middle Way? The Wesleyan Witness in a Pluralistic World." *Wesleyan Theological Journal* 48, no. 1 (2013): 7-27.

Young, Carlton R. "John Wesley's 1737 Charlestown Collection of Psalms and Hymns [map, music]." *The Hymn: A Journal of Congregational Song* 41 (October 1990): 19-27.

Young, Frances. "Grace and Demand: The Heart of Preaching." *Epworth Review* 12, no. 2 (1985): 46-55.

---. "Suffering and the Holy Life." *Wesleyan Theological Journal* 43 (2008): 7-21.

Young, Josiah. "Some Assumptions and Implications Regarding John Wesley's View of the Trinity: 'The Root of All Vital Religion' [paper presented at 10th Oxford Inst. of Methodist Theological Studies, August 12-22 1997]," *Quarterly Review: A Journal of Theological Resources for Ministry* 18 (Summer 1998): 139-53.

Young, Norman. "Wesley's View of Catholic Spirit and the Ecumenical Situation Today." *Uniting Church Studies* 5 (March 1999): 59-66.

Yrigoyen, Charles, Jr. "[John Wesley-200th Anniv. Studies]." *Methodist History* 29, no. 2 (January 1991): 63-121.

Yrigoyen, Charles. ""I Was in Prison and You Visited Me": The Prison Ministry of John and Charles Wesley and the Early Methodists." *Evangelical Journal* 29, no. 1 (2011): 11-23.

Zehrer, Karl. "The Relationship between Pietism in Halle and Early Methodism; trans. by James A Dwyer." *Methodist History* 17 (July 1979): 211-24.

Dissertations

Ahn, Hee-Sook Esther. "The Soup of Salvation: John Wesley's Recipe for Conversion and the Beloved Women in His Life." Litt.D. dissertation, Drew University, 2014.

Arnett, William Melvin. "John Wesley: Man of One Book." Ph.D. dissertation, Drew University, Madison, New Jersey, 1954.

Banza, Pierre Alain. "To 'Men of Reason and Religion': John Wesley as an Apologist for 'Methodism': With Special Reference to His Debates with Josiah Tucker, Thomas Church, and 'John Smith.'" Ph.D. dissertation, The University of Manchester (United Kingdom), 2010.

Beedle, Edward E. "Preaching Wesley's Ordo Salutis: A Study in Wesleyan Theology Today." D.Min. dissertation, Asbury Theological Seminary, 2017.

Bence, Clarence. "John Wesley's Teleological Hermeneutic." Ph.D. dissertation, Ann Arbor, Michigan: University Microfilms International, 1982.

Benner, Forest T. "The Immediate Antecedents of the Wesleyan Doctrine of the Witness of the Spirit." Ph.D. dissertation, Temple University, Philadelphia, Pennsylvania, 1966.

Bennett, E. Fay. "The Call to God in the Ministry of John Wesley." Ph.D. dissertation, Southwestern Theological Seminary, 1963.

Black, Robert Edwin. "The Social Dimensions of John Wesley's Ministry as Related to His Personal Piety." Ph.D. dissertation, Union Seminary of Virginia, 1984.

Blaising, Craig Alan. "John Wesley's Doctrine of Original Sin." Th.D. Thesis, Dallas Theological Seminary, 1979.

Blevins, Dean Gray. "John Wesley and the Means of Grace: An Approach to Christian Religious Education." Ph.D. dissertation, Claremont School of Theology, Ann Arbor, 1999.

Boraine, A. L. "The Nature of Evangelism in the Theology and Practice of John Wesley." Ph.D. dissertation, Drew University, Madison, New Jersey, 1969.

Bosch, L. C. "The Ethical Implications of the Concept of Faith as Freedom From Society in the Theology of John Wesley." Ph.D. dissertation, University of South Africa, 1995.

Boshears, Onva K. "John Wesley the Bookman: A Study of his Reading Interests in the Eighteenth Century." Ph.D. dissertation, University of Michigan, 1982.

Brendlinger, Irv A. "A Study of the Views of Major Eighteenth Century Evangelicals on Slavery and Race, with Special Reference to John Wesley." Ph.D. dissertation, University of Edinburgh, 1982.

Brightman, Robert Sheffield. "Gregory of Nyssa and John Wesley in Theological Dialogue on the Christian Life." Ph.D. dissertation, Boston University, 1969.

Brooks, Gennifer Benjamin. "An Ecclesial Homiletic: The 'Pure Word of God' on Holy Living in the Sermons of John Wesley." Ph.D. dissertation, Drew University, 2005.

Bryant, Barry Edward. "John Wesley's Doctrine of Sin." Ph.D. dissertation, King's College, University of London, 1992.

Burns, Michael T. "John Wesley's Doctrine of Perfect Love as a Theological Mandate for Inclusion and Diversity." Ph.D. dissertation, The University of Manchester (United Kingdom), 2009.

Campbell, Ted Allen. "John Wesley's Conception and Uses of Christian Antiquity." Ph.D. dissertation, Southern Methodist University, 1984.

Cannon, William R. "The Doctrine of Justification in the Theology of John Wesley." Ph.D. dissertation, Yale University, 1942.

Casto, Robert Michael. "Exegetical Method in John Wesley's Explanatory Notes Upon the Old Testament: A Description of His Approach, Uses of Sources, and Practice." Ph.D. dissertation, Duke University, 1977.

Cho, John C. "A Study of John Wesley's Doctrine of Baptism in the Light of Current Interpretations." Ph.D. dissertation, Emory University, 1966.

Coggin, James Earl. "John Wesley's Doctrine of Perfection and Its Influence on Subsequent Theology." Ph.D. dissertation, Southwestern Baptist Theological Seminary, 1950.

Coleman, Jim. "The Antithetical Homiletic of John Wesley's Sermons on Several Occasions, i-Iv." Ph.D. dissertation, The University of Manchester (United Kingdom), 2016.

Collins, Kenneth J. "John Wesley's Theology of Law." Ph.D. dissertation, Drew University, 1984.

Colon-Emeric, Edgardo Antonio. "Perfection in Dialogue: An Ecumenical Encounter between Wesley and Aquinas." Ph.D. dissertation, Duke University, 2007.

Conolly, Katherine Simmons. "A Wesleyan Understanding of Grace as Responsible and Therapeutic: A Path to Transformational Spirituality." D.Min. dissertation, George Fox University, George Fox Evangelical Seminary, 2002.

Cooper, Alan Lamar. "John Wesley: A Study in Theology and Ethics." Ph.D. dissertation, Columbia University, 1962.

Cox, Leo. "John Wesley's Concept of Perfection." Ph.D. dissertation, State University of Iowa, 1959.

Crofford, James Gregory. "Streams of Mercy: Prevenient Grace in the Theology of John and Charles Wesley." Ph.D. Thesis, University of Manchester, 2008.

Crow, Earl P. "John Wesley's Conflict with Antinomianism in Relation to the Moravians and Calvinists." Ph.D. dissertation, The University of Manchester, Manchester, England, 1964.

Cubie, David Livingstone. "John Wesley's Concept of Perfect Love: A Motif Analysis." Ph.D. dissertation, Boston University, 1965.

Dale, James. "The Theological and Literary Qualities of the Poetry of Charles Wesley in Relation to the Standard of His Age." Ph.D. dissertation, Cambridge University, 1960.

Dean, William Walter. "Disciplined Fellowship: The Rise and Decline of Cell Groups in British Methodism." Ph.D. dissertation, University of Iowa, 1985.

Derr, Colleen R. "John Wesley and the Faith Formation of Children: Lesson for the Church." Ed.D. dissertation, Regent University, 2013.

Dicker, Gordon Stanley. "The Concept `Simul Justus et Peccator' in Relation to the Thought of Luther, Wesley and Bonhoeffer, and its Significance for a Doctrine of the Christian Life." Th.D Thesis, Union Seminary, 1971.

Dorr, Donal J. "The Wesleyan Doctrine of Sin and Salvation." D.D. Thesis, St. Patrick's College (Maynooth), 1964.

Downes, James Cyril Thomas. "Eschatological Doctrines in the Writings of John and Charles Wesley." Ph.D. dissertation, Edinburgh University, 1960.

Dunlap, E. Dale. Methodist Theology in Great Britain in the 19th Century. Doctoral dissertation, Yale University, 1956. Ann Arbor, MI: University Microfilms, 1968.

Eaton, David Eugene. "Arminianism in the Theology of John Wesley." Ph.D. dissertation, Drew University, 1988.

Edgar, Frederick Russell. "A Study of John Wesley from the Point of View of the Educational Methodology Used by Him in Fostering the Wesleyan Revival in England." Ph.D. dissertation, Columbia University, 1952.

Eicken, Erich Von. "Rechtfertigung und Heiligung bei Wesley dargestellt unter Vergleichung mit Anschauungen Luthers und des Luthertums." Ph.D. dissertation, Heidelberg, 1934.

English, John C. "The Historical Antecedents and Development of John Wesley's Doctrine of Christian Initiation." Ph.D. dissertation, Vanderbilt University, 1965.

Evans, Arthur C. "John Wesley and the Church Fathers." Ph.D. dissertation, St. Louis University, 1985.

Evans, Deborah E. "The Leadership of John Wesley." Ph.D. dissertation, Alvernia University, 2016.

Felleman, Laura Bartels. "The Evidence of Things Not Seen: John Wesley's Use of Natural Philosophy." Ph.D. dissertation, Drew University, 2004.

Fraser, M. Robert. "Strains in the Understandings of Christian Perfection in Early British Methodism." Ph.D. dissertation, Vanderbilt University, 1988.

Fuhrman, Eldon R. "The Concept of Grace in the Theology of John Wesley." Ph.D. dissertation, University of Iowa, 1963.

Fujimoto, Mitsuru S. "John Wesley's Doctrine of Good Works." Ph.D. dissertation, Drew University, 1986.

Gallaway, Craig B. "The Presence of Christ with the Worshipping Community: A Study in the Hymns of John and Charles Wesley." Ph.D. dissertation, Emory University, 1988.

Garlow, James L. "John Wesley's Understanding of the Laity as Demonstrated By His Use of the Lay Preachers." Ph.D. dissertation, Drew University, 1979.

Gerdes, Egon W. "John Wesley's Attitude Toward War." Ph.D. dissertation, Emory University, 1960.

Gray, Wallace G. "The Place of Reason in the Theology of John Wesley." Ph.D. dissertation, Vanderbilt University, 1953.

Greve, Lionel. "Freedom and Discipline in the Theology of John Calvin, William Perkins, and John Wesley: An Examination of the Origin and Nature of Pietism." Ph.D. dissertation, Hartford Seminary, 1976.

Hammond, Geordan. "Restoring Primitive Christianity: John Wesley and Georgia, 1735-1737." Ph.D. dissertation, University of Manchester, 2008.

Hansen, William Albert. "John Wesley and the Rhetoric of Reform." Ph.D. dissertation, University of Oregon, 1972.

Harper, Steve. The Devotional Life of John Wesley, 1703-1738. Doctoral dissertation, Duke University. Ann Arbor, MI: University Microfilms International, 1981.

Heitzenrater, Richard Paul. "John Wesley and the Oxford Methodists." Ph.D. dissertation, Duke University, 1972.

Henderson, David Michael. "John Wesley's Instructional Groups." Ph.D. dissertation, Indiana University, 1980.

Hiatt, Robert Jeffrey. "Salvation as Healing: John Wesley's Missional Theology." Ph.D. dissertation, Asbury Theological Seminary, 2008.

Hicks, Robert Cyrus. "The Theological Worlds of John Wesley's Soteriological Leadership." Ph.D. dissertation, Gonzaga University, 2015.

Hillman, Robert J. "Grace in the Preaching of Calvin and Wesley: a Comparative Study." Ph.D. dissertation, Fuller Theological Seminary, 1978.

Hoffman, Thomas G. "The Moral Philosophy of John Wesley: The Development of His Moral Dynamic." Ph.D. dissertation, Temple University, 1968.

Hohenstein, Charles R. "The Revision of the Rites of Baptism in the Methodist Episcopal Church, 1784-1939." Ph.D. dissertation, University of Notre Dame, 1990.

Holsclaw, David F. "The Declining of Disciplined Christian Fellowship: The Methodist Class Meeting in Nineteenth-Century America." Doctoral dissertation, University of California, Davis. Ann Arbor, MI: University Microfilms International, 1979.

Hoon, Paul W. "The Soteriology of John Wesley." Ph.D. dissertation, Edinburgh University, 1936.

Hopper, Isaac. "'Christ Alone for Salvation': The Role of Christ and His Work in John Wesley's Theology." Ph.D. dissertation, The University of Manchester (United Kingdom), 2017.

Horst, Mark L. "Christian Understanding and the Life of Faith in John Wesley's Thought." Ph.D. dissertation, Yale University, 1985.

Hosman, Glenn Burton. "The Problem of Church and State in the Thought of John Wesley as Reflecting his Understanding of Providence and his View of History." Ph.D. dissertation, Drew University, 1970.

Hucks, John T. "John Wesley and the Eighteenth Century Methodist Movement: A Model for Effective Leadership." Ph.D. dissertation, Regent University, 2003.

Hynson, Leon O. "Church and State in the Thought and Life of John Wesley." Ph.D. dissertation, University of Iowa, 1971.

Im, Seung-An. "John Wesley's Theological Anthropology: A Dialectic Tension Between the Latin Western Patristic Tradition (Augustine) and the Greek Eastern Patristic Tradition (Gregory of Nyssa)." Ph.D. dissertation, Drew University, 1994.

Ireson, Roger W. "The Doctrine of Faith in John Wesley and the Protestant Tradition: A Comparative Study." Ph.D. dissertation, University of Manchester, 1973.

Johnson, Christine L. "Holiness and Death in the Theology of John Wesley." Ph. D. dissertation, The University of Manchester (United Kingdom), 2014.

Johnson, Steve. "John Wesley's Liturgical Theology: His Sources, Unique Contributions and Synthetic Practices." Ph.D. dissertation, The University of Manchester (United Kingdom), 2016.

Jones, Scott. "John Wesley's Concept and Use of Scripture" Doctoral dissertation, Southern Methodist University. Ann Arbor, MI: University Microfilms International, 1992.

Jordan, Eric Evans. "The Ideal of Sanctify in Methodism and Tractarianism with Special Reference to John Wesley and John Henry Newman." Ph.D. dissertation, University of London, 1958.

Keefer, Luke L., Jr. "John Wesley: Disciple of Early Christianity." Ph.D. dissertation, Temple University, 1982.

Kellett, Norman L. "John Wesley and the Restoration of the Doctrine of the Holy Spirit to the Church of England in the 18th Century." Ph.D. dissertation, Brandeis University, 1975.

Kerr, Aaron K. "John and Charles Wesley's 'Hymns on the Lord's Supper' (1745): Their Meaning for Methodist Ecclesial Identity and Ecumenical Dialogue." Ph.D. dissertation, Duquesne University, 2007.

Kim, Hong Ki. "The Theology of Social Sanctification Examined in the Thought of John Wesley and in Minjung Theology: A Comparative Study." Ph.D. dissertation, Drew University, 1991.

Kim, Kwang Yul. "A Tension Between the Desire to Follow the Example of Jesus' Life and the Desire to Trust in His Redemptive Work: The Theology of John Wesley Reflected in his Christian Library." Ph.D. dissertation, Westminster Theological Seminary, 1992.

Kim, Young Taek. "John Wesley's Anthropology: Restoration of the Imago Dei as a Framework for Wesley's Theology." Ph.D. dissertation, Drew University, 2006.

Kingdon, Robert W. "The Development of John Wesley's Social Gospel." Ph.D. dissertation, Chicago Theological Seminary, 1928.

Knight, John Allan. "John William Fletcher and the Early Methodist Tradition." Ph.D. dissertation, Vanderbilt University, 1966.

Kwak, Ju-Hwan. "The Work of the Holy Spirit in Preaching: Focusing on John Wesley and Karl Barth." Ph.D. dissertation, School of Theology at Claremont, 1994.

Kwon, Ohoon. "Toward a Contextualized Church in a Unified Korea/Corea: Exploring Resources in Wesleyan Theology and Eastern Philosophies." Ph.D. dissertation, Asbury Theological Seminary, 2006.

Kwon, Tae Hyoung. "John Wesley's Doctrine of Prevenient Grace: Its Import for Contemporary Missiological Dialogue." Ph.D. dissertation, Temple University, 1996.

Lawson, Albert B. "John Wesley and Some Anglican Evangelicals of the Eighteenth Century. A Study in Cooperation and Separatism; With Special Reference to the Calvinistic Controversies." Ph.D. dissertation, Sheffield University, 1974.

Lee, Hoo-Jung. "The Doctrine of New Creation in the Theology of John Wesley." Ph.D. dissertation, Emory University, 1991.

Lee, Peter A. "The Political Ethics of John Wesley." Ph.D. dissertation, Yale University, 1940.

Lee, Sung-Duk. "Der Deutsche Pietismus Und John Wesley." Ph.D. dissertation, Brunnen, 2003.

Lee-Koo, SunAe. "Humility as a Key Component of John Wesley's Understanding of a Christian's Spiritual Development." Ph.D. dissertation, The Catholic University of America, 2011.

Lelos, Ingrid Goggan. "The Spirit in the Flesh: The Translation of German Pietist Imagery into Anglo-American Cultures." Ph.D. dissertation, The University of Texas at Austin, 2009.

Lerch, David. "Heil und Heiligung bei John Wesley [Salvation and Sanctification According to John Wesley]." Ph.D. dissertation, University of Zurich, 1941.

Leupp, Roderick Thomas. "The Art of God: Light and Darkness in the Thought of John Wesley." Ph.D. dissertation, Drew University, 1985.

Lowery, Kevin Twain. "Constructing a More Cognitivist Account of Wesleyan Ethics." Ph.D. dissertation, University of Notre Dame, 2004.

Loyer, Kenneth M. "Spirit of Love: The Holy Spirit and the Christian Life in Thomas Aquinas and John Wesley." Ph.D. dissertation, Southern Methodist University, 2010.

Luby, Daniel Joseph. "The Perceptibility of Grace in the Theology of John Wesley. A Roman Catholic Consideration." Ph.D. dissertation, Pontificia Studiorum Universitas A.S. Thomas Aquinas in Urbe, 1984.

Maddix, Mark. "Reflecting John Wesley's Theology and Educational Perspective: Comparing Nazarene Pastors, Christian Educators, and Professors of Christian Education." Ph.D. dissertation, Trinity Evangelical Divinity School, 2001.

Madron, Thomas W. "The Political Thought of John Wesley." Ph.D. dissertation, Tulane University, 1965.

Magallanes-Tejeda, Hugo. "The Preferential Option for the Poor: A Wesleyan Liberation Ethics." Ph.D. dissertation, Drew University, 2002.

Manifold, Orrin Avery. "The Development of John Wesley's Doctrine of Christian Perfection." Ph.D. dissertation, Boston University, 1945.

Marino, Bruce. "Through a Glass Darkly: The Eschatological Vision of John Wesley." Ph.D. dissertation, Drew University, 1994.

Matthews, Rex D. "Religion and Reason Joined: A Study in the Theology of John Wesley." Th.D. Thesis, Harvard University, 1986.

Mayo, Harold Jonathon. "John Wesley and the Christian East: On the Subject of Christian Perfection." Masters Thesis, St. Vladimir's Orthodox Theological Seminary, 1980.

McCormick, Kelly S. "John Wesley's Use of John Chrysostom on the Christian Life: Faith Filled with the Energy of Love." Ph.D. dissertation, Drew University, 1983.

McEldowney, James E. "John Wesley's Theology in its Historical Setting." Ph.D. dissertation, University of Chicago, 1943.

McEwan, David B. "An Examination of How John Wesley's Theological Methodology Functions in Pastoral Practice, Illustrated by His Doctrine of Christian Perfection." University of Queensland, 2006.

McGever, Michael Sean. "Early Evangelical Conversion Theology: John Wesley and George Whitefield's Theologies of Conversion." University of Aberdeen, 2018.

McGonigle, Herbert. "John Wesley-Evangelical Arminian." Ph.D. dissertation, Keele University, 1994.

McIntosh, Lawrence D. "The Nature and Design of Christianity in John Wesley's Early Theology." Ph.D. dissertation, Drew University, 1966.

McNulty, Frank J. "The Moral Teachings of John Wesley." STD Thesis, Catholic University of America, 1963.

Mealey, Mark Thomas. "Taste and See That the Lord Is Good: John Wesley in the Christian Tradition of Spiritual Sensation." Ph.D. dissertation, University of St. Michael's College (Canada), 2006.

Meistad, Tore. "To Be a Christian in the World: Martin Luther's and John Wesley's Interpretation of the Sermon on the Mount." Ph.D. dissertation, University of Trondheim, Norway, 1989.

Mercer, Jerry L. "A Study of the Concept of Man in the Sermons of John Wesley." Ph.D. dissertation, Claremont University, 1970.

Meredith, Lawrence. "Essential Doctrine in the Theology of John Wesley, With Special Attention to the Methodist Standards of Doctrine." Th.D. Thesis, Harvard University, 1962.

Meyers, Arthur C. "John Wesley and the Church Fathers." Ph.D. dissertation, St. Louis University, 1985.

Miller, Richard A. "Scriptural Authority and Christian Perfection: John Wesley and the Anglican Tradition." Ph.D. dissertation, Drew University, 1991.

Mitchell, Renee O. "John Wesley and John Henry Newman on the Nature and Function of Ecclesial Authority." Ph.D. dissertation, Southern Methodist University, 2013.

Mitchell, Robert Daniel. "The Wesleyan Quadrilateral: Relocating the Conversation." Ph.D. dissertation, Claremont School of Theology, 2007.

Mobley, Matthew Alan. "Common Bound: The Small Groups of Methodism." D.Min. dissertation, Duke University, 2016.

Moore, Don Marselle. "Immediate Perceptual Knowledge of God: A Study in the Epistemology of John Wesley." M.Ph. Thesis, Syracuse University, 1993.

Moyer, Bruce Eugene. "The Doctrine of Christian Perfection: A Comparative Study of John Wesley and the Modern American Holiness Movement." Ph.D. dissertation, Marquette University, 1992.

Mussman, Robert Byron. "A Study and Evaluation of the Primary Non-Scriptural Influences on John Wesley's Doctrine of Christian Perfection." Ph.D. dissertation, Southern Baptist Theological Seminary, 1959.

Naglee, David Ingersoll. "The Significance of the Relationship of Infant Baptism and Christian Nurture in the Thought of John Wesley." Ph.D. dissertation, Temple University, 1966.

Naumann, William H. "Theology and German-American Evangelicalism: the Role of Theology in the Church of the United Brethren in Christ and the Evangelical Association." Doctoral dissertation, Yale University. Ann Arbor, MI: University Microfilms International, 1966.

Neff, Blake J. "John Wesley and John Fletcher on Entire Sanctification: A Metaphoric Cluster Analysis." Ph.D. dissertation, Bowling Green State University, 1982.

Nygren, Ellis Herbert. "John Wesley's Interpretation of Christian Ordination." Ph.D. dissertation, New York University, 1960.

Oh, Gwang Seok. "John Wesley's Ecclesiology: A Study in Its Sources and Development." Ph.D. dissertation, Southern Methodist University, 2006.

Park, Chang Hoon. "The Theology of John Wesley as 'Checks to Antinomianism.'" Ph.D. dissertation, Drew University, 2002.

Park, Kyoung-Shin Joseph. "The Influence of John Wesley's Standard Sermons on the 18th Century Methodist Society." Ph.D. dissertation, Southwestern Baptist Theological Seminary, 2014.

Pask, Alfred H. S. "The Influence of Arminius upon the Theology of John Wesley." Ph.D. dissertation, University of Edinburgh, 1939.

Pennington, Chester A. "The Essentially Wesleyan Form of the Doctrine of Redemption in the Writings of Emil Brunner." dissertation, Drew University, 1948.

Peterson, Brent David. "A Post -Wesleyan Eucharistic Ecclesiology: The Renewal of the Church as the Body of Christ to Be Doxologically Broken and Spilled out for the World." Ph.D. dissertation, Garrett-Evangelical Theological Seminary, 2009.

Powe, Frederick Douglas. "John Wesley and James Cone on the Rhetoric and Practice of Justice." Ph.D. dissertation, Emory University, 2004.

Quantrille, Wilma Jean. "The Triune God in the Hymns of Charles Wesley." Ph.D. dissertation, Drew University, 1989.

Rakestraw, Robert. "The Concept of Grace in the Ethics of John Wesley." Doctoral dissertation, Drew University, 1985. Ann Arbor, MI: University Microfilms International, 1985.

Randall, Rory R. "Towards an Open Theist Renewal Theology." Ph.D. dissertation, Regent University, 2015.

Renshaw, John R. "The Atonement in the Theology of John and Charles Wesley." Ph.D. dissertation, Boston University, 1965.

Rogers, Charles A. "The Concept of Prevenient Grace in the Theology of John Wesley." Ph.D. dissertation, Duke University, 1967.

Roy, James. "Catholicity or Methodism: or, The Relation of John Wesley to Modern Thought." Ph.D. dissertation, University Microfilms; Ann Arbor, Michigan, 1981.

Russell, Bernard C. "The Theory and Practice of Christian Discipline According to John Wesley: Its Theological Bases and its Modern Relevance." Ph.D. dissertation, Drew University, 1951.

Sanders, Paul S. "An Appraisal of John Wesley's Sacramentalism in the Evolution of Early American Methodism." Ph.D. dissertation, Union Theological Seminary, NY, 1954.

Scanlon, Michael J. "The Christian Anthropology of John Wesley." S.T.D. Thesis, Catholic University of America, 1969.

Sherman, P. Young. "The Doctrine of the Holy Spirit in Relation to Methodist Theology." Ph.D. dissertation, Drew University, 1930.

Score, John N. R. "A Study of the Concept of Ministry in the Thought of John Wesley." Ph.D. dissertation, Duke University, 1963.

Scott, Leland. "Methodist Theology in America in the 19th Century." Ph.D. Doctoral dissertation, Yale University, 1954.

Selleck, J. Brian. "The Book of Common Prayer in the Theology of John Wesley." Ph.D. dissertation, Drew University, 1983.

Shermer, Robert Charles. "John Wesley's Speaking and Writing on Predestination and Free Will." Ph.D. dissertation, Southern Illinois University, 1969.

Shimizu, Mitsuo. "Epistemology in the Thought of John Wesley." Ph.D. dissertation, Drew University, 1980.

Shipley, David C. "Methodist Arminianism in the Theology of John Fletcher." Ph.D. Doctoral dissertation, Yale University, New Haven, 1942.

Smith, Mark Anthony. "John Wesley: A Pattern of Monastic Reform." Ph.D. dissertation, University of Kentucky, 1992.

Staples, Rob L. "John Wesley's Doctrine of Christian Perfection: A Reinterpretation." Ph.D. dissertation, Pacific School of Religion, 1963.

Starkey, Lycurgus. "The Work of the Holy Spirit in John Wesley's Theology." Ph.D. dissertation, Columbia University, 1962.

Stuart, William J. "Theology and Experience: A Reappraisal of Wesley's Theology." Ph.D. dissertation, University of Zurich, 1974.

Sweetland, William E. "A Critical Study of John Wesley as Practical Thinker and Reformer." Ph.D. dissertation, Michigan State University, 1955.

Tews, Jane A. "The Origin and Outcome of the Liturgies of John Wesley." D.Min. Thesis, Claremont School of Theology, 1978.

Thomas, Howe O. "John Wesley's and Rudolf Bultmann's Understanding of Justification by Faith Compared and Contrasted." Ph.D. dissertation, University of Bristol, 1990.

Thompson, Andrew Carl. "John Wesley and the Means of Grace: Historical and Theological Context." Th.D. dissertation, Duke University, 2012.

Thorsen, Donald A. "Theological Method in John Wesley." Ph.D. dissertation, Drew University, 1988.

Townsend, James Arthur. "Feelings Related to Assurance in Charles Wesley's Hymns." Ph.D. dissertation, Fuller Theological Seminary, 1979.

Turner, George Allen. "A Comparative Study of the Biblical and Wesleyan Ideas of Perfection to Determine the Sources of Wesley's Doctrine." Ph.D. dissertation, Harvard University, 1946.

Tuttle, Robert G. "The Influence of Roman Catholic Mystics on John Wesley." Ph.D. dissertation, University of Bristol, 1969.

Tyson, John H. "The Interdependence of Law and Grace in John Wesley's Teaching and Preaching." Ph.D. dissertation, University of Edinburgh, 1991.

Tyson, John Roger. "Charles Wesley's Theology of the Cross: An Examination of the Theology and Method of Charles Wesley as Seen in His Doctrine of the Atonement." Ph.D. dissertation, Drew University, 1983.

Wade, William N. "A History of Public Worship in the Methodist Episcopal Church and Methodist Episcopal Church, South from 1784 to 1905." Ph.D. dissertation, University of Notre Dame, 1981.

Wagner, Paul S. "John Wesley and the German Pietist Heritage: The Development of Hymnody." Th.D. dissertation, University of Trinity College (Canada), 2004.

Walker, G. Clinton. "John Wesley's Doctrine of Justification in Relation to Two Classical Anglican Theologians: Richard Hooker and Lancelot Andrewes." Ph.D. dissertation, Baylor University, 1993.

Watson, David Lowes. "The Origin and Significance of the Early Methodist Class Methodist Meetings." Ph.D. dissertation, Duke University, 1978.

Watson, Kevin M. "The Early Methodist Band Meeting: Its Origin, Development, and Significance." Ph.D. dissertation, Southern Methodist University, 2012.

Welch, Barbara Ann. "Charles Wesley and the Celebration of the Evangelical Experience." Ph.D. dissertation, University of Michigan, 1971.

Westerfield-Tucker, Karen Beth. "'Till Death Us Do Part': The Rites of Marriage and Burial Prepared by John Wesley and Their Development in the Methodist Episcopal Church, 1784-1939." Ph.D. dissertation, University of Notre Dame, 1992.

Whited, Harold Vaughn. "A Rhetorical Analysis of the Published Sermons Preached by John Wesley at Oxford University." Ph.D. dissertation, University of Michigan, 1958.

Willhauck, Susan E. "John Wesley's View of Children: Foundations for Contemporary Christian Education." Ph.D. dissertation, Catholic University of America, 1992.

Williams, Colin. "Methodism and the Ecumenical Movement." Ph.D. dissertation, Drew University, 1958.

Williams, George Homer. "'The Word Came with Power': Print, Oratory, and Methodism in Eighteenth-Century Britain." Ph.D. dissertation, University of Maryland, College Park, 2002.

Williams, L. Brian. "Religious-based Managed Care: A Wesleyan Paradigm for Reforming Health Care." Ph.D. dissertation, University of Southern California, 1998.

Williams, Ronald Gordon. "John Wesley's Doctrine of the Church." Th.D. Thesis, Boston University, 1964.

Wilson, David D. "The Influence of Mysticism on John Wesley." Ph.D. dissertation, Leeds University, 1968.

Wilson, Kenneth A. "The Devotional Relationship and Interaction Between the Spirituality of John Wesley, the Methodist Societies, and the Book of Common Prayer." Ph.D. dissertation, Queens University of Belfast, 1984.

Yeich, Stephen Brian. "Christian Perfection as a Vision for Evangelism." Ph.D. dissertation, The University of Manchester (United Kingdom), 2015.

Zele, Adam Scott. "John Wesley's America." Ph.D. dissertation, Duke University, 2008.

www.ingramcontent.com/pod-product-compliance
Lightning Source LLC
LaVergne TN
LVHW011343080426
835511LV00005B/111
* 9 7 8 1 6 2 1 7 1 9 4 3 4 *